AS BEFITS A LEGEND

As Befits

Building a

a Legend

Tomb for Napoleon,

1840–1861

MICHAEL PAUL DRISKEL

The Kent State University Press

Kent, Ohio, and London, England

© 1993 by THE KENT STATE UNIVERSITY PRESS, Kent, Ohio 44242
All rights reserved
Library of Congress Catalog Card Number 93-12099
ISBN 0-87338-484-9
Manufactured in the United States of America

Library of Congress Cataloging–in–Publication Data

Driskel, Michael Paul.
    As befits a legend : building a tomb for Napoleon, 1840–1861 /
Michael Paul Driskel.
        p.   cm.
    Includes bibliographical references and index.
    ISBN 0–87338–484–9 ∞
    1. Napoleon I, Emperor of the French, 1769–1821—Tomb.
2. Neoclassicism (Architecture)—France—Paris.   3. Paris (France)—
Buildings, structures, etc.   4. Visconti, Louis, 1791–1853—
Criticism and interpretation.   5. Sepulchral monuments—France—
Public opinion.   6. Public opinion—France.   7. Art and state—
France—History—19th century.   8. Dôme des Invalides (Paris,
France)   I. Title.
NA6165.D75   1993
726′.8′0944361—dc20   93–12099
                                                     CIP

British Library Cataloging-in-Publication data are available.

Table of Contents

List of Illustrations   vii

Preface   xi

Acknowledgments   xvii

1   The Monument and Its Architect   1

2   Politics of Representation and Location   17

3   The "Contest"   76

4   The Process   129

5   Authorship, Meaning, and Method   180

Appendixes   206

Notes   220

Selected Bibliography   244

Index   248

List of Illustrations

1   Jules Hardouin-Mansart, facade of the dome of
    the Invalides   xx

2   *Perspectival View of the Hotel of the Invalides*   2

3   *Elevation and Longitudinal Section of the Hôtel
    des Invalides*   3

4   *Tomb of Napoleon*   4

5   *Floor Plan of the Dome of the Invalides*   5

6   View toward the altar of the dome of the Invalides   6

7   *Tomb of Napoleon, Longitudinal Section*   7

8   *Tomb of Napoleon, Entry into Crypt*   7

9   Statues of *Civil Force* and *Military Force*   8

10 Sarcophagus of Napoleon   9

11 View across the crypt toward Victory Figures   9

12 Statue of Napoleon in imperial regalia   10

13 Bas-relief, *Exhumation of the Body of Napoleon by
    the Prince de Joinville*   11

14 Bas-relief, *Louis-Philippe Receiving the Remains
    of Napoleon at the Dome of the Invalides on
    15 December 1840*   11

15 Pierre-Jean David d'Angers, untitled drawing   20

16 Gustave Tassaert, *France and the Prince de Joinville
    at the Tomb of Saint Helena*   23

17 Anonymous, *Tremble All! Kings in League with One
    Another! Because of his Open Tomb . . .*   24

18 Nicolas-Toussaint Charlet, *The Marseillaise*   26

19 Nicolas-Toussaint Charlet, *The Advice of the Master* 27

20 Napoléon Thomas, *The Translation of the Ashes of
    Napoleon to the Invalides*   30

21	Victor Adam, *Arrival of the Funeral Cortege at the Esplanade of the Invalides*	31
22	Aimé Lemud, *The Return to France*	33
23	Gustave Tassaert, *The Final Return of Napoleon*	34
24	View of the Vendôme Column, Place Vendôme	37
25	Emile Seurre, *Napoleon on the Column 28 July 1833*	38
26	Nicolas-Toussaint Charlet, *Make Them Sing to the Column! . . .*	40
27	Eugène André, *It is thus that he would be delivered to our wishes and our admiration*	41
28	View of the July Column, Place de la Bastille	43
29	Church of the Madeleine, Paris, south facade	45
30	Jules-Claude Ziegler, *The History of Christianity*	47
31	The Panthéon, Paris, west facade	50
32	*Project to Crown the Arch of Triumph*	53
33	Camille Moret, *Project for a Tomb of Napoleon on the Hill at Chaillot*	55
34	Léon Vaudoyer, letter with drawing of Duban's project for the tomb of Napoleon	59
35	Adolphe Lafosse, *Allegory of the Civil and Military Triumphs of the Emperor Napoleon*	62
36	*Marochetti's Second Project for a Tomb of Napoleon*	63
37	Antoine Etex, *Project for a Monument to Napoleon*	66
38	Antoine Etex, *Project for a Tomb of Napoleon*	67
39	Nicolas-Toussaint Charlet, frontispiece illustration for de Las Cases, *La Mémorial de Sainte-Hélène*	68
40	François Bosio, *Equestrian Statue of Louis XIV*	69
41	Bonino da Campione, *Tomb of Cansignori della Scala*	71
42	Jean Goujon (?), *Tomb of Louis de Brézé*	72
43	Charles Marochetti, *Equestrian Statue of Philibert Emmanuel, Milan*	73
44	Antoine Allier, *Project for a Tomb of Napoleon*	89
45	Clément Pruche, *The Contest for the Tomb of Napoleon*	91
46	Jean-Baptiste Débéban, *Project for a Monument to Napoleon*	93
47	Alexandre Colin, *Nocturnal Convoy*	94
48	P. F. Geslin, *The Historical Clock*	96
49	Horace Vernet, *The Apotheosis of Napoleon*	99

50	Louis Auvray, *Project for a Tomb of Napoleon*	101
51	Louis Auvray, *Maquette for a Tomb of Napoleon*	102
52	Jules Bouchet, *Project for a Tomb of Napoleon*	104
53	Félix Duban, *Project for a Tomb of Napoleon*	105
54	Louis Petitot, *Project for a Monument to Napoleon*	106
55	Louis Moreau, *Project for a Tomb of Napoleon*	107
56	Henri de Triqueti, *Model for a Tomb of Napoleon*	108
57	Henri de Triqueti, *Project for a Tomb of Napoleon*	109
58	Henri de Triqueti, *Project for a Bas-relief Running around the Sarcophagus of the Tomb of Napoleon* (left half)	111
59	Henri de Triqueti, *Project for a Bas-relief Running around the Sarcophagus of the Tomb of Napoleon* (right half)	111
60	Achille Devéria and Hippolyte Maindron, *Project for a Tomb of Napoleon*	112
61	François Thiollet, *Floor Plan for a Tomb of Napoleon at the Invalides*	114
62	Edmond Lévêque and Louis Buhot, *Project for a Monument to Napoleon*	115
63	Hector Horeau, *Project for a Tomb of Napoleon*	117
64	Antoine Rivoulon, *Project for a Monument to Napoleon*	118
65	Antoine Etex, *Project for a Tomb of Napoleon for the Contest of 1841*	119
66	Henri Labrouste, *Project for a Tomb of Napoleon*	120
67	Théodore Labrouste, *Project for a Tomb of Napoleon*	121
68	Théodore Labrouste, *Statue of Napoleon for Tomb Project*	122
69	Théodore Labrouste, *Floor Plan for Tomb Project*	123
70	Louis Visconti, *Project for the Tomb of Napoleon*	125
71	Longitudinal Section of the Invalides	127
72	J.-A.-D. Ingres, *Sketch of a Tomb of Napoleon*	135
73	Honoré Daumier, *Future Monument of Napoleon at the Invalides*	139
74	Louis Visconti, *Longitudinal Section for the Tomb of Napoleon*	140
75	Louis Visconti, *Elevation of the Entry to the crypt, the Dome of the Invalides*	142
76	Charles Marochetti, *Project for the Equestrian Statue of Napoleon*	143

77 Louis Visconti, *Project for the Pedestal for the Equestrian Statue of Napoleon, Frontal View*   144

78 Louis Visconti, *Project for the Pedestal for the Equestrian Statue of Napoleon, Profile View*   145

79 James Pradier, *Victory Figure: The Italian Campaign*   149

80 James Pradier, *Victory Figure: The First Austrian Campaign*   151

81 Henri de Triqueti, *Christ on the Cross*   152

82 Charles Simart, *The Civil Code*   155

83 Cham, *The Monument of the Emperor*   163

84 Edouard Hollier, *Saint Napoleon, Patron of Warriors*   169

85 Antoine Etex, *The Tomb of Vauban*   170

86 E. E. Viollet-le-Duc, *Floor Plan for Restoration of Saint-Denis*   174

87 E. E. Viollet-le-Duc, *Plan for Restoration of Saint-Denis*   175

88 Anonymous, *Translation of the Remains of Napoleon Ier*   176

89 Tomb of Louis Visconti, cemetery of Père Lachaise, Paris   181

90 Fountain of the Four Bishops, Place Saint-Sulpice, Paris   188

91 Daniel Buren, *Column Monument*   192

92 George W. Keller, *The James A. Garfield National Memorial*   195

93 Philip Johnson, *The Kennedy Memorial*   197

94 Philip Johnson, *Cenotaph in The Kennedy Memorial*   199

95 Daniel Chester French, *Lincoln Enthroned*   200

96 Bernard Kliban, *The Nixon Monument*   203

Preface

What is an architect? Or in what sense is the architect of a public monument its "author"? These questions might at first sight seem straightforward, admitting relatively simple answers. In reality, however, they are fraught with difficulty when the point of reference is a project of great complexity and social significance, such as the tomb of Napoleon at the Church of the Invalides in Paris. Therefore, one challenging problem to be explored in this book is the origin of the design for a major public monument and its successive elaborations, or the question of who, if anyone, should be given personal, authorial credit for this landmark in the history of nineteenth-century architecture.

As usually practiced, architectural history is principally concerned with the creativity of individual architects, design problems solved by significant works, and the historical or contextual influences that determined particular architectural forms or solutions. In short supply is detailed attention to the actual interpersonal process within which buildings and monuments are constructed. This study will fill this gap to some small degree and contribute to what one might describe as a phenomenology of the nuts and bolts of architectural praxis. In closely examining the activities of Ludovico-Tullis (Louis) Visconti, the official architect of the tomb of Napoleon, and his interaction with all the parties involved in the monument, one will gain a much better idea of what constituted the *vie quotidienne* of a successful nineteenth-century architect or the mundane reality of the nonaesthetic matters that occupied the greater part of his professional life. Therefore, in this regard the present study might be seen as a contribution to the sociology of the architectural profession.

It is often assumed that a successful and harmonious architectural monument must reflect a harmonious relationship between its patron, architect, and decorative sculptors. However, that is certainly not the case with this project, which painfully developed within a network of conflict. From beginning to end, the monument was beset by the clash of individual egos and entangled in a continuous series of more-or-less acrimonious conflicts between the various participants. Thus, the section of this book that concerns the decoration and embellishment of the structure will explore at some length the nature and causes of these struggles, as well as how they were resolved.

In *De-architecture*, a spirited, postmodern critique of the assumptions of modernist architecture, James Wines has discussed the failure of the twentieth century to create a viable public art and to integrate art and architecture in public monuments. He finds that most public works of art today bear little relation to their architectural environment and that architects and artists are continually at odds because of their differing concepts of both "publicness" and the creative act: "There has been no conceptual common ground for collaboration, no philosophical reason to engage in a dialogue, no higher mandate . . . to link the two enterprises to a shared goal."[1] According to Wines, this lack of a shared vision of art for the public sphere can be traced to the end of the last century. For various socioeconomic reasons, artists at that time created an identity for themselves that positioned them in opposition or open hostility to the middle classes and the state's administrative machinery, the patrons of public art. Closely associated with this stance is the ideology of avant-gardism. On the other hand, architects have tended to provide functionalist, nonartistic, or impersonal reasons for the employment of sculpture or painting within the context of architecture. As a result, the contemporary sculptor, when asked to execute a public work or collaborate with an architect, basically enlarges and installs his own private art or private vision in a public space.

While there is some truth to this broad generalization, the problem that Wines isolates can be traced back much earlier in the century. One might say that while Visconti, as a faithful administrator as well as architect, was attempting to work within what he conceived as the public sphere, certain sculptors he employed, who were affiliated with the academic art institutions of the day, were already intent on projecting their private art into a communal space. And the concept of the "avant-garde" never entered the picture.

The process of building a monument to Napoleon will be closely scrutinized, but the problem of its social meanings will be given equal importance in my discussion. More specifically, an attempt will be made to answer difficult questions such as: What political or ideological motivations underpinned the choice of its location? What social meanings were inscribed in its form or style? How was it received and perceived by its contemporary audience? In attempting answers to these questions, I will begin by examining the public debate over the proper location for the tomb, since this discourse provides a means of immediate access to the field of meanings engaged by it.

When the government formally announced in 1840 that Napoleon's body was to be returned to France, it also decreed that his tomb was to be constructed in the Church of the Invalides. But this autocratic decree was hotly disputed in the ensuing months. Fundamental issues in this contentious discourse were closely interrelated ones of the most appropriate location for a monument to this singular individual, the degree of its prominence or visibility, and whether it should be incorporated into an existing structure or have an autonomous presence, i.e., where this monument was to be located and how conspicuous a part it was to have in the urban fabric of the capital. These questions were, of course, directly related to the widely differing and baldly contradictory conceptions of the meaning of Napoleon or the Napoleonic legend. The use of the term *legend* stresses the way the collective imagination of the period, viewing him through the filters of myth and nostalgia, reworked the memory of Napoleon. But more than simply revealing how the choice of the Invalides as the burial site was perceived by the public, study of this discourse provides a valuable map of the social values attached to other monuments and public spaces during the July Monarchy. Assuming that political significance, like linguistic meaning, is the product of difference, the differential relation of the Invalides to other places and monuments in the symbolic economy of Paris must be given careful scrutiny.

Another means of understanding the meanings embedded in Visconti's design is by study of the public competition held for the tomb in 1841 and the discourse it provoked. The contest, or "pseudocontest" as it was called by many observers, furnished an occasion for an intensely acrimonious critical discourse on the nature and function of the sepulchral monument. The way this contest was conducted also provided a convenient means to criticize the government of Louis-Philippe, thereby illustrating the way in which aesthetic judgments and political ideology can become intertwined. But more than just studying the critical discourse surrounding the projects in the contest, I will also examine closely a number of the designs or models that served as alternatives to Visconti's plan. By surveying these other proposals one can gain a sense of the uniqueness and difference of his solution, and at the same time form a clear idea of the range of imaginative possibilities and typologies for architectural monuments at one particular moment in nineteenth-century France. Thus, from a close reading of both the criticism of these entries in the contest and the projects themselves, considered as participants in this discourse, I will propose that Visconti's project was selected because it performed as a symbolic mediation of the terms in the debate and the visual conceptions of how a funeral monument of this kind should be represented.

Remarkably astute in dealing with the enormously complex politics and the changes in government during the period the tomb was under construction, Visconti managed to keep the project moving toward completion and inauguration despite the many obstacles. However, after his death, which occurred in the first years of the Second Empire, he was unable to control further the fate of his monument. Therefore, the final section of this book will deal with a question that has been avoided in all previous literature on this subject, that is to say the reasons underlying the refusal of Napoleon III to inaugurate the tomb for more than nine years after its completion.

A few words may be in order concerning the process of constructing the present book and my methodology. "Neopositivism" is certainly one rubric (or pejorative, depending on one's position in debates pervading the humanities today) that might be used to characterize my endeavor. The aptness of the term would, first of all, derive from reliance throughout most of the text on hard evidence, that is the concrete, material record left by the process of construction, which consists in large part of musty documents hidden away in decrepit archival containers. Secondly, the empiricist nature of this enterprise also stems from my subscription to the principle that hypotheses and conjectures are only as good as the facts upon which they are grounded. But, during the present reign of the theories of poststructuralism and deconstruction in the humanities, the very existence of such entities as facts is often called into question. Therefore, it is perhaps appropriate to specify how this now-suspect concept is being (mis?)used here. To do this I might invoke a distinction made by John Searle between "brute" and "institutional" facts. In his account, the former are susceptible to simple empirical investigation and supply the raw material for the inductive method of the natural sciences. On the other hand, the latter "are indeed facts, but their existence, unlike the existence of brute facts, presupposes the existence of certain human institutions."[2] These institutions, then, are constitutive systems of rules, often unstated or implicit, that govern human social life. From the perspective of this book, brute facts are those discovered in the various libraries, archives, and museums of France; their material existence is indubitable, but they certainly do not speak for themselves. These kinds of facts only acquire deeper historical meaning when explained in terms of institutional facts, and these second-order facts do not, needless to say, possess the same density as the first. In the latter group the art of interpretation plays a significantly larger role in their explication, and there is greater room for error.

Of course, I could not have even begun to assemble my hard evidence or bring a rudimentary organization to it without having preexisting master ideas about its relevance and meaning, and in this regard my interpretations of institutional facts are conditioned by my own historical position to an inescapable degree. I should admit that my understanding of the institutional facts has been influenced by the related disciplines of structural linguistics and structural anthropology. When studying this monument, I have considered it as a representation of an elementary network of relationships or system of signs pervading French social life at the time, whose parts receive meaning through their differential relation to one another and have employed the concepts of binary analysis and symbolic mediation, central to the work of Lévi-Strauss, to account for its form. That is to say my means of description, my conceptualizations of the important issues, and even the ways in which I have posed my questions are a function to some extent of the brute spatio-temporal fact of my date of birth.

But, I should stress again that as much old-fashioned legwork as thought and theory went into the production of my text. In order to locate the drawings of Visconti for this project, the various alternative proposals for the tomb, and images of the projects in the contest of 1841, which were dispersed after its close, it was necessary to go to extraordinary lengths, and this part of the research has been decidedly the most time-consuming. Most surprisingly, even after finding and consulting with keepers of the archives for several of the families of architects or sculptors in the contest (Baltard and Rochet, for example) and contacting individuals who have written recent Ph.D. dissertations on the architects whose projects were acclaimed in the contest of 1841, no trace was found of their efforts. Equally disturbing is that in the preparation of the recent Visconti bicentenary exhibition by an international team of scholars, all sorts of drawings and documents relating to the architect's career were uncovered, but not a clue was found in family or public archives as to the present location of the original drawing he submitted to the contest of 1841. This project is only known from one tracing in very poor condition and his written description. The disappearance of these projects, however, is very revealing as to our ambiguous conception of the ontological status of architectural drawings and models for structures that were never realized and to the problem of their category or classification.[3] Because in the past they have generally not been considered aesthetic objects of a very high order, museums and the art market have had relatively little interest in them; on the other hand, being artwork in some vague sense, they have not been considered serious historical or archival documents, worthy of cataloguing and preserving in nonartistic contexts. Of course, this becomes all the more problematic when one considers that in this case they were directly related to an individual who occupies one of the most prominent positions in world history (there exists, after all, an active market for any personal memorabilia, as well as an avid band of collectors seeking bibelots of no aesthetic worth that he may have touched). Clearly this project has fallen through the interstices in our system of organization of knowledge and value.

Acknowledgments

The origin of of this book lies in a Graduate Loan exhibition I directed at Brown University in 1982, a project that proved to be at once greatly frustrating and immensely rewarding. I owe a debt of gratitude to all the students who participated in that project. Entitled *All the Banners Wave: Art and War in the Romantic Era*, the exhibition had of necessity to deal with a vast quantity of Napoleonic imagery of all sorts and a copious literature concerned with the death of Napoleon in 1821 and the return of his body to France in 1840. In working on this project, I came to realize that there was one major lacuna in this writing: no substantial account existed of the process of building his tomb in the Church of the Invalides in Paris, or of the problems and social meanings that are implicated in it—despite the facts that this is a work of a major nineteenth-century architect, and it is housed in one of the most prestigious works of architecture in France. Following this exhibition I spent a summer in France, where I made a survey of the enormous quantity of archival documents and primary sources pertaining to the project, and determined to write a detailed study on the subject. At that point I sat down and compared notes with Jacques de Caso, who had himself done work on the monument and generously offered to share his research with me. Thus, it is to him that I owe the first of many scholarly debts. At the same time Meredith Shedd shared with me the research she had done on Simart and other sculptors involved with the monument. I also had several stimulating and encouraging discussions about this undertaking with David Van Zanten, who has been very supportive of this study for a number of years. But the best laid plans of this sort cannot be realized without obtaining financial support for them, and it is the J. Paul Getty Foundation that made this book possible by extending me a Post Doctoral Fellowship in 1985–86, which permitted the conclusion of my research in France and the writing of the first draft of the book.

I cannot begin to list all the museum curators and archivists in France who aided my research in one way or another, but I should acknowledge the help of Jean-Marcel Humbert, Conservator at the Musée de l'Armée in Paris and Gérard Hubert, Conservator of the Château of Malmaison. Special thanks are also due to Jean Simon and Anne Gavois, archivists of the Assemblée nationale, who uncovered Visconti's official drawings for the project and facilitated the process of having them photographed. For providing a rare photograph and useful information concerning the monument, I am likewise indebted to Philip Ward-Jackson of the Courtauld Institute, London. Among museum professionals who made exceptional efforts to help me uncover projects for the contest for the tomb, Geneviève Lacambre, Curator of the Musée Moreau in Paris, comes readily to mind. I also must thank Françoise Hamon and Charles MacCallum, editors and directors of the exhibition and catalogue *Louis Visconti 1791–1853*, for permitting me to participate and for facilitating my research. Finally, I should express my gratitude to Julia Morton, Senior Editor at Kent State University Press, for her enthusiastic support of this project, and Linda Cuckovich, whose copyediting skills have made this book both more readable and more accurate in its presentation of facts.

AS BEFITS A LEGEND

CHAPTER 1

The Monument and Its Architect

Among the more surprising and momentous public announcements during the nineteenth century must be that made by Charles de Rémusat, France's minister of the interior, to the Chamber of Deputies on 12 May 1840. During the humdrum process of introducing appropriation bills for public works, Rémusat created a sensation by requesting the funds necessary to bring the body of Napoleon back from the distant island of Saint Helena, where it had rested since his death on 5 May 1821, and to construct a tomb befitting the former ruler of the nation.[1] In one bold stroke he revealed that the government had concluded an agreement with the English permitting the return of the emperor and that his tomb was to be constructed in the Church of the Invalides in Paris. This fateful decision to construct the tomb of Napoleon in this location immediately posed a major problem that was to be finally solved by the design of Louis Visconti (1791–1853), the architect who was given the commission for this monument in 1842 and who supervised its construction until his death in 1853.

At issue was the question of how this structure was to be incorporated harmoniously into the famous domed, central-plan church of Jules Hardouin-Mansart, one of the greatest architects in the history of France (fig. 1). Begun shortly before 1680 and finally inaugurated in 1706, the "dome," as it is generally referred to in the literature on the project, is one of the great domed spaces of the baroque era—not far behind Saint Peter's in Rome and Saint Paul's in London in scale and technical virtuosity—and is the capstone and crowning element in the group of buildings designed as a rest home and hospital for the veterans of the

Fig. 1 (*opposite*)
Jules Hardouin-Mansart. Facade of the dome of the Invalides, Paris. Photo courtesy of Lauros-Giraudon.

wars of Louis XIV (fig. 2). After the château at Versailles, it is the most ambitious architectural program sponsored by the Sun King.

The original commission for the complex of buildings in which the dome is situated was given in the early 1670s to Libéral Bruant, who based his design on El Escorial, Philip II's royal monastery outside Madrid. When Bruant died, the secular buildings were nearing completion and his basilican-plan church was well underway, but plans for the dome had apparently not yet been given final form. At this point Hardouin-Mansart was invited to construct the dome, which was intended to complete Bruant's church and to be the most significant architectural component of the complex. An engraving, executed before construction of the dome was started, provides a longitudinal section of both Hardouin-Mansart's dome and Bruant's basilican-plan church and shows their rather incongruous juncture (fig. 3).[2] Al-

Fig. 2
Perspectival View of the Hotel of the Invalides, c. 1680s. Anonymous engraving. Photo courtesy of the Bibliothèque Nationale, Département des Estampes.

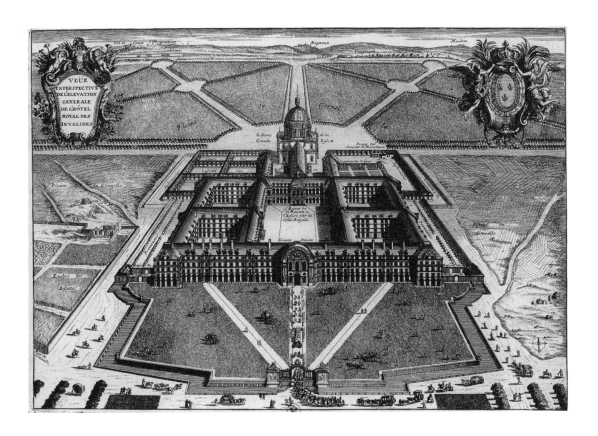

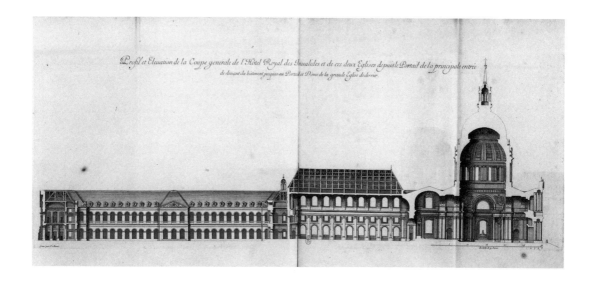

Fig. 3
Elevation and Longitudinal Section of the Hôtel des Invalides. Engraving by J. Marot. Illustration for Le Jeune de Boulencourt. *Description générale de l'hostel royal des Invalides,* Paris, 1683. Photo courtesy of the Bibliothèque Nationale, Département des Estampes.

though the two buildings were evidently intended to work as a single architectural ensemble, they are essentially two different building types, sharing only a common wall, and originally served much different functions: the church of Bruant was used for daily religious ceremonies, while the dome was reserved for great ceremonial occasions.[3]

Today, when one enters Hardouin-Mansart's structure by the south door, not the entry of Louis XIV, who would have traversed the *cour d'honneur* and entered through Bruant's church, there is an unobstructed view of the altar and baldachin. At first sight the interior appears to have changed little from the way it looked in the beginning of the eighteenth century. From the doorway the view to the altar is interrupted only slightly by the simple stone coping around the sunken crypt, located directly under the cupola, that contains Napoleon's sarcophagus and a rich program of sculptural decoration. Only as one comes near the opening in the floor under the cupola does the sarcophagus and sculpture surrounding it become visible. Stepping away from the crypt and surveying the interior of the building, it is apparent that the structure is completely integrated with its architectural matrix and in close harmony with the dominant architectural rhythms of this great example of French baroque classicism, a perception better captured by a lithograph of a nineteenth-century artist than by

Fig. 4
Tomb of Napoleon. Lithograph by
P. Benoist, 1864. Photo courtesy
of the Bibliothèque Nationale,
Département des Estampes.

modern photographic means (fig. 4). A drawing of the floor plan
shows that while the sarcophagus may be invisible from the entryway, it is at the exact center of the bilaterally symmetrical greek
cross plan—fifty-four meters in both directions—and the four
main axes of the structure (fig. 5). It also forms a negative space
that is answered by the four raised spatial volumes that constitute
the auxiliary chapels.

At the end of the principal axis beginning at the south entry
is located the raised altar, which is part of the tomb complex.
Surmounted by a highly naturalistic figure of the crucified Christ
by Henri de Triqueti, a major sculptor of the day, and a colossal

Fig. 5
*Floor Plan of the Dome of the
Invalides.* Anonymous drawing.
Photo courtesy of the Caisse
Nationale des Monuments Histo-
riques © 1992 ARS, New York/
SPADEM, Paris.

Fig. 6
View toward the altar of the dome
of the Invalides. Photo courtesy of
Lauros-Giraudon.

baldachin, obviously based on the famous prototype at the Vatican and fabricated from bronze and rare marbles, this structure also contains the entry into the tomb complex (fig. 6). Access to the crypt, as can be seen in a cross-section from one of the first published descriptions of the tomb, is gained by descending the staircase behind the altar and baldachin (figs. 7, 8). On either side of the entry door to the crypt stand two monumental bronze caryatid figures signifying Napoleon's civil and military positions, which employed the most advanced metallurgical techniques of the day and were fabricated after the models by Francisque Duret (fig. 9). Above this door is inscribed the famous declaration or request supposedly made by Napoleon on the island of Saint Helena shortly before his death: "Je désire que mes cendres reposent sur les bords de la Seine au milieu de ce peuple Français que j'ai

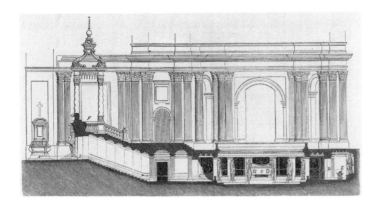

Fig. 7
Tomb of Napoleon, Longitudinal Section. Illustration from A. Lenoir, *Le Tombeau de Napoléon.* Paris, 1853. Photo courtesy of the Bibliothèque Nationale.

Fig. 8
Tomb of Napoleon, Entry into Crypt. Lithograph by Jules Arnout, n.d. Photo courtesy of the Bibliothèque Nationale, Département des Estampes.

Fig. 9
Entry into the crypt of the tomb of
Napoleon. Statues of *Civil Force*
and *Military Force* by Francisque
Duret. Photo courtesy of Roger-
Viollet.

tant aimé" (I desire that my ashes rest on the banks of the Seine,
amid the French people whom I loved so much).

Descending into the interior of the crypt, one confronts the
monumental and enormously costly porphyry sarcophagus en-
capsulating the body of the emperor (fig. 10). Then moving
around the peristyle and looking across the circular opening, one
encounters twelve victory figures executed after the models of
James Pradier (fig. 11). These monumental statues, which face
the sarcophagus, assume similar hieratic poses but are differenti-
ated by the organization of their drapery and attributes. Along the
inner wall of the peristyle, in the space between the piers supporting the victory figures, are ten allegorical bas-reliefs illustrating various aspects of Napoleon's contribution to French society,

Fig. 10
The sarcophagus of Napoleon. Design by L. Visconti. Porphyry, completed 1853. Photo courtesy of the Caisse Nationale des Monuments Historiques © 1992 ARS, New York/SPADEM, Paris.

Fig. 11
View across the crypt toward Victory Figures. By James Pradier. Photo courtesy of the Caisse Nationale des Monuments Historiques © 1992 ARS, New York/SPADEM, Paris.

carved after the models of Pierre-Charles Simart. On the side of the crypt directly opposite the entry door is a small chamber, or *cella* as it was referred to at the time, containing a statue of Napoleon in imperial regalia (fig. 12), also a product of Simart, who was considered at the time to be the Ingres of sculptors. From the door of this shrinelike space one has a direct line of sight to the figure of Christ on the cross above the altar, a juxtaposition that appears to be more than fortuitous, as even a brief survey of the myth of Napoleon would reveal.

Throughout the sculptural program contemporary dress is eschewed. While the imperial costume of the freestanding figure of Napoleon is faithful to history, it would not have been considered modern by viewers during the period. Abjuration of contempo-

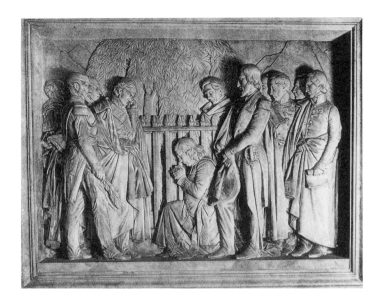

Fig. 13
Augustin Dumont, *Exhumation of the Body of Napoleon by the Prince de Joinville*. Bas-relief, marble. Tomb of Napoleon. Illustration from Niox, *Invalides*. Photo courtesy of the Bibliothèque Nationale.

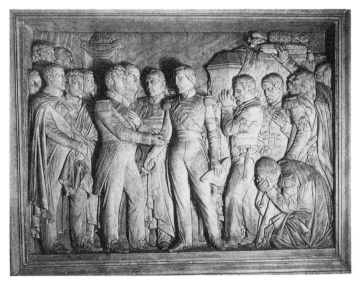

Fig. 14
François Jouffroy, *Louis-Philippe Receiving the Remains of Napoleon at the Dome of the Invalides on 15 December 1840*. Bas-relief, marble. Tomb of Napoleon, illustration from Niox, *Invalides*. Photo courtesy of the Bibliothèque Nationale.

rary costume is broken only in the case of the two reliefs juxtaposed on either side of the lower entry into the crypt. On the right is seen a relief by Augustin Dumont representing the moment before the exhumation of Napoleon's body began at the Valley of Geraniums on the island of Saint Helena (fig. 13).

Kneeling before the tomb is abbé Félix Coquereau, and standing behind him is the Prince de Joinville, the son of Louis-Philippe and person charged with the mission. Opposite this scene is a relief by François Jouffroy representing Louis-Philippe receiving the remains of Napoleon under the dome of the Invalides on the afternoon of 15 December 1840 and inviting General Bertrand to place the fabled sword on the coffin (fig. 14). These two moments in the saga of the *retour des cendres* were intended to remind the beholder who was responsible for the return and under whose rule the tomb was begun.

Louis Visconti, the official architect of this project, was born in 1791 in the Chigi Palace at Rome, where his father, Ennius-Quirnius, served as the librarian and personal secretary of Prince Sigismondo Chigi.[4] The most highly esteemed classical archaeologist in Italy, Ennius-Quirnius Visconti was generally considered to be the successor of Winckelmann. As a consequence, he had an immediate entrée into the private collections of the aristocracy and many friends and protectors in aristocratic circles in both Italy and France. Regardless of this favored position in the social hierarchy of his time, Visconti was a sympathizer with the aims and ideals of the French Revolution and consequently was named minister of the interior of the new Roman Republic in 1798. However, after this short-lived adventure in republican government failed the following year, the Visconti family was forced to seek refuge in France. Immediately upon his arrival in Paris, Visconti was made a curator of antiquities at the Louvre; in 1802 he was elected to the Institut de France where, until his death in 1818, he produced a series of studies that made him the preeminent archaeologist in Europe and one of the luminaries of French intellectual life. These facts alone suggest that his son entered the world with a proverbial silver spoon in his mouth.

In his recently discovered and previously unpublished autobiography, Louis Visconti states that his father wished him to follow in his footsteps and become an archaeologist; having a strong aversion for ancient languages, he chose an artistic career instead.[5] In 1806 he entered the atelier of François Vincent, a major history painter and member of the Institut. After more than a year in Vincent's studio, Visconti decided to study architecture and was quickly admitted to the Ecole des Beaux-Arts as a student of Charles Percier, a member of the Institut and the most favored architect of Napoleon. He remained at the école until 1818; while winning some minor prizes, he was never successful in winning the grand prix, which would have entitled him to further his education by study in Rome. After his last attempt to win the coveted prize, he was given an uninspiring bureaucratic post at the State Wine Depot in Paris and two years later became an inspector for the construction of the Ministry of Finances on the rue de Rivoli. From there he began a multifaceted career, serving in a number of important administrative posts for the city of Paris, receiving commissions for a series of important public buildings and monuments, and conducting a lucrative private practice. He also married well, and his private residence, which the journal L'Artiste described in 1842 as a model for the home of an artist or enlightened lover of the arts, became an important cultural salon during the July Monarchy.[6] In sum, his career provides a paradigm of success for an architect and man-of-the-world in the first half of the nineteenth century.

Visconti's first major private commission was an *hôtel* in the quartier known as the Nouvelle Athènes. Begun in 1821 for the General Gouvion Saint-Cyr, the unfinished building was purchased in 1824 by Mademoiselle Mars (pseudonym for Anne Boutet), the most famous actress of the day. She then commissioned Visconti to modify the structure and complete it according to her tastes.[7] When the sumptuous residence was finished, Visconti had a very conspicuous exemplar of his architectural talent to add to his portfolio. During the next two decades he proceeded to secure a number of commissions for private residences in prestigious sections of Paris, including the Hôtel Pontalba (1839), which is today part of the American Embassy. In addition to his private dwellings, he also designed a number of funeral monuments for his wealthy clientele, the most important of which was the tomb of General Suchet (1829) at the cemetery of Père Lachaise.

Visconti launched the public half of his career in 1826 when he was appointed a member of the group responsible for the reconstruction of the Bibliothèque Nationale in Paris. Two years later he became the chief architect of the project and was closely involved with its development until 1853. On the rue de Richelieu, directly across from this national library, stood an expiatory monument begun by the Bourbon Monarchy that was unfinished at the time of the July Revolution of 1830. Naturally this project of the previous regime, loaded with reactionary implications, was destined for demolition, and in 1834 Visconti received the commission for a monumental fountain, known as the Louvois Fountain, to replace it. Shortly after commencing work on this monument, Visconti was awarded the commission for another important fountain on the rue de Richelieu, one dedicated to the great playwright Jean-Baptiste Molière. This fountain, inaugurated in 1842, was followed by yet another that is the largest in size and prominence among those he executed in Paris, the so-called Fountain of the Four Bishops, which was finally inaugurated in 1848 and is located in the square directly across from the Church of Saint-Sulpice. Although he was involved with the construction or restoration of a number of government buildings, he received the most prestigious state commission from Napoleon III in 1852 for the completion of the Louvre, or construction of galleries that would link this building with the Tuileries Palace.[8] However, he was to die the following year at the height of his power and prestige, and his plans were never to be realized in the manner he had envisioned.

In addition to his architectural practice, Visconti had a complex career as an administrator, sitting on many governmental committees and performing numerous bureaucratic functions for both the State and the city of Paris. Among these tasks was his service in the Conseil des Bâtiments civils, the state agency that reviewed the plans of all public buildings in France before authorizing their construction. However, the most important of these positions was his 1826–48 service as a *commissaire-voyer* or *architecte-voyer* for several arrondissements of Paris, an institution peculiar to France. The most literal translation of the term *architecte-voyer* is probably "architectural overseer," although in American municipal governments, "zoning commissioner" is the title of the position closest to it in function. The position of architecte-voyer was established in Paris early in the seventeenth century, but the responsibilities involved greatly expanded in the nineteenth century with the dramatic growth of the city. Among the duties of this functionary were those concerned with determining the width and direction of streets, controlling the safety and salubrity of new construction sites, and, most important, imposing regularity in height and style of buildings in the interest of aesthetic harmony.[9] The existence of this office, then, is one of the reasons Paris has its remarkable appearance of organic unity today. As can be well imagined, this position entailed endless negotiations with property owners, builders, and architects and required diplomatic skills of a high order as a primary prerequisite. The qualities Visconti brought to this job have been succinctly described by architectural historian David Van Zanten, who writes, "The fact that he exercised for twenty years the role of architecte-voyer is not foreign to his success: intermediary between the demands of the architectural project and those of the urban form, his position—which suited him admirably—was that of a negotiator. His discourse could not therefore be autocratic, nor his response intransigent: that is what made him progress (and what assured his success)."[10] It can be added that these special talents also made him the ideal person to negotiate the complex social, political, artistic, and administrative forces that surrounded the construction of the tomb of Napoleon.

However, this concept of the architect as an administrator runs contrary to deeply held ideas, both then and now, about the artistic or creative nature of the architectural profession. It was a common complaint during Visconti's lifetime that he sacrificed his individual artistic vision to the administration of a large staff of subordinates who carried out the practical work of the profession, and that his social and entrepreneurial skills overshadowed his artistic gifts. Concerning the tomb of Napoleon, many questioned how much of an artistic contribution he could be said to have made to the structure, how much of his own personal vision is embodied in it and how much was supplied by his collaborators and unseen functionaries in the fine arts bureaucracy. This verdict was recorded in 1872 in the most important architectural dictionary of the century, written by Adolphe Lance, one of Visconti's former students and assistants.

> As a man Visconti had some of the qualities and defects of his compatriots: gifted with an intelligent and gentle physiognomy, which evoked sympathy, he had in his own manner a sort of amiable cordiality, caressing and communicative, more Italian perhaps than French, which rarely failed to attain its effect . . . . Visconti was armed from head to foot to enter the battle of life, especially against we French, whose diplomatic renown is not of the first rank in the

world. . . . All this was a great strength for him and one cannot fail to recognize that this strength counted for much in his success. . . . He was not able to be and was not—in the true sense of the word— "an architect."[11]

Among the nonaesthetic abilities that made Visconti a successful architect was an understanding of the political realities of the period, the capacity to deal with a wide variety of individuals possessing strong personalities, and an ability to negotiate a range of conflicting political forces. Therefore, irrespective of the truth value of charges of lack of creativity brought against him or the problematic nature of his personal artistic contribution to the design of the tomb of Napoleon, these qualities made him the ideal choice to direct and see to completion this embattled project.

CHAPTER 2

Politics of Representation and Location

Knowledge of the political climate in France during the July Monarchy and of the diverse ways in which the hydra-headed myth of Napoleon functioned within it is of cardinal importance in excavating the meanings embedded in the tomb at the Invalides, since they directly or indirectly conditioned the choice of its design, expression, and location. Appearances being what they are, we should be skeptical of any claim that the delirious masses who lined the Champs-Elysées for Napoleon's funeral procession on 15 December 1840 necessarily represented a consensus of opinion among the French populace on the retour. There was certainly no such agreement among the members of the legislative body, many of whom had serious reservations about the wisdom of bringing Napoleon's body back to France at all. These dissenting voices, the most eloquent of which belonged to Alphonse de Lamartine, were clearly heard in the debate that took place over the funding of the project. Poet, writer, social reformer, and member of both the Academy and the Chamber of Deputies, Lamartine was someone whose opinion was greatly respected by both liberal and conservative factions in the legislature.[1] He began his discussion, which was met with great anticipation, by tactfully questioning the decision to remove Napoleon's remains from their tranquil resting place far from France, voicing the concern that perhaps not enough time had elapsed to cool the dangerous passions his memory evoked. Not being one of those who wished to substitute "the cult of force for the cult of liberty," and believing that "peace is the happiness and glory of the world," he admitted his misgivings that the return would be perceived as a glorification of war and violence. He further confessed that he did not like "men who have an official doctrine of *liberty, legality, and progress* and who take for their symbol *a sword and despotism.*" But in conclusion, since the decision had already been irrevocably made, he acquiesced and voted to allocate all the funds requested by the government.[2] Similar misgivings were expressed by Alexandre Glais-Bizoin, deputy from Loudéac and voluble member of the opposition throughout the July Monarchy. Addressing the Chamber from the benches on the extreme Left, he declared that he could support the return of Napoleon's body only on the condition that when it was disinterred, one "left in the grave bonapartist ideas, napoleonic ideas, that I consider one of the gravest wounds to our social order, as they have been the most deadly for the emancipation of the people, and as they are still today the most contrary to the independence of the human spirit."

These grave reservations concerning the decision to bring the imperial remains back to France foreshadow serious problems of representation, ones that were inevitably to arise concerning the degree of prominence or visibility of his tomb and the message that its decoration should convey. These problems were again voiced seven years later in another parliamentary address, this time before the Chamber of Peers. Count Charles de Montalembert, prolific writer, Catholic polemicist, and member of important government bodies concerned with the preservation of historic monuments, declared that he was adamantly opposed to the program for Simart's monumental bas-reliefs in the tomb representing only Napoleon's civil career: "It seems to me that these are not the memories that one should preserve; I like and admire the civil life of the consul, but not that of the emperor, who substituted despotism for order. . . . In our era, there is no need to preach despotism to us, even in public monuments."[3] Unlike Lamartine, he saw more danger residing in the civil career of Napoleon than in the carnage that his military one wreaked on Europe. The issue raised by these comments—that is, which side of Napoleon's career should be given emphasis in his funereal monument—was to trouble this project throughout its course.

David d'Angers, a vocal supporter of democratic principles and an important member of the Institut de France, likewise saw a potential danger in the return of the emperor and the values he represented. Writing in 1840 for the left wing *Almanach populaire de la France*, David, a sculptor, let his own conception of the appropriate kind of monument for Napoleon intrude upon his general discussion of the principles of sculpture:

> If one wished to erect a monument to Bonaparte, this parricidal son of the Revolution, it would be necessary to represent him with his arms crossed on the peak of a mountain formed of cadavers, cannons, flags and broken caissons; all this debris would be piled up in such a way as to give a throne to each of the members of his family. At the base of this mountain one would sculpt the soldiers of the Republic cursing and threatening him with menacing gestures.

Later in the essay he returned to the subject of Napoleon, maintaining that "under the Empire, the despotism of this new Caesar gave the arts a direction entirely opposed to their true aim."[4] And in a letter written during the 1840s the sculptor expressed similar views:

> I don't regret not receiving the commission for the monument to Napoleon; That man did so much damage to Liberty! He showed so little nobleness toward the nation that confided to him its most precious interests, with so much generosity! In truth, there is in his memory enough to paralyze the heart of a republican. However, considering Napoleon from a poetic point of view, he is a great man and will occupy a large place in history. From this point of view he enters the domain of the arts, which will perpetuate his features.

A visual equivalent of this written condemnation is found in an undated sketch by David, which represents megalomaniacal ambition and its dreadful human consequences (fig. 15).[5] On the left one sees the mountain of cadavers and cannons heaped up in the form of a hill. At the pinnacle of this testimony to the destructive forces of war stands Napoleon Bonaparte, arms crossed and confidently surveying the carnage for which he is responsible. But at the same time this sketch reveals the deep-seated ambiguity in David's attitude to the memory of Napoleon that was shared by many of his compatriots, possibly a harbinger of the difficulties that were to arise in choosing the appropriate design for his tomb or deciding how he was to be represented for the ages to come. In the upper right of David's drawing is found a different and totally contradictory aspect of the myth of the emperor. Sitting atop the lonely rock of Saint Helena, as it was commonly referred to at the time, isolated against the starry sky and the ocean in the background, he is here represented under the

Fig. 15
Pierre-Jean David d'Angers, untitled drawing, c. 1840. Musée
d'Angers. Photo courtesy of
J. de Caso.

sign of the outcast Prometheus, a figure often invoked in prose
and poetry of the day celebrating Napoleon's memory. As the
mythical Prometheus, Napoleon was condemned to suffer for either human progress or for France's military glories, depending
upon who was recounting the myth. An example of this equation
of the ancient and the modern god is found in Edgar Quinet's
epic poem of 1835, entitled "Napoléon":[6]

> Du nouveau Prométhée ils ont ouvert le flanc;
> Le vautour d'Albion boit lentement son sang.
> Au loin, le roc est nu; la maremme, homicide;
> L'arbre à gomme africain y jette une ombre aride;
> Et debout sur le seuil, comme fait un geôlier,
> L'Océan, sans dormir, garde son prisonnier.

They have opened the side of the new Prometheus;
The vulture of Albion slowly drinks his blood.
In the distance, the rock is naked; the marsh, homicide;
The african gum tree casts an arid shadow on it;
And standing on the threshold, like a jailer,
the ocean sleeplessly guards its prisoner.

Below this section of David's sketch is another representing a
still different aspect of the Napoleonic myth: the great man tilling
the fields on the island of Saint Helena. This vignette makes a
direct reference to an anecdote recounted in Count de Las Cases's
famous *Mémorial de Sainte-Hélène* (1823) in which, during a
horseback ride on the island, Napoleon dismounted, took a plow
from a peasant, and tilled a perfect furrow, demonstrating his
closeness to both the soil and those who work it. In so doing he
placed his myth under the sign of the *soldat-labourer* or the sad
Cincinnatus, a powerful topos in French culture from the Restoration until the end of the century.[7] The anecdote summons up
the figure of the legendary Roman general Cincinnatus, who after achieving many victories on the field of battle returned to his
plow to cultivate the peaceful art of agriculture and pastoral virtues. This story is also emblematic of the main thrust of Las
Cases's book, which was to rewrite the Napoleonic legend, laying
stress on the democratic sympathies and ideals of the emperor as
revealed in conversations during his exile. It also dovetails with
the outpouring of popular literature during the Restoration representing Napoleon as a man of the people, an example being
Béranger's *chanson* "Les Souvenirs du peuple," which was republished numerous times during the century and illustrated by
Raffet, Charlet, and other graphic artists. Thus, abutting one another on the sketch are various aspects of the Napoleonic myth
and its positive and negative poles, between which opinion continually oscillated in discussions of his legacy. One might see this
either as David's lucubration over the difficulties of finding any
one form appropriate for a monument to Napoleon or as his attempt to sketch the parameters of the problem.

While some in France brought Greek mythology to bear on
the fate of Napoleon, others invoked Egypt and its monuments as
more appropriate to describe his place in world cosmologies.
Such was the case of Louis Geoffroy, who in a lengthy tome,
Napoléon apocryphe: Histoire de la conquête du monde et de la

monarchie universelle, first published in 1836 and reissued in 1841, provided his imaginary account of the appropriate funeral monument for the immortal Napoleon. Geoffroy described a tomb that Napoleon might have chosen for himself had he not had the misfortune to die a prisoner of the English: it would have been constructed by carving Mont Valerian, a large hill on the banks of the Seine just outside Paris, into the form of a colossal pyramid decorated only with Napoleon's name in gold letters, a monument scaled to the size of the colossus it honored. Thus, France would have been provided with a pharaonic monument to rival those at Giza and one suitable to honor a descendant of the sun god Ra. More than being just an interesting fantasy, this passage reveals what many in France believed: that an appropriate monument to Napoleon, before all else, must be colossal.

The supernatural aspects of Napoleon were celebrated in reams of cheap newsprint and popular images, and many of widely different professions and backgrounds seriously believed that the divine principle had been reincarnated in the nineteenth century in the person of Napoleon. Equations of Christ and Napoleon were commonplace in all manner of popular literature in the 1830s and 1840s. The lonely rock at Saint Helena was frequently compared with the hill at Calvary upon which Christ met his end. Among the many evocations of the Christ-Napoleon of the period, one might cite a verse from an anonymous popular song:

Jésus, par sa puissance
Sauva le paien par le péché perdu.
Napoléon sauva la France;
Comme Jésus il fut vendu
A la suite d'odieuses peines,
Jésus sur une croix mourut:
Napoléon, à Sainte-Hélène,
A souffert comme Jésus.[8]

Jesus, by his strength
Saved the pagan, lost in sin,
Napoleon saved France;
Like Jesus he was sold
After odious sufferings,
Jesus died on the cross:
Napoleon at Saint Helena,
Has suffered like Jesus.

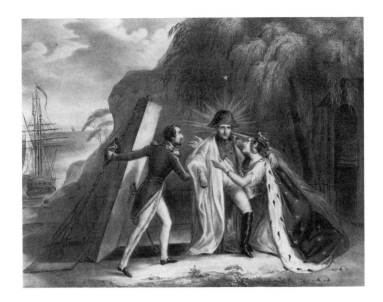

Fig. 16
*France and the Prince de Joinville
at the Tomb of Saint Helena.*
G. Tassaert, design. A. Urrty,
lithograph, 1840. Photo courtesy
of the Bibliothèque Nationale,
Département des Estampes.

Horace Vernet adopted this christological comparison when he
executed a painting to commemorate the retour des cendres,
which was modeled on the Christian prototype of the Resurrection. The iconography of the Resurrection was used in many Napoleonic prints of 1840, an example being one by Gustave
Tassaert representing the Prince de Joinville assisted by a dia-
demed figure of France (fig. 16).

Another anonymous lithograph of the period, intended for a
large audience, modified the iconography of the Resurrection to
give it a different function and meaning (fig. 17).[9] This image
relates directly to the political climate in France at the time and
to its foreign policy. As he rises from the tomb, Napoleon proffers
a sword to the waiting personification of France. In the background, partially obscured by the light of his star, is the dome
of the Invalides. The caption makes it clear that the sword should
be used to confront France's enemies and that the legend of
Napoleon is one that could erupt over them like a volcano:

Tremblez tous! Rois ligués!! . . . car de sa tombe ouverte,
S'élance le volcan, qui sur vous fulmina.
L'épée du grand héros, à la France est offerte! . . .
Tremblez!! . . . qu'il vous souvienne! Austerlitz, Jéna!!

Fig. 17
Anonymous, *Tremble All! Kings in League with One Another! Because of his Open Tomb* . . . Lithograph, 1840. Photo courtesy of the Bibliothèque Nationale, Département des Estampes.

Tremble everyone! Kings united!! . . . because from his open tomb, the volcano erupts, which will explode over you.
The sword of the great hero is offered to France! . . .
Tremble!! . . . he will remember you! Austerlitz, Jena!!

Why individuals such as the publisher of this print believed and hoped that the retour des cendres would promote a foreign war can be explained by what was known as "The Eastern Question."[10] In 1839 war had broken out once again in the Middle East between the Sultan of Turkey and Mehemet Ali, Pasha of Egypt, who was an ally of France and, for various reasons, something of a legend in his own right. When the allied powers—England, Austria, Prussia, and Russia—signed a treaty on 15 July 1840 to support the Sultan with military force if necessary, an outcry of protest erupted in France in favor of Mehemet Ali along with a chorus of hatred for France's former conquerors. A demand that France enter the war on the side of the Egyptian accompanied this outpouring of bile. The odious treaty was likened by many to the Treaty of Paris of 1815 with which the same four powers inflicted heavy penalties on France. Among these were the loss of the lower Rhenish valley and the territory conquered by the Revolutionary Army of 1792. Thus, the widespread war fever in favor of the pasha was largely motivated by the nationalist desire for revenge. But the demand that France go to war to regain the Rhineland and her lost possessions contained criticism, whether implicit or explicit, of the government of Louis-Philippe for its passive acceptance of this state of affairs. This was the thrust of Edgar Quinet's pamphlet *1815 et 1840*, published in November 1840, which charged that the July Monarchy had "voluntarily put a seal on the defeat" by its pusillanimous refusal to take action against its foreign enemies.[11]

While many caught up in the rabid nationalism of the period were undoubtedly acting on a purely visceral level, a substantial number of figures on the Left looked upon a war in the Middle East or in the Rhineland as an occasion for a social revolution within the borders of France herself, one that would create an alliance between the army and the proletariat and also turn the guns around and overthrow the bourgeois monarchy of Louis-Philippe. Heinrich Heine, perceiving this to be the ulterior motive of many calling for France to go to war, wrote from Paris in November 1840:

> Threats of war with the new coalition endanger not only the throne of the king, but also the reign of the bourgeoisie, which Louis-Philippe represents in law and in fact. . . . The bourgeoisie . . . would certainly be too weak to withstand the shock if the enemy attacked with forces four times greater. Before an invasion ever occurred, the bourgeoisie would abdicate; the lower classes would assume their place once again, as in the frightful nineties, but better organized, with a clearer conception of their goal, with new doctrines, new gods, new earthly and celestial forces. . . .

One should qualify Heine's generalization to some degree, however, by stressing that there were many members of the middle classes who were as bellicose as any member of the revolutionary Left, and that the opposition to a war against the allied powers was strongest among those who had the most to lose, the industrial bourgeoisie.[12]

This belligerent discourse received its most memorable visualization in the work of Nicolas-Toussaint Charlet, an ardent bonapartist and the best-known graphic artist in France. His prints were in a series of lithographs published by Villain in the fall of 1840. One of these overt calls for war, entitled *La Marseillaise* after the famous martial hymn, depicts a soldier on the shoulders of a burly worker ripping down a poster with the words "Treaties of 1815" written on it, while another soldier points to graffiti on a wall proclaiming "Our old frontiers or death" (fig. 18). The

Fig. 18
Nicolas-Toussaint Charlet. *The Marseillaise*, Lithograph, 1840. Photo courtesy of the Bibliothèque Nationale, Département des Estampes.

censor found this too inflammatory and, on 22 August 1840, forbade its publication, but this did not prevent Charlet from continuing his campaign in support of war in both the Middle East and the Rhineland in numerous other prints, only some of which passed the censor. A print approved by the censor on 13 October 1840 represents an old soldier, bearing the features of Charlet himself, in the studio of a young painter criticizing a military painting on his easel on the grounds that "Your figure of France raises her arm but doesn't strike" (fig. 19).[13] Directly behind the military man is a bust of Napoleon.

Fig. 19
Nicolas-Toussaint Charlet, *The Advice of the Master*. Lithograph, 1840. Photo courtesy of the Bibliothèque Nationale, Département des Estampes.

Although Charlet considered himself an *homme du peuple* and a supporter of the cause of the proletariat, his art was greatly admired by certain influential members of the upper bourgeois such as Adolphe Thiers.[14] An enthusiast for the legend of Napoleon and a prolific historian who eulogized the French victories during the Empire, and as one of the most bellicose statesmen of the century, Thiers felt a natural affinity for the content of Charlet's lithographs. It is clear that in both intemperate rhetoric and exercise of the powers of his office he abetted the war hysteria during the crisis over the Eastern Question. However, inasmuch as Thiers's militarist rhetoric was completely contrary to the desire for peace of the industrial bourgeoisie and the so-called Doctrinaire party, which represented their interests in parliament, one could have predicted that his days in office would be numbered.

When the clamor for war reached alarming proportions, Louis-Philippe finally refused to support Thiers's attempts to obtain additional funds for the military buildup; this act forced the resignation of Thiers. He then appointed François Guizot as minister of foreign affairs and unofficial prime minister on 29 October 1840. At the same time Duchâtel, an able administrator and member of the Doctrinaire party, replaced Rémusat as interior minister. Guizot promptly instituted a policy known as the *paix armée* (armed peace) and diligently pursued a peaceful foreign policy. This shift in direction combined with military reverses suffered by Mehemet Ali, which made it evident that the media in France had greatly exaggerated his strength, cooled the fever for war to some degree.

One question immediately posed by the retour des cendres is why Louis-Philippe, a constitutional monarch of the Orléans line, brought Napoleon's body back to France at all instead of leaving it in the poetic isolation of Saint Helena. It seems unlikely that, despite the popular sentiment that Napoleon's corpse should be wrested from the English, he thought it a matter of necessity inasmuch as he must have known that many would have serious reservations about the adventure. Rather than being an instigator, he appears to have acquiesced to the suggestions of his chief minister, Adolphe Thiers, an opinion commonly advanced in the press of the day.[15]

But the act also falls within the deliberate political strategy adhered to by Louis-Philippe and by politicians such as Thiers and

Guizot, who labeled it the *juste milieu*. Advocates of this political philosophy held that the wisest course for a government that wished to stay in power was to attempt to occupy a *via media* between competing political and social ideologies and to promote a representation of the July Monarchy as a regime that encompassed and mediated opposing political positions. The single most conspicuous visual representation of this strategy is the great museum that Louis-Philippe began at Versailles in 1831. When he came to power, the château of Versailles was in a state of great disrepair and in need of restoration. However, instead of restoring it to its original state at the end of the reign of Louis XVI, he proceeded to convert the complex of buildings into a museum illustrating the history of France from the reign of Clovis to that of his own. Within the museum separate rooms were dedicated to the career of Napoleon and to the Empire period. The motto above the entrance summarized the official policy behind the project: *To All The Glories Of France*. The implicit message in the program was that the July Monarchy was strong enough to display the glories of its ideological adversaries and of encompassing within its juste-milieu synthesis *all* aspects of the past and all the social divisions it had witnessed. It said that unity could be achieved by remembering rather than forgetting the past, and that Napoleon was a major part of that past. Thus, the act of bringing Napoleon's body back to France might be considered Louis-Philippe's assertion that he was strong or secure enough to bring a major ideological adversary into his synthetic embrace.

Louis-Philippe also probably believed that relatively little threat was posed to his reign by bonapartists, despite the emotional charge surrounding the memory of Napoleon, because bonapartism was an amorphous belief system, not a coherent political theory, and it had no specific program—other than to put a member of the Bonaparte family in a position of power in France and restore France's tarnished glory—and no specific organizational structure. He would have been further confirmed in his belief that bonapartism had little effective political force after the miserable failure of Louis-Napoleon—exiled uncle of Napoleon I and next in line in the order of succession of the Bonaparte dynasty—to stage a *coup d'état* in 1836. However, even if bonapartism was not an effective political force at the time, the rampant chauvinism that the Eastern Question evoked

Fig. 20
Napoléon Thomas, *The Translation of the Ashes of Napoleon to the Invalides.* Lithograph, 1840. A. S. K. Brown Collection, Brown University. Photo: the author.

proved that the myth of Napoleon could be appropriated and turned to dangerous ends by various opposition groups. Thus, by the fall of 1840, Louis-Philippe must have had second thoughts about his decision. But once the agreement had been signed with the English, he had no choice but to return Napoleon's body in a manner befitting his myth.

In striking contrast to the paucity of literature on the construction of the tomb, the retour des cendres has been the subject of much scholarship, the work of Jean Boisson being the definitive study.[16] The first act was the departure of the Prince de Joinville, Louis-Philippe's third son, for Saint Helena from the port of Toulon on 7 July 1840 to repatriate the body. This mission finally accomplished, the ship and the remains of the emperor returned to the harbor of Cherbourg on 30 November. There the body and casket were transferred to a steamboat and carried up the Seine, stopping at several cities en route, finally arriving at its destination at Courbevoie on the morning of 15 December. Leaving Courbevoie, the funeral cortege passed under the Arc de Triomphe and continued down the Champs-Elysées, across the Seine and on to the Church of the Invalides. All social classes lined the route of the parade; they stood for hours to get the best view on one of the coldest winter days most could remember. More than ten meters high, drawn by sixteen black horses, and covered with allegorical sculpture, the funeral chariot transported the casket in its interior, while a cenotaph, supported by twelve victory figures executed after the models of Jean-Jacques Feuchère, was displayed at the top of the assemblage (fig. 20).[17] Finally, upon reaching the Church of the Invalides, the casket was removed from the mobile sculpture and placed in a monumental catafalque directly under the central cupola. It remained there, on display for enormous numbers of visitors, for a short time before being moved to the chapel in the dome dedicated to Saint Jerome, where it was to rest for another two decades.

Enhancing the pomp and circumstance were scores of temporary plaster statues of allegorical figures and historical personages executed by sculptors from the full spectrum of artistic talent of the day. These lined the Champs-Elysées, the Place de la Concorde, and the esplanade of the Invalides (fig. 21). A fact

Fig. 21
Victor Adam, *Arrival of the Funeral Cortege at the Esplanade of the Invalides*. Lithograph, 1840. A. S. K. Brown Collection. Photo: the author.

significant for the later construction of the tomb is that Louis Visconti was charged with supervising this sculptural program and the temporary decoration for the great ceremony. He was assisted by fellow architect Henri Labrouste, who appears to have developed the details for the ensemble. The program consisted of three parts: on the Champs-Elysées the statues represented the Napoleonic victories, stressing the career of Bonaparte the soldier; on the bridge linking the Place de la Concorde and the Chamber of Deputies were placed standard allegorical figures of virtues and aspects of social life; and on the esplanade of the Invalides was arranged an encyclopedic assemblage of figures from French history. In the center of the esplanade stood the plaster model for François Bosio's huge standing statue of Napoleon in imperial regalia, installed on the Column of the Grande Armée at Boulogne in 1841.[18]

From an aesthetic point of view the most important part of the sculptural decoration was the collection of thirty-two plaster statues, each five meters in height, distributed on either side of the esplanade before the Invalides complex. The strategy for selecting famous individuals from French history to be represented seems to have been the same one informing the decoration at Versailles: to include all aspects of French history from Clovis to the present. Thus, one saw effigies of such personages as Jeanne d'Arc, Louis XIV, and Henri IV, as well as Napoleonic generals such as Mortier, who had died five years earlier in the assassination attempt against Louis-Philippe. That an intent to honor Napoleon specifically was not behind the sculptural program might be inferred from the inclusion of the duc d'Enghien, the seventeenth-century soldier better known as the Grand Condé; among the more notorious deeds of Napoleon was the assassination of the Grand Condé's direct lineal descendant in 1804. Thus, the message of the works chosen for the esplanade seems to have been that Napoleon was part of this serial history, not a being apart from or above it, as many wished to believe.

The ceremony, which had the structure of a liturgical ritual, was at odds with the outpouring of emotion and jingoist rhetoric from many of the observers and certain military units who lustily sang *La Marseillaise* all along the route. This militaristic euphoria was captured by Aimé Lemud's lithograph *Le Retour en France*, executed more than two weeks before the actual event

Fig. 22
Aimé Lemud, *The Return to France*. Lithograph, 1840. Photo courtesy of the Davison Art Center, Wesleyan University, Middletown, Connecticut.

(fig. 22).[19] In this visionary print, the casket of the emperor is borne directly on the shoulders of veterans of the Grand Armée, and the use of a mediating triumphal carriage is dispensed with as spectral warriors swarm around it evoking the sound and fury of the battlefield. To amplify the message of the image a legend was provided in the form of three lines from Victor Hugo's jingoist poem "A La Colonne," written in October 1830, in which the poet had imagined the return of Napoleon's body and the resurgence of militarist *élan* it would provoke.[20]

The retour des cendres generated a veritable deluge of prints and popular illustrations of all kinds, among them many diametrically opposed visual interpretations of its significance. In contrast to images such as Lemud's, celebrating the dynamism of the Napoleonic myth and excluding any reference to monarchical traditions, others took a very different tack. An image that contains a message much different from Lemud's is a lithograph after a drawing of Gustave Tassaert, a sequel to his representation of the resurrection of Napoleon (fig. 16). Here the Prince de Join-ville sits calmly at the tiller of the allegorical funeral vessel, while Napoleon's body is depicted rigidly horizontal in a profile view that stresses his immobility (fig. 23). The verse in the caption underneath amplifies its meaning: Napoleon, having opened his eyes, sighs, "My force is exhausted, everything is becoming dim." In contrast, the verse concludes by declaring that "One day the Prince will recount his exploits / Worthy, everything promises it, of an offshoot of Kings." The prince, representing the Orleans Monarchy of Louis-Philippe, has clearly taken over the ship of state formerly under the control of Napoleon and steadfastly guides it to its destination, represented by the dome of the Invalides, where the usurper will be laid permanently to rest.

Fig. 23
The Final Return of Napoleon.
Gustave Tassaert, design. A. Urrty, lithograph, 1840. Photo courtesy of the Bibliothèque Nationale, Département des Estampes.

Hence, this image and that of Lemud represent different political ideologies and aspirations of differing political factions and class loyalties in France, but the message in each work is conveyed by form as well as imagery. Lemud's print is animated by a rising diagonal movement that moves from the lower right to upper left and gives the work its expression of ascendency. On the other hand, the image of Tassaert, with the ship and the body of Napoleon aligned parallel to the horizontal frame of the print, expresses stasis and inertia. Put more simply, the one represents Napoleon under the sign of verticality and the other horizontality—a distinction important to remember in the later debate over the proper form of the tomb.

That the terminal point or destination of this funeral cortege was the Church of the Invalides seems to have provoked little dissent, but when the question was raised as to whether it should be the temporary resting place or the final one, there was widespread disagreement among the respondents. The issue of the location was to become the subject of intense debate in the following months and to remain one until the final inauguration of the monument.

Alternative sites for the tomb and the implications they contained were weighed carefully in the famous address of Lamartine to the Chambers on 26 May. He declared that the site chosen by the government was not final, despite the finality of tone in Rémusat's proclamation, and proceeded to rule out the Invalides as a site. His reason was not its unsuitability but his belief that bonapartists would be constantly agitating to have it moved if it were placed at the Invalides:

> No, his last tomb will not be there; his fanatics tell us that in advance. He is legitimate; they wish a royal tomb for him, a unique tomb. To place their emperor among the soldiers, that is beautiful for a warrior, but is too little for a sovereign. . . . they see only the forfeiture of the throne in this choice of a sepulcher.

Next, he addressed the Vendôme Column. In his opinion its central position in the city would make it a focal point for all sorts of seditions and invite bonapartist rallies. For the same reasons he discounted the Church of the Madeleine. He was equally opposed to the Basilica of Saint-Denis on the grounds that it asserted too forcefully his links with France's royal past, "relations that history and even the stones ought to avoid." The Arc de Triomphe was judged to be too pagan, and his tomb there would prevent any future displays of military triumph: "What future general would dare pass in triumph over the tomb of Napoleon?"[21] The July Column, which had been proposed by some, was similarly discarded as inappropriate, since there was no obvious relation between Napoleon and the July Revolution.

Having eliminated most of the locations that were being bruited about at the time, he proposed as the best solution a new monument "to Napoleon alone on the Champ de Mars . . . where his statue and his spirit will still be passed by revues of our soldiers departing and returning." In his opinion, Napoleon's tomb should be isolated in whatever location was chosen; for one reason, he was singular and deserved a singular monument. Most of all, he should be separated from other national traditions. This would demonstrate that France could judge as well as honor its great men, that she knew how "to separate herself . . . from those who menace her in his name, and that in raising a monument she wishes to resuscitate the cinders neither of war, nor tyranny, nor the legitimists, nor the pretenders, nor the imitators."[22] The covert message beneath Lamartine's carefully chosen words was that the appropriate location for the tomb should be an isolated one on the periphery of the city, removed from its daily life. In short, for him the monument would dramatically affect, or pollute, any central place in the city in which it was placed. Thus, the ideal location was one that would serve as a place of *quarantine.*

In the months following Lamartine's speech the tomb was to become a subject of intense polemic. In this passionate discourse the fundamental issues were the closely interrelated ones of the location of the monument, the degree of its prominence or visibility, and whether it should be incorporated into an existing structure or have an autonomous presence. All three of these issues were directly related to the crucial question of how conspicuous a part it was to have in the urban fabric and symbolic economy of Paris. They were also closely connected to the meanings that the monument would express or embody.

If the aim of the government had been simply to stress Napoleon's military exploits at the expense of his civil career

and his dynastic claims, the choice of the Vendôme Column as a tomb site might have served this end well. The column, commemorating the victory at the Battle of Austerlitz, was commissioned by Napoleon in 1806 and inaugurated in 1810 (fig. 24). On the summit was placed Chaudet's colossal statue of Napoleon dressed as a Roman emperor. One of the first acts of the Bourbon restoration in 1814 had been to remove Chaudet's statue from this hated monument and replace it with a flag bearing *fleurs de lis*. When he assumed power in 1830, Louis-Philippe was almost obliged to negate this act of the Bourbons by placing Napoleon's effigy on the column once again, but significantly in Emile Seurre's effigy he was dressed as Bonaparte the General rather than Napoleon I, Emperor of France (fig. 25). In the program for the 1831 contest held to select a sculptor, it was specifically

Fig. 24
View of the Vendôme Column, Place Vendôme. Lepère and Gondoin, architects. Photo courtesy of Lauros-Giraudon.

Fig. 25
Emile Seurre, *Napoleon on the Column 28 July 1833*. Engraving after his statue, from A. Tardieu, *La Colonne*. A. S. K. Brown Collection. Photo: the author.

stated that inasmuch as the figures on the bas-reliefs on the column were in military dress, the figure of Napoleon should be likewise.[23]

Locating the tomb at the Place Vendôme would have satisfied a popular demand heard as early as 1821 in a pamphlet by an old soldier of the Grande Armée that discussed the various possible sites and concluded that the Vendôme Column was "the only monument worthy to receive your ashes."[24] But Thiers and Rémusat were probably dissuaded from this location for several rea-

sons. The column occupied a large open area near the center of
Paris that was close to the major boulevards and had already been
the scene of mass demonstrations during the Revolution. In one
of these demonstrations the equestrian statue of Louis XIV, occupying the center of the square, had been pulled down; as a consequence the Place Vendôme had acquired a democratic
coloration that was only heightened in 1832, when it was the focus of demonstrations against the government. Because of these
populist associations, Frédéric Soulié, the prolific novelist, sympathizer with liberal causes, and founder of the periodical, *Napoléon; journal anecdotique et biographique de l'Empire et de la
Grande Armée,* urged that it be selected for the burial site in a
brochure he published in 1840.[25] Soulié preferred to promote the
part of the Napoleonic myth that made Napoleon the Emperor of
the People, or the Father of Equality. Under this guise the hallowed column was the most appropriate place for his body:

> Remember also that equality was the law under his reign; it is because
> of this that he is our hero; it is for this reason that he has remained so
> great and so revered in our memories; it is for this that there is in our
> hearts an enthusiastic and profound cult for his memory; for this rea-
> son his tomb ought to be equally accessible to the smallest and to the
> largest person, to the poorest and the richest, to the last as well as to
> the first in our nation; it is for this reason that we men of the people,
> we do not wish to need a special favor to be able to go and kneel by
> the sepulcher of our emperor of all.[26]

A visual equivalent of this populist rhetoric directed toward the
Vendôme Column might be found in a lithograph by Charlet
that was approved by the censor on 22 September 1840 (fig.
26).[27] A burly man-of-the-people, ubiquitous in Charlet's prints,
salutes the statue of Napoleon on the column, giving it biblical
significance by proclaiming it to be the people's "Song of Songs."
Attempting to ignore this homage to the great man is a teaching
brother of the LaSalle order, who serves as a reminder of the
alliance of throne and altar during the Restoration. Given the
timing of this print, it might be considered Charlet's vote for a
tomb site.

The hope or fantasy held by many that Napoleon's body would
be permanently installed in the base of the Vendôme Column
was illustrated in a book of poetry published in 1840, but at the

Fig. 26
Nicolas-Toussaint Charlet, *Make Them Sing to the Column!* . . . Lithograph, 1840. Photo courtesy of the Bibliothèque Nationale, Département des Estampes.

same time given a sinister turn (fig. 27). The chief irony in this image of Napoleon peacefully sleeping in his coffin lies in the contrast between the caption, "It is thus that he would be delivered to our wishes and our admiration," and the content of the accompanying poem, part of which was reproduced below it. Instead of being a celebration of Napoleon, this *Lune parisienne* by an active but obscure author named Cuisin is a warning about the violent potential that the act would carry. The poet hoped that Napoleon's return would not engender war and violence or put his heirs on a throne—that "in evoking the giants of the

C'EST AINSI QU'IL SERAIT RENDU A NOS VOEUX ET A NOTRE ADMIRATION!!

Eug. André

Craindrait-on que ce voeu, qu'il fit à son trépas,
Se changeât dans l'Europe, en signal de combats,
Que son coeur ranimé sous ce bronze de gloire,
Ne palpitât encor de rêves de victoire;
Que dans la nuit, de bout, armé de ses regards,
Il ne plongeât le globe en de nouveaux hasards,
Où un lambris trop étroit pour ce squelette immense,
Ne craquât en débris sous sa vaste puissance,
Que d'un coude athlétique ébranlant son tombeau,
A son crâne il ne mît son magique chapeau,
Et qu'évoquant enfin les géants de l'empire,
Il fît de la colonne un trône à son délire!!...y.

4e lune parisienne.

Lith. de C. Adrien, R. Richer g.

Fig. 27
Eugène André, *It is thus that he would be delivered to our wishes and our admiration*. Illustration in P. Cuisin, *Les lunes poétiques*, 1840. Photo courtesy of the Bibliothèque Nationale.

Empire/ He would make the column a throne for his delirium."
In issuing this warning, Cuisin was only giving an ironical twist to the message found in several of his anti-Napoleonic tracts written during the Restoration that contain condemnations of such things as "the criminal magic of imperial terrorism."[28]

Although Cuisin concluded the section in his Lune parisienne with the judgment that the power of the Napoleonic myth had passed—"Its luster is lost for having shined too much"—such was not the opinion of the agent who supplied Rémusat with police reports on the reaction in Paris to the announcement of the retour and the choice of the Invalides as the place of final repose. Before the bill was voted on in the Chambers, he warned that for a variety of different reasons, republicans, legitimists, and bonapartists were all opposed to the selection of the Invalides and would attempt to use it as an issue to provoke demonstrations. In a report on the opinions of the student population in the Latin Quarter, he maintained that the republican opposition demanded that the Vendôme Column be the site; "if you do the contrary," they declared, "take care, the people are of our opinion."[29]

It is difficult today to visit the Place Vendôme, where one finds a center of the international diamond trade and the Hotel Ritz, and imagine that it could have been perceived as a public space of "Le Peuple." Even in the eighteenth century this square and the immediately adjacent buildings had housed the wealthy and was a place of opulence. However, this concentration of the affluent was immediately subtended by one of the more sinister slums in Paris, a situation that occurred in other areas of the city as well.[30] This lower-class section lay between the rue de Richelieu and the present Avenue de l'Opéra. Hence, one of the effects of Hausmann's creation of the Avenue de l'Opéra in the Second Empire was to segregate the area from the Place Vendôme. What seems clear then is that the government's rejection of the Place Vendôme was based on both political and pragmatic reasons. The site was much too visible, and there was too little remove from the life of the city and the social classes to whom the myth of Napoleon of the People most appealed.

Some writers suggested another column in a more proletarian quarter as an appropriate site. This is the Colonne de Juillet, occupying the center of the Place de la Bastille, which was inaugurated on 28 July 1840. The monument, begun on the designs of Jean-Antoine Alavoine and then revised and completed by Louis Duc, was intended to commemorate the Revolution of 1830 and be a mausoleum for those who died in the fighting (fig. 28). The meaning of the monument is summarized by the flam-

Fig. 28
View of the July Column, Place
de la Bastille. Alavoine and Duc,
architects. Dedicated 1840. Photo:
the author.

boyant corinthian capital, crammed with exuberant, symbolic detail, which crowns the column. An article published in *Magazin
pittoresque* in 1840 captured its dominant expression:

one can see that which is elegant and triumphal in this column; this
part is the capital. The Vendôme Column, covered with rich sculptures, does not need this ornament. Mr. Duc, on the contrary, has
put all the exuberance of his column in the coiffure that he designed

for it. . . . The lower part of this capital is ornamented with a row of palm fronds which are like the echo of a mournful cry rising to the heavens; above this begins a melange of victory symbols. In the middle of bounding vegetation, which gives support to the volutes of the angles, one sees the extremities the basket of which we have recognized the trace in the lower regions of the column. It is from the interior of this basket that are deployed the powerful thrusts that support the abacus. But around this festive basket four children with an audacious allure do an animated round dance, placing their feet on the funereal leaves, holding in their hands celebratory garlands, holding their heads up above those of the lion, which are flanked by two triumphal leaves comprising the finials.[31]

Judging from this description, it was clearly recognized at the time that this monument was basically celebratory in nature, with the civilians who fell in July 1830 while attempting to overturn the Bourbon Monarchy being those celebrated. This festive and decorative capital establishes the monument as an antitype to the severe architecture and sculptural decoration of the Vendôme Column and austere military values it represents.

The opposed systems of values exemplified by these columns was expressed in an imaginary dialogue between the two monuments published in 1840 in the radical republican *Almanach populaire de la France*. In the skit the columns hold an animated conversation, each explaining what it represents.[32] The July Column claims as its greatest accomplishments "the protection we have accorded to industry, which has sunk mines and established railroads everywhere . . . the institution of stock shares, the steam engine, the daguerreotype," and continues, "we have no exterior politics, we love peace at any price." Thus, the author of the dialogue juxtaposes austerity and self-sacrifice for communal and national goals, suggested by the Vendôme Column, with celebration of abundance and wealth brought by peaceful free enterprise, a metonomy of which might be Duc's capital. The incongruity of suggesting that Napoleon be interred in this monument, conceived as an antithesis to the Vendôme Column, was readily apparent, and proposals that he be buried there can be considered as either a challenge to the ruling ideology of the July Monarchy or as an attempt to bring the Napoleonic legacy within its eclectic embrace. However, given the strong opposition to the rule of Louis-Philippe at the time, one can well imagine the outcry that would have occurred had the citizen-king converted this monument to the heroic citizenry of Paris into the tomb of an emperor. On the other hand, it is inconceivable that Louis-Philippe would have chosen to dedicate this monument, honoring a revolution he claimed to represent, to the memory of a much different kind of ruler.

The Church of the Madeleine was another site some believed appropriate to receive Napoleon's remains (fig. 29). This church, whose present form is that of a roman peripteral temple, was begun in 1764 by Contant d'Ivry and was under construction at the same time as the Place Louis XV, today known as the Place de la Concorde, which it overlooks down the rue Royale. At the time of the French Revolution the church was not finished, and work on it was suspended as much discussion took place over its most appropriate function. Under the Empire, Napoleon considered

Fig. 29
Church of the Madeleine, Paris, south facade. Vignon, architect. Photo courtesy of Lauros-Giraudon.

several different destinations for the unfinished building and finally determined to erect on the site a "Temple de la Gloire," or a military pantheon to celebrate the heroes of Napoleonic victories. He then commissioned Pierre Vignon to redesign the building. However, when the Restoration came to power it was decided to convert Vignon's structure to a church and place in it an expiatory monument to Louis XVI. The building was essentially complete at the inauguration of the July Monarchy, and after some hesitation it was finally decided to retain its original religious function. The church was then richly embellished with a decorative program of mural painting and sculpture. It should be stressed, however, that at the time of the return of Napoleon's remains, it had not been inaugurated and was still able to be used for another function.

The history of this building conferred strong Napoleonic associations upon it, but its close proximity to the Place de la Concorde heightened them even more when the famous Obelisk of Luxor, a gift of Mehemet Ali, was erected there in 1836. Looking north down the rue Royale, it directly bisects the facade of the Madeleine and occupies one of the four cardinal points on the great cross axis where the July Monarchy concentrated most of its decorative energies and financial resources. It was commonly believed at the time that the erection of the monument fulfilled a project originally conceived by Napoleon himself, a fact insisted on by many popular broadsheets distributed all over France. One of these illustrated brochures, for example, proclaimed that the obelisk "had been constructed under Ramses II, king of Egypt . . . a reign that can be compared in all its aspects to the one of Napoleon."[33]

The relationship of the Madeleine to Napoleon was only accentuated when Jules-Claude Ziegler's mural painting was unveiled in the apse in 1838 (fig. 30). The commission for this work of truly heroic dimensions was originally given to Paul Delaroche in 1833 but for various reasons was withdrawn two years later by Adolphe Thiers—then minister of the interior—and given to Ziegler, one of Ingres's most promising students.[34] There seems to be little doubt that Thiers had a significant role in the formulation of the program that represents the triumph of christianity in the east and west. Despite the all-embracing theme of the work and its panoply of historic personages, the most conspicuous fig-

ure is that of Napoleon in the immediate foreground, who forms the cameo of the historical bracelet and is juxtaposed to Christ at the opposite pole. Napoleon's relationship to the Catholic church is represented by two historic acts combined in one vignette: the coronation of Napoleon by Pius VII and the conclusion of the Concordat in 1802, which re-established Roman Catholicism as the religion of the French and restored certain traditional prerogatives. After the completion of this mural, the imprint of Napoleon was stamped on the edifice in the most graphic way.

If the intent were to honor Napoleon with a monument linked to his persona alone, the Madeleine would have been a much better choice than the Invalides, where Saint-Louis is the central historical figure in the mural painting in the cupola. Charles Gauguier, deputy from the Vosges, soldier in the Napoleonic armies, and member of the Chambers since 1831 (where he usually voted with the Left opposition), proposed this as the most

Fig. 30
Jules-Claude Ziegler, *The History of Christianity*. Mural, Church of the Madeleine, 1838. Photo: the author.

suitable location during the 26 May debate. Rather than condemning Napoleon's totalitarianism, he defended his repressive acts as measures to suppress anarchy and civil war and declared, to the audible objections of some of his listeners, that "God seemed to be astonished by the superhuman genius of the great Napoleon." As for the location of the tomb, he argued that it should be in a place apart, so as not to be confused with those of former kings or other soldiers. The Church of the Madeleine was the only edifice he deemed suitable. If one were to rule that location out, it would mean that one should construct a new building to house the tomb. This was also an argument used by others on the opposite end of the ideological spectrum, such as one ardent legitimist who produced a long pamphlet in defense of the location. He went on to argue that the July Monarchy had declared Napoleon to have been a legitimate ruler of France; therefore, he deserved a tomb worthy of a king. Since he was not part of a genuinely legitimate royal line, however, he must have a monument apart. Thus, a tomb at the Madeleine that was "royal, unique and the last" would be most appropriate.[35] This is to say that the author wished to honor the principle of royalty but separate Napoleon from any dynastic claims. In advocating this location he also seems to have been urging that the principle of royalty itself be given a position of prominence in the system of symbols comprising the city.

César Daly, founder of *Revue générale de l'architecture*, was one of the most knowledgeable commentators on contemporary architecture and its institutional milieu. Writing in late 1841, he declared that the choice of the Invalides had been placed in limbo and that the Madeleine was being reconsidered as a site for the tomb. He further reported that the painters Horace Vernet and Paul Delaroche had visited the king with a plan for a new mural cycle for the building, if it were chosen for the tomb of Napoleon.[36] Upon learning of this, Ziegler responded that his own composition in the apse had been executed in anticipation of this destination and that a few modifications in his mural would make it suitable for this new function. His assertion has a certain plausibility in that the composition is unique for a religious edifice in France and that its program was designed by Thiers, who had undoubtedly dreamed, since the advent of the

July Monarchy, of the day that Napoleon's remains would be returned to France.

Daly continued by pointing out one major problem with the Madeleine: the State had already expended an enormous amount on the sculptural and painted decoration and the whole program would have to be redesigned at an even greater expense. From a practical standpoint this was a larger obstacle than any resistance that might have come from the Catholic church over the change in destination. It is important to remember that the building was not turned over to the archbishop of Paris until 1842 and that the Catholic press was in agreement that the architecture of this church was either "unchristian" or pagan. For the loss of this church, the clergy would have undoubtedly accepted compensation in the form of another edifice they viewed as more religious in character. The view that the architecture of this building was unsuitable for a church was shared by many others as well, such as the prominent architect Jacques-Ignace Hittorff. In his 1834 article on the church's architectural precedents, he began by expressing his personal wish that, like the Panthéon or the former Church of Sainte-Geneviève, the structure be given a secular function.[37]

Regardless of the logical force behind the arguments in favor of this location for the tomb, it appears that the government of Louis-Philippe ruled it out partly on the basis of the expenditure involved, but more importantly, because the edifice was not isolated enough, or did not put the emperor at great enough remove from contemporary life in the capital—that is to say, because of its conspicuous place in the urban fabric and the high visibility that would have been given to the Napoleonic legacy in the symbolic order of Paris. In addition, those in power may have shared Lamartine's fear that if it were chosen, "fanaticism and disorder would be able to exit from its doors and spread through our boulevards."[38]

Although the Panthéon was another edifice frequently mentioned in discussions of prospective sites for the monument, it is probable that the administration was filled with dread at the thought of the problems this would create. Soufflot's grand building had already been subjected to major reversals in destination. Originally constructed as the Church of Sainte-Geneviève, it had been rededicated to France's great men during the Revolution, only to be returned to the Church during the Restoration. In an effort to appease his republican opposition, make a display of his liberalism, and respond to the tide of anticlericalism that followed the overthrow of the Bourbons, Louis-Philippe ordered the church to be once again turned into a secular Panthéon. In keeping with the new destination, David d'Angers was commissioned to execute a frieze for the pediment that would announce its function.[39] His frieze, representing the distribution of laurel crowns to France's great men from the civil sphere on one side and the military on the other, was completed in 1837, but the government refused to inaugurate it without changes in its cast of characters (fig. 31). The ostensible reason that the minister of the interior gave for his dissatisfaction was that on the military side of the composition, David had failed to include any recog-

Fig. 31
The Panthéon, Paris, west facade. Soufflot, architect. Photo courtesy of Lauros-Giraudon.

nizable military hero other than Napoleon. The real reason was probably because of the inclusion of certain republican figures on the civil side but most of all because of the prominence of Voltaire, whose presence on the facade of this former church was bound to enrage Catholics. The government's attempt to prevent David's composition from being unveiled provoked a storm of criticism in the opposition press, and the administration finally caved in and let the work remain as it was. The unveiling of this secular sculpture in July provoked the expected outrage from militant Catholics and in particular that of Monsignor de Quélen, the legitimist archbishop of Paris, who issued a *mandement* condemning it and proclaiming a day of prayers and expiation. Given the controversy and criticism from both Left and Right that this commission unleashed, one can understand why Rémusat would have wanted to steer clear of any further modification of the function or decoration of this monument.

As for the Arc de Triomphe, which was as distant from the center of the city as the Invalides, it was probably excluded not only because it did not offer the possibility of controlling the projected masses of fervent bonapartists in the same way as the Invalides but also because of political problems it would have posed. Like the Panthéon, this colossal monument had undergone several major changes in destination and program that correspond to changes in the regimes ruling France, and its final form was still not completely determined in 1840.

Begun in 1806, it was originally intended to commemorate the victories of the French armies, but in 1823 the Restoration decided to consecrate it to the victories of the duc d'Angoulême in the Spanish campaign. Then in 1831, the July Monarchy resolved to complete the decoration and commissioned an ambitious sculptural program commemorating French victories of the Napoleonic era. But even this program displayed a glaring conflict as to who was being celebrated—Napoleon or the soldiers of his armies. Two gargantuan reliefs at the base of the arch on the side facing the center of Paris vividly illustrate this: on the left is Cortot's sculpture of Napoleon in classical dress being crowned by Victory, while opposite it is Rude's famous *Le Départ* or, as it is more commonly called, *La Marseillaise*. Thus, the emperor cohabits with the salt of the earth who filled the ranks of the French armies, and the principles of authority and democracy are displayed side by side. This same conflict is seen in the attempts to decide upon a sculptural group to crown the monument. It was generally agreed that the arch would be incomplete without such a sculptural group placed on top, and to that end in 1838, a full-scale temporary model of a classical quadriga containing an allegorical figure celebrating "La France constitutionnelle triomphante" was installed (fig. 32, *top*).[40] But after it was removed, no decision was made as to whether the work should be made permanent. Then, in 1840 for the retour des cendres, it was decided that another sculptural capstone should be hoisted atop the arch; several different sculptors were consulted about the project and made drawings of their conceptions. When the temporary monument was actually erected on top of the arch in December 1840, Napoleon was represented standing on a pedestal and dressed in imperial regalia (fig. 32, *bottom*). Since the group crowning the monument would ultimately determine to whom it was dedicated, major political problems were posed by the choice between France and Napoleon. Choosing one or the other was sure to bring widespread criticism. Putting the tomb of Napoleon at this location would have complicated the decision even more. Hence, it was eventually decided to neither place the tomb there nor add a crowning sculpture on top of it.

Of all the proposed sites, the one that seemed to have the strongest claim to house the imperial remains was abbé Suger's famous Basilica of Saint-Denis. Not only was it on the banks of the Seine, but it was also the location that Napoleon, when emperor, chose as a burial site for himself and his dynasty. On 20 February 1806 he signed a decree consecrating the church as a burial place for emperors and kings. According to the decree, four chapels were to be built in the church, with three housing the tombs of the three different lines of French kings and the fourth devoted to the imperial dynasty, of which he was the founding member.[41] Although the ministers of Louis-Philippe, not wishing to legitimize dynastic claims of the Bonaparte family, probably would have preferred to forget these facts, a number of the residents of Saint-Denis persisted in reminding them. On 17 May 1840 they sent Clauzel a petition demanding that the tomb be placed there, along with a copy of the decree of 1806.[42] Regardless of the associations with Napoleon, its availability, and the fact that the basilica satisfied the government's desire to place the

Fig. 32
Project to Crown the Arch of Triumph. Engraving from J. D. Thierry, *Arc de Triomphe de l'étoile,* 1845. Photo courtesy of the Bibliothèque Nationale, Département des Estampes.

tomb in a quiet area away from the center of Paris, the thought of burying Napoleon with legitimate kings of France outweighed these considerations, and it appears never to have been seriously considered by Rémusat or Thiers. But even had the government been willing to take this step, the question of how large a place in the structure should be reserved for Napoleon would have created great difficulty.

Finally, one location not mentioned in the Clauzel report that had close associations with Napoleon found many supporters. This was the site most favored by those who believed Napoleon's tomb should not cohabit with any existing building or monument. The hill at Chaillot, overlooking the Champ de Mars and the Ecole militaire, had been selected by Napoleon in 1810 as a locale for a grand palace to honor his dynasty; he enlisted his two court architects, Pierre Fontaine and Charles Percier, on the project. When his only legitimate son was born in 1811, he decided to dedicate the palace to his heir, the Roi de Rome. At the time of Napoleon's fall Fontaine had designed the building, but only the foundations had actually been constructed. The site was then abandoned until 1823 when the Bourbons began plans to construct a "Villa Trocadero" in honor of the duc d'Angoulême. This project in turn came to nothing when the Revolution of 1830 swept Louis-Philippe into power.[43]

Throughout the 1830s the disposition of the hill at Chaillot was a matter of debate, and one of the proposals for its use was given graphic form by architect Camille Moret when he sent a large-scale lithograph to the Salon of 1839. More than a year before the announcement of the return of Napoleon's remains, he exhibited a plan, section, and elevation of a colossal mausoleum to house them on the hill (fig. 33).[44] He also proposed an accompanying complex sculptural program that would have corresponded to the three different phases of Napoleon's career. He was probably aware that critics would declare that judging by its siting and numerous figures of Napoleon's generals, only his military career was being honored. Apparently to offset this criticism, he placed an imperial crown at the top of the conical structure and inscribed it with "Empereur et Roi."

Hector Horeau is another architect who appears to have envisioned a tomb for Napoleon on the Trocadero. In a drawing of 1841 he recorded his ideas for a colossal statue of Napoleon in

Fig. 33
Camille Moret, *Project for a Tomb
of Napoleon on the Hill at Chaillot*, 1839. Photo courtesy of the
Bibliothèque Nationale, Département des Estampes.

military dress, described in his notes as to be more than thirty
meters high and carved from a single piece of granite, that would
have been erected on the spot. Although the text accompanying his drawing does not specifically state that this monument
would also serve as his tomb, this is the way it would have been
interpreted by those knowledgeable about the debate over the
location.[45]

The most important of the partisans of the hill at Chaillot,
however, was probably Louis Vitet, whose thoughts on the matter
appeared in an essay published in *Revue des Deux Mondes* in
September 1840.[46] He began with an exposition of the limits

imposed upon the sculptor by the style of Mansart's structure at the Invalides and its association with the Bourbon dynasty. As a solution to this quandary, Vitet urged that the tomb be erected in splendid isolation on the hill overlooking the Champ de Mars. The importance of Vitet's article stems less from the dialectical skills of its author than from the role he played in the cultural and political life of his time, being at once a member of the Chamber of Deputies, the Conseil d'Etat, and the Commission des Monuments Historiques, in addition to being a prolific scholar and critic. Regardless of Vitet's influence and others' support for this location, there is no evidence that either Rémusat or his successors seriously considered a change in plans. The reason seems to be that while the site had the necessary remove from the center of the city, the prominence of a monument on this hill would have given it too large a place among the city's monuments: its low proximity to the center of power would have been offset by its extremely high visibility.

The government's choice of the Invalides as the site for the tomb of Napoleon received a solemn justification in Rémusat's announcement of 12 May:

> This august sepulcher should not remain exposed on a public place, in the middle of a clamorous and disturbing crowd. It is appropriate that it be placed in a silent and venerable location, where all those who respect glory and genius, grandeur and misfortune, can visit it in tranquility.

> He was an Emperor and a King; he was the legitimate ruler of our country. In this regard, he could be interred at Saint-Denis. But an ordinary sepulcher of kings is not appropriate for Napoleon. It is necessary that he still reign and command in the precincts where the soldiers of our country go to repose, and where those who are called to defend it will always go for inspiration. His sword will be placed on his tomb.[47]

However, the response of the press to the choice of the Invalides was one of general dissatisfaction. Among the few articles praising the wisdom of the choice and defending the government was one published in *Revue des Deux Mondes* several days after the vote. After explaining why the other proposed locations were unsuitable, Louis de Carné, a liberal member of the neo-

Catholic movement, described the kind of monument he would like to see constructed under Mansart's cupola. His article, praising Napoleon for having "pulled society from an abyss and established an empire of beliefs and laws," was an extended plea for recognition of the legitimacy of the Empire of Napoleon.[48] In proclaiming the legitimacy of Napoleon's reign and declaring that the choice of the Invalides was intended to confirm it, he set himself in opposition to many who viewed the location as a blatant attempt to delegitimate his rule. One of these was Eugène Pelletan, who, writing for a Saint-Simonian journal, succinctly expressed what was the view of many in the opposition:

> The place was not chosen in vain. . . . The hidden intention was to contest, by means of the place where he is interred, the legitimacy of Napoleon's reign. They wished to say: the emperor has never been more than a general of the Bourbon armies, and we are giving him a place alongside the great captains who have served the only royal dynasty which was legitimate, in one or the other of its branches. In deposing the body of Napoleon in an edifice uniquely consecrated to the services and glories of the military, they wish to honor in the great soldier only his merit on the fields of battle. They do not wish to sanctify his first application of the right of popular sovereignty. They attempt to avoid . . . the memory of the dynasty which held . . . the crown. . . . Under the pretext that quiet and repose are necessary for the mortuary bed of the great man, that one must distance it from all the clamor and agitation of the crowd, they removed his coffin from Saint Helena and placed it in the Invalides.[49]

What was unstated but understood in the comments of Pelletan is that the constitutional monarchy of Louis-Philippe, continually worried about its own legitimacy, did not wish to validate any dynastic claims or aspirations of the heirs and relatives of Napoleon.

This assumption provides a plausible explanation for the government's commitment to the Invalides. But there were other factors that must have entered into the decision as well. One of these is that, of all the suggested sites, the location, architecture, and function of the Invalides provided the greatest security for the tomb and guarantee of controlling any demonstrations or disruptions that might originate at the emotionally charged funeral monument. The Invalides was in a sparsely populated section of Paris, relatively distant from the center, making it difficult for mass demonstrations to assemble there quickly. The complex had large open spaces on all four sides that prevented demonstrators any easy escape from the cavalry, such as was possible in the labyrinthine system of narrow passageways in the more populous quarters of Paris. Likewise, it was impossible to erect barricades across narrow cobblestone streets, a feat easy to accomplish in the center of the city. When the large bronze doors of the south portal of Mansart's dome were closed, it was impenetrable from that side, and the access to the church from the north side was through a veritable fortress. In addition, there was always a sizeable contingent of soldiers of the regular army stationed there that could be readily put to use to quell any disturbances. Furthermore, the dome of Mansart was one of the most conspicuous and prestigious monuments in the city of Paris, and the government could not be charged with failing to give Napoleon his due. And while the tomb could be isolated in the dome, the massive structure could in no way be considered a mausoleum for Napoleon alone. In short, the dome of the Invalides had the best balance of visibility and remove.

After declaring that the emperor's remains were to be installed at the Invalides, Rémusat, regardless of the disagreement over the location of the tomb, wasted little time in engaging an architect to design the tomb to receive them. As related in his *mémoires*, he picked Félix Duban, "then regarded as the best of our architects," to adapt the site in the dome to its new destination. Duban, in turn, quickly accepted the invitation and, only thirteen days after Rémusat's announcement, submitted a program, an estimate of the cost of the project, and a drawing of his proposal. [50] His letter further reveals that he had discussed the design with the minister of the interior and was incorporating not only his suggestions but also those of Thiers, which had been communicated to him by the sculptor Charles Marochetti. Marochetti had already been chosen to execute a large-scale "figure impériale," presumably an equestrian statue for the courtyard. Concerning this aspect of the project, Duban had undisguised reservations: "I will accept it only on the hypothesis of the most marvelous execution." Marochetti was also probably designated to execute other parts of Duban's sculptural program. Writing later, Rémusat explained that Duban not only opposed the idea of collaboration with Marochetti but also expressed his desire to design the entirety of the work himself, leaving the execution of the sculptural decoration not to an established sculptor with an exaggerated sense of his own importance but to a simple *practicien* instead.[51] These remarks portend a jurisdictional problem that was to plague the project throughout its course. At stake were the sensitive issues of control and authorial credit and the question of whether the monument was to be the expression of an individual's artistic genius or a collective product.

Although the sketch that accompanied his letter has disappeared, Duban's next design for the tomb is known from a second-hand source. In a letter written at the end of July 1840, architect Léon Vaudoyer revealed that Duban was about to present his latest idea to the interior minister and drew a quick sketch of Duban's project (fig. 34). In this conception of the tomb

Fig. 34
Léon Vaudoyer, letter with drawing of Duban's project for the tomb of Napoleon. Archives Nationales. Photo: the author.

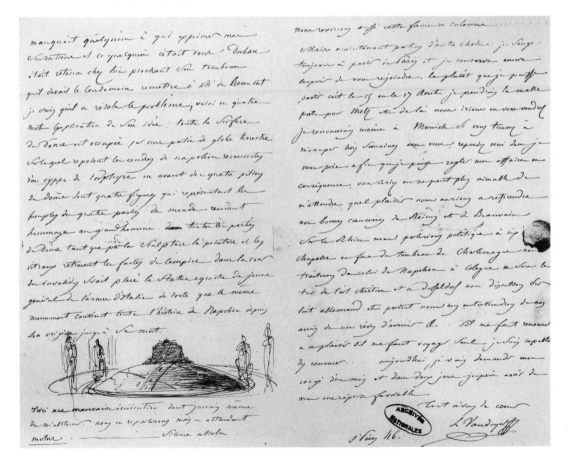

the space under the dome would have been occupied by a semi-spherical tumulus representing the globe and would have been surmounted by an ornamented sarcophagus. The part left for Duban's collaborators was the execution of four allegorical statues on the periphery of the tomb, representing the four continents paying homage to Napoleon, and a series of bas-reliefs and mural paintings illustrating the principal events in the career of Napoleon. That Rémusat did not find this design acceptable is known from another letter by Vaudoyer, written a few days later.[52]

Although the choice of Duban was predictable, the selection of Marochetti to execute the equestrian monument surprised many observers, since the sculptor was a foreigner who had not yet been naturalized as a French citizen. Furthermore, while Marochetti had studied at the Ecole des Beaux-Arts, as a student of Bosio, he had not distinguished himself there, winning only one honorable mention in the competitions for the coveted *Prix-de-Rome*. But after making a study voyage to Italy at his own expense, Marochetti returned to France where he was favored with several important state commissions during the early years of the July Monarchy, the most notable being a bas-relief for the Arc de Triomphe and a monumental group sculpture for the altar of the new Church of the Madeleine in Paris.[53] Far and away the most important sculptural work he had completed to date was an equestrian monument honoring Emmanuel Philibert of Savoy, which was executed in Paris in 1837 and erected in a public square in Turin. However, before this statue was transported to Italy, it was exhibited briefly in the central courtyard of the Louvre where it attracted some critical attention, if not the entirely enthusiastic acclaim the artist would have wished.[54]

Exactly what motivated the administration to risk controversy and provoke widespread disagreement over its choice of Marochetti is not clear, but it may have had something to do with the fact that the sculptor had the full support of Thiers. The latter, in his position as director of Travaux Publics in 1833 and 1834, personally selected the sculptors for the commissions at the Madeleine and the Arc de Triomphe, and Marochetti was favored with the state's beneficence in both instances. Another indication that Thiers had more than a passing acquaintance with the artist may be implied by the fact that as early as 1836 he spent an afternoon in the sculptor's château seeking respite from the cares of office. But a different explanation of how the Italian came to be awarded the prestigious commission is one proposed by Léon Vaudoyer, which might be titled "the Latin Lover Scenario," in a letter written at the time of the commission. According to Vaudoyer, someone privy to gossip in administrative circles, Marochetti was involved in an illicit, amorous relationship with Madame Dosne, the wealthy mother-in-law and lifelong advisor of Thiers in artistic matters.[55]

All the evidence indicates that Marochetti and Duban were intent on working independently of one another from the very beginning of the endeavor, making any collaboration extremely difficult. Exactly when Duban withdrew from the project is unclear, but by the middle of July 1840 Marochetti was clearly in charge and at work on his own conception of the monument. By choosing a foreigner to execute the tomb, a choice that passed over many far more prominent French sculptors, Rémusat must have suspected that the government was asking for trouble. And indeed, heated opposition to this decision was quick to form in the Parisian art community. An indication of the resistance to this choice is seen in several letters written by sculptors who had won the Prix de Rome and were studying at the French Academy in Rome at the time. Auguste-Louis Ottin, for example, wrote to his parents on 16 June 1840, complaining bitterly that "French artists were very depressed to have such a work stolen by a charlatan like this one, who, in addition, isn't even French." Another *laureat* at the Academy, Jean-Marie Bonnassieux, in a letter to Augustin Dumont dated 21 October 1840, expressed the resentment of all his colleagues in Rome over the audacious act that had insulted France by giving this commission to "a foreigner, who had only his wealth and origin to legitimatize this favor."[56]

Marochetti's design, known today only from descriptions in the contemporary press, was tried for its effect when, according to Rémusat, Thiers proposed that a full-scale simulacrum be erected in the church in order that one might judge its merits. Thus, a jerry-built structure of wood and canvas, intended to approximate the appearance of the monument, was duly erected *in situ* in late July and presented to certain critics and government functionaries for a single day before being quickly dismantled. This project was savagely ridiculed in the press by many who were certainly not in attendance at its display, and the duc d'Orléans, representing the absent Louis-Philippe, was overtly displeased. This design consisted of an aedicular tomb in the manner of Renaissance prototypes, such as that of Louis XII at the Church of Saint-Denis. On top of this structure was to be placed an effigy of Napoleon on horseback, in effect bringing Marochetti's equestrian statue from the courtyard into the dome. Juxtaposed to this representation of the living figure of Napoleon was an effigy of his cadaver in the open, vaulted interior space below. At the corners of the structure were placed four colossal allegorical figures on the same scale as the equestrian statue.[57] This conception is the one that seems to have been illustrated in a popular print of 1840 that celebrated and summarized the principal events in the career of Napoleon (fig. 35). In the sky on the

Fig. 35
Allegory of the Civil and Military Triumphs of the Emperor Napoleon. Drawing by Charles Rony. Lithograph by Adolphe Lafosse, 1840. Photo courtesy of Bibliothèque Nationale, Département des Estampes.

Fig. 36
*Marochetti's Second Project for a
Tomb of Napoleon.* Lithograph,
published in *L'Artiste*, 1840.
Photo: the author.

right of the print and between the Vendôme Column and the dome of the Invalides is a tomb surrounded by a crowd of adulators that seems to be based on Marochetti's well-publicized *première pensée*. This design was to be short-lived, as in the course of discussion about its merits, the idea of a double effigy was discarded. In lieu of this conception, a decision was made to give its four surfaces a detailed allegorical program of relief sculpture, enclose the sarcophagus within a closed, rectangular base, and surmount the structure with an equestrian statue that was in keeping with the desired gravity and severity of the monument. By the end of October, Marochetti had revised his abortive project sufficiently to permit lithographs to be made of it, copies of which were quickly published in different Parisian art journals (fig. 36).[58]

The most visible problem with this conception lies in the four vastly overscaled allegorical figures cantilevered out over the base of the tomb that completely dwarf the entry door below. And the four rigid figures of symbolic eagles, which one journalist likened to vultures, are also strangely overscaled in that they are far larger than the door opening. Thus, this version seems to be an attempt to combine references to the monumental figures in Michelangelo's Medici Chapel in Florence with the severe architecture of Egyptian funeral monuments.[59] But the most serious failing was the lack of any attempt to harmonize this structure with Mansart's architecture in which it was to have been placed.

Many questions were raised by this clumsy structure, in particular, why it was decided to crown it with an equestrian statue in the first place. This might be explained in part by the May 1840 vote of the Chamber of Deputies over allocation of funds for the return of Napoleon and the construction of his monument. After Rémusat's *projet de loi* had been introduced, along with its request for one million francs to accomplish the task, a commission was appointed, as customary, to study the bill and make a report on it. Directing this committee was General Bertrand Clauzel, an influential deputy and a controversial figure during the wars in North Africa.[60] When this report was finished, discussion of its recommendations began before the full legislative body on 26 May. The most significant departure of the Clauzel report from Rémusat's original bill was that it proposed to double the sum of money for the ceremony and tomb and included a provision for an equestrian statue of Napoleon to be erected in some unnamed place. This new recommendation provoked both confusion and consternation among the deputies. Before the voting began on the first part of the bill, namely the allocation of funds, Armand Des Longrais, a deputy from the Vire demanded that a vote be taken for the original proposal and not the revised one sponsored by Clauzel. The president of the Assembly agreed, and protests arose immediately, the loudest of which came from Clauzel and Adolphe Thiers, the unofficial prime minister and person responsible for initiating the original bill. Thiers adamantly proclaimed that he and the government threw their full support behind Clauzel's recommendations.[61] This protest was to no avail, however, as the Chamber quickly voted for only the one-million-franc allocation and rejected the idea of an equestrian statue. Since this addition had the support of Thiers, its denial could only be interpreted as a political defeat for the minister. Thus, denied this equestrian monument, it appears that Thiers decided to retaliate or to reassert his authority by incorporating one in the design of the tomb itself. Thiers had also personally given the commission for the equestrian monument to Marochetti before funding was approved for it, and asking the sculptor to execute an equestrian tomb was a way of fulfilling this commitment. This meant, of course, that Duban was forced to retire from the project.

It should be noted, however, that before the Clauzel report was ever written, Antoine Etex had already executed a design that combined the desired equestrian monument and a tomb. This project was a simple variant of a monument he had already designed for the Place d'Europe in Paris in 1839 (fig. 37). In his conception of this public monument, Napoleon, mounted on a battle-horse and dressed in his military uniform, seems on the verge of leaping from the symbolic bronze sphere on which he is supported. The famous victories of the emperor on the fields of battle across Europe would have been inscribed around the marble base, further amplifying his achievements. This representation of Napoleon appears to have been proposed by the directors of the railway company that had agreed to share the expense of constructing the monument with the State and the city of Paris. However, Louis-Philippe cancelled the project when the idea was proposed to him. Etex in his memoirs related that the news of

PROJET DE MONUMENT A ERIGER SUR LA PLACE DE L'EUROPE EN 1839

Fig. 37
Antoine Etex, *Project for a Monument to Napoleon*. Drawing, 1839. Photo courtesy of the Musée Carnavalet.

this rejection was broken to him in a conspiratorial tone by Thiers: "My dear Etex, they are too *con* at the moment to place such a monument to Napoleon on a public place; it is together that we will construct this monument, but later." Upon hearing of Rémusat's proclamation that the emperor was to be permanently installed at the Invalides, Etex, who could never be accused of lacking persistence or entrepreneurial zeal, lost no time in converting this design from a fountain to a tomb. A highly finished watercolor, dating only three days after the announcement of the retour, illustrates his conception (fig. 38).[62] Thus, it appears that even though Etex was not awarded the commission for the tomb, his idea of a monument serving a dual purpose was the type adopted by Marochetti and tentatively approved by Rémusat. Another similarity between the projects of the two sculptors lies in the costume given the hero; in his first project Etex had dressed Napoleon in his military uniform, but in the tomb project he selected imperial dress, deriving from the Roman Empire and recalling that of the figure of Marcus Aurelius on the famous equestrian statue on the Capitoline hill in Rome.[63] In a like manner, Marochetti chose to clothe his figure in another Roman costume. These changes in costume are only indicative of the question that was to endure throughout the

Fig. 38
Antoine Etex, *Project for a Tomb of Napoleon.* Drawing, 1840. Photo courtesy of the Musée Carnavalet.

Fig. 39
Nicolas-Toussaint Charlet, frontispiece illustration for de Las Cases,
La Mémorial de Sainte-Hélène,
1842. Photo: the author.

construction process of the monument: was the military or the
civil Napoleon to be represented by the tomb?

When Charlet executed the frontispiece for de Las Cases's
Mémorial de Saint-Hélène (1842), which represents Napoleon
seated on a rearing horse in a costume that is partly modern,
partly antique, he probably had Etex's project in mind (fig. 39).
But there was another monument that both artists could have
used as a prototype: François Bosio's equestrian statue of Louis
XIV, erected in 1822 at the Place des Victoires in Paris (fig. 40).
In this work, designed to replace the one that had been destroyed
during the Revolution and to commemorate the return of the

Fig. 40
François Bosio, *Equestrian Statue
of Louis XIV.* Bronze. Place des
Victoires, Paris, 1822. Photo courtesy of Lauros-Giraudon.

Bourbons to power, the "roi soleil" wears his famed periwig but is
otherwise garbed as a Roman warrior, a choice of dress that was
considered by at least one critic in 1827 to be an "anachronism"
and a "strange folly." This work also seems to make deliberate reference to the famous statue of Louis XIV, which Bernini executed for the château at Versailles and which was subsequently
reproduced and reworked in 1687 under the direction of
Girardon.[64] But the dynamic pose was the most memorable characteristic of the monument; it meant to suggest the energy and
vitality that the notoriously sedentary Louis XVIII was bringing
back to France. While it appears that Etex and Marochetti both

responded to this conspicuous Bourbon paradigm for a dynamic equestrian monument, Etex seems to have instated his prototype in the choice of pose and dress and exceeded its implied dynamicism, while conversely Marochetti took just the opposite tack and created an antitype to the work of Bosio, his mentor.

Any equestrian monument to Napoleon would have inevitably been compared with that in the Place des Victoires. This might be confirmed by the comments of the deputy Glais-Bizoin in the debate over the funding of the tomb in the Chamber of Deputies on 26 May 1840. Opposed to the requested additional funding for an equestrian monument, he stated that it was ridiculous to bring Napoleon down from his lofty position on the Vendôme Column and place him on the same level as the "cavalier of the Place des Victoires"; if Napoleon was really without equal, as bonapartists argued, this was a contradictory act.[65] One might say then that rather than making the two figures equal, an act the deputy thought another equestrian statue would suggest, Marochetti attempted to establish their differences formally by his choice of a pose of hieratic immobility, or by placing both horse and rider in a rigidly frontal position and firmly anchoring all four legs of the latter on the pedestal. This interpretation becomes more plausible when one remembers that the destination of Marochetti's statue was a church commissioned by the Sun King and executed by his preferred architect.

As a historian, Thiers was undoubtedly aware that Louis XIV had commissioned a series of monuments in public places across France—primarily Paris, Rennes, Montpellier, Lyon, Toulouse, Dijon, and Marseilles—as political propaganda during and for his reign and that Mansart was the individual who issued the directives concerning the erection of these monuments.[66] Thus, the architecture of Hardouin-Mansart at the Invalides and the equestrian monument Bosio created to summon up the glory of the *grand siècle* are referents against which Marochetti's static sculpture established its difference.

In developing his concept Marochetti would have been able to appeal to several well-known prototypes or precedents to legitimate his project. He was probably familiar with the Scaliger tombs erected during the fourteenth century at the Church of S. Maria Antica in Verona. The most complex and elaborate funeral monument in the burial plot outside the church is that

Fig. 41
Bonino da Campione, *Tomb of
Cansignori della Scala*. Marble,
c. 1374. S. Maria Antica, Verona.
Photo courtesy of Giraudon-
Alnari.

honoring the memory of Cansignori della Scala, executed by
Bonino da Campione around 1374 (Fig. 41). Like Marochetti's
first conception, this tomb features an arcaded tabernacle containing a sarcophagus and a funeral effigy of the dead warrior and
is surmounted by an equestrian statue rendered with heraldic ri-
gidity of pose. Another work by the sculptor, likewise rendered in
a severely hieratic idiom, is the equestrian tomb of Bernabò Visconti, executed for the church of S. Giovanni in Conca at Milan.
Still another precedent, although placed against a wall and not
freestanding, is the tomb of Bartolommeo Colleoni in Bergamo
executed by Giovanni Amadeo between 1470 and 1476. However, the existence of these prototypes did not prevent critics from

Fig. 42
Jean Goujon (?), *Tomb of Louis de Brézé*. Marble, c. 1535–44. Rouen Cathedral. Photo courtesy of Lauros-Giraudon.

complaining that Marochetti's type of equestrian funeral monument was without precedent in Catholic churches in France.[67] But again the sculptor could have cited an important monument in the cathedral of Rouen: the tomb of Louis de Brézé, executed between 1535 and 1544, whose equestrian statue—sometimes attributed to Jean Goujon—is juxtaposed to the *transi* figure below (fig. 42). This sculptural ensemble is placed against a wall. While the mounted figure lacks the extreme stiffness of the Scaliger effigies, it nonetheless could be cited as a French precedent.[68] Thus, one might consider Marochetti's innovation in his first conception to be the combination of the prototypes at Verona and Rouen with the freestanding aedicular tomb of the kind found in numerous examples at Saint-Denis. It should be stressed, however, that the existence of these prototypes does not

Fig. 43
Charles Marochetti, *Equestrian Statue of Philibert Emmanuel, Milan*. Lithograph by Alophe, from *L'Artiste*, 1839. Photo: the author.

lessen the dialectical relationship between his project and that of Bosio at the Place des Victoires.

Other factors can also be adduced to account for the equestrian statue in Marochetti's project, among which may be the sculptor's wish to execute it in a mode radically opposed to the work for which he was best known, thereby advertising his versatility. This is his intensely movemented equestrian monument honoring Philibert Emmanuel (fig. 43). Those familiar with contemporary sculpture who were viewing Marochetti's project for the Invalides would have been forced to compare it with this work, which was exhibited in Paris and might be considered its expressive counterpole. Finally, the hieratic immobility of the pose of the equestrian figure could be considered an attempt to concretize the prescription of Rémusat, describing his own conception of the proper monument before the Chamber of Deputies on 12 May 1840: "This monument ought to have a simple beauty, large forms and an appearance of unshakeable solidity that will withstand the action of time. For Napoleon, a monument as durable as his memory."[69]

The critics of the major art journals were merciless in condemning Marochetti's proposal, but it is clear from the context that their contempt was directed as much at the autocratic method by which he was chosen to undertake the project as his plan for the monument itself. The "dubious" means by which he was favored with this commission were to haunt the critical reception of his other works throughout the remainder of the July Monarchy. A less direct and more diplomatic protest against Marochetti's project was to emanate from the Académie des Beaux-Arts in the form of a letter to the interior minister written on 29 July 1840 by Raoul-Rochette, its perpetual secretary. Subsequently published in the pages of the two scourges of Rémusat, L'Artiste and Journal des Artistes, the letter offered the Academy's assistance in the selection of an artist to execute the monument and in choosing a project that would be in harmony with the architecture of the location for which it was destined. Although politely worded, it passed unequivocal judgment on the manner in which Marochetti was selected and on the project he had produced: "It seems that for this kind of project . . . one cannot choose for its execution talents too often tested and too *national*, capacities too elevated or too French." The commentary that accompanied the letter when published in *L'Artiste* was quick to point out that while he was not mentioned by name, this constituted a direct condemnation of the Italian favorite of the minister of the interior and the manner in which he was chosen. [70]

Of all the discussions of Marochetti's project, the longest, most thoughtful, and by far the most sympathetic was that in Louis Vitet's article on the tomb, which appeared while the various trials were in progress at the Invalides. Although the object of Vitet's arguments was to have the location shifted from the Invalides, he had much praise for the originality of Marochetti's conception. He claimed that it resembled no other tomb that he knew of, though he pointed out the other equestrian tombs that might be seen as distant precedents. Hence he proposed that Marochetti be given the commission to erect the monument on the hill at Chaillot and made a few suggestions as to how the design might be modified to make it more suitable for its new location. Vitet seems to have been one of the few individuals whose opinion Rémusat solicited regarding the tomb, but according to Rémusat's own account, Vitet only half-approved of Marochetti's design, and his praise was only part of his strategy to have the monument erected at Chaillot. [71]

Given the controversy surrounding the choice of Marochetti and the illustrations of his design that survive, it was perhaps fortunate for his reputation that he was never to execute any of the proposed projects. His chances of actually erecting his tomb at the Invalides were all but extinguished when the government of Thiers and Rémusat, his two protectors, was forced to resign in October 1840, largely because of their handling of the Eastern Question and the internal disruption it had created in France. Thus, at the time of the retour des cendres, questions of the design of the monument, the architect or sculptor to whom the commission was to be given, and even its location, were still unresolved.

CHAPTER 3

The "Contest"

The issue that excited even more controversy than the location of Napoleon's tomb was one of how its architect should be chosen, or who should choose him. Very shortly after Rémusat's dramatic announcement of the return of the imperial remains, a chorus of voices began to be heard in the press demanding an open competition for this national monument. This clamor only increased as news of Marochetti's experiments at the Invalides became widespread.

The demand for a public contest for the tomb of Napoleon should certainly not be considered a new development in France. On the contrary, it was the continuation of a discourse begun at least four decades earlier.[1] As might be expected, during the early months of the French Revolution the call for public contests for works of art, as a countermeasure to the autocratic system of patronage of the *ancien régime*, became a standard part of republican rhetoric. Possibly the most carefully formulated example of this revolutionary demand is a petition submitted to the Constituent Assembly by the Commune des arts on 9 May 1792. Signed by forty-one members of the group, it specified in great detail the procedures for publicizing and judging contests for public works of art and at the same time condemned the arbitrary and autocratic decision that had recently given Jean-Antoine Moitte the commission for the sculptural relief on the pediment of the Panthéon. Ironically, the person responsible for delegating this commission to Moitte was Quatremère de Quincy, the esteemed archaeologist and sculptor, who, in an essay of 1791, had enthusiastically endorsed the idea of *concours publiques*. But subsequently Quatremère focused his energies on reform of the

Salon system and demonstrated little enthusiasm for the idea of competitions for public monuments.[2]

This new priority which Quatremère gave to the Salon as a site of patronage and his relative lack of support for contests for monumental art after publication of his treatise mirrors a shift in thinking in France as a whole. In the introduction to the catalogue for the Salon of 1795, the anonymous author extolled the benefits to be derived from competition among artists, yet promptly qualified this remark by stating that there were "different species of contests, some more salutary than others." Principal among the less salutary kinds were those for public monuments among established artists. This shift in emphasis is also clearly seen in the writing of the archaeologist and rival of Quatremère, T.-B. Emeric-David, who in his celebrated book *Recherches sur l'art statuaire*, written between 1798 and 1801 in response to a contest sponsored by the Institut national, praised the benefits to be gained from "emulation" and struggle among first-rate artists, but was opposed to the idea of contests open to all.[3]

Despite the persistence of republican ideas among the opposition during the reign of Napoleon as first consul and emperor and then during the Bourbon restoration, commissions for public monuments remained almost exclusively matters of administrative decree rather than competitive events. Notable exceptions to this rule were the contests under the consulate for the conversion of the Church of the Madeleine in Paris into a Temple of Glory for paintings celebrating the Treaty of Amiens and the signing of the *Concordat* with Pope Pius VII, which re-established the Church in France, and the contest in 1807 for a painting to commemorate the battle of Eylau. Under Charles X, there were only two significant contests for public works held in 1829. The first was for the pediment of the Church of the Madeleine and the second for the redesign of the Place Louis XV, which was soon to become the Place de la Concorde. The Madeleine competition was restricted to six sculptors who were invited by the government to submit sketches of their proposals. There was no detailed program provided. For the contest for the Place Louis XV, ten architects were asked to submit their designs; the competition was then opened to any other architects who desired to exhibit their proposals. Thirteen architects took advantage of this option, but the two who won the laurels were, as could be expected, among the invitees. What is significant about the latter contest is that a detailed and carefully written program was published.[4]

After the Revolution of 1830 and the installation of the hybrid monarchy of Louis-Philippe, the debate over the nature of public contests became more heated than at any time since the great Revolution. This debate quickly found a well-defined focus in the series of three contests held in the opening months of the July Monarchy for history paintings to decorate the Salle des Séances at the Chamber of Deputies. These contests prompted both praise of the administration and charges of incompetence, but most importantly they generated discussion of the larger political and philosophical implications in the concept of the contest itself. The issue of public competitions was given even more topicality in May 1831, when the State announced that another important contest was to be held—this one for a statue of Napoleon to replace the one by Chaudet atop the Vendôme Column that had been removed during the Restoration.[5] While supporters of the practice of open contests were not entirely satisfied with the general level of projects submitted, they nonetheless praised the State for taking a step in the right direction and expressed hope that this would become standard operating procedure.

However, a major shift occurred in the State's policies for awarding commissions for public monuments as Adolphe Thiers gradually assumed greater power in the government of Louis-Philippe. Appointed Minister of Public Works in October 1830, Thiers slowly proceeded to institute a much more autocratic procedure for awarding commissions in the months that followed.[6] The first controversial decision of Thiers's tenure arose over the commission for the monument that was to be erected at the Place de la Bastille and dedicated to the victims of the July Revolution. The *Journal des Artistes* had already made its position on the matter quite clear several months before Thiers took office: "If ever a monument ought to be the object of a contest, this is surely the one." But when Thiers appeared before the Chamber of Deputies on 18 December 1832 to speak for the allocation of funds for its construction, he expressed his strong opposition to the idea of a contest and was supported by a vote of the deputies.[7] Encouraged by this, he continued to dispense commissions on his own authority with little consultation from the general art community. In the process, rather than defusing the issue, he generated even more support for contests.

Thiers's opposition to the use of public competitions certainly did not reflect the views of the majority of the artistic community in the months following the Revolution of 1830. Representative of the majority opinion is an essay by the critic Jal, published in January 1831. In response to the argument that contests produce only mediocre works and that the best artists usually refuse to compete in them, he offered an obvious solution: "Never give public works to men who disdain or flee contests, and they will want to compete until the bitter end."[8] As far as he was concerned, the jury system was the only means to avoid the institutionalization of an old-boy network in which commissions were obtained by paying court to those in positions of power. Similar anti-autocratic views turned up in many contexts not ostensibly concerned with the question, such as the *Manuel du peintre et du sculpteur*, which was published as part of the Roret series in 1833. The author, an obscure painter named L.-C. Arsenne, after presenting all the arguments given by opponents of contests, declared that there was no reason to believe that the taste of a government functionary was more enlightened than that of anyone else: "Taste is that which is most arbitrary and the most despotic; public opinion is the only legitimate force."[9] For him the issue clearly was not aesthetic, but political.

Among the strongest advocates of public contests was the journal *L'Artiste*. One instance of its support of open competitions is found in its announcement of the public contest that was to be held in Strasbourg in 1834 for a dual monument and tomb for Kléber, the famous general of the Revolutionary armies. This contest was described as a "recompense, very feeble it is true, for all the deceptions which our hopes for public contests in Paris have encountered," and the article concluded with the declaration that all sculptors in France must enter the contest and "by the solemnity that their unanimous presence will give to this contest, embarrass the government for the shameful mystery in which it rules over the distribution of public works to several incompetent favorites."[10] It then reprinted the very detailed program for the contest, one which could serve as a model for the government of Louis-Philippe.

At Strasbourg there was even more opposition rhetoric tied to the contest. In its discussion of the entries, the *Courrier du Bas-Rhin*, a voice of the republican opposition in the city and one of the strongest sponsors of the monument, set forth in most emphatic terms its belief in the necessity for contests and the ultimate wisdom of the judgment of le peuple, or the masses, rather than that of specialists or appointed functionaries:

> The best judge [of contests] is the crowd with its instinctive feeling for the beautiful; with that ideal that it bears, confused and obscure, in itself; the crowd belongs to no school, no party, no coterie; the work of art that is the most perfect is that which awakens in the crowd the sentiment of the beautiful, common to all men, and which strikes it the most vividly.[11]

This is an extreme form of the populist beliefs that underlay the demands for public contests being voiced in many different cities in France.

Regardless of the democratic or republican political values inextricably tied to the idea of the public contest, the most vocal and powerful group demanding open competitions had no ostensible political coloration at all. This body was the newly founded Société libre des Beaux-Arts, an independent organization of artists, architects, and musicians whose ranks numbered almost two hundred members. In the first five years of its existence the topic of *concours* was a recurrent matter of discussion at its meetings.[12] When in 1831 the State established a commission to study the problem of the administration of the arts, the society addressed its detailed recommendations to it and to the minister of the interior, paying particular attention to the problem of contests and to how an impartial jury might be selected to judge them. It proposed that a master-jury of not more than 120 members should be elected, not appointed, and when individual competitions were to be judged, a lottery would be held to determine which of the electees should serve.[13]

The society was particularly concerned with the contests for the history paintings for the Salle des Séances of the Chamber of Deputies and viewed them as a vindication of and support for their efforts to make the practice universal.[14] Their satisfaction was undoubtedly heightened by the fact that two of the winners in the competition for the decoration of the Chambers, Coutan and Vinchon, were members of their organization. And when Thiers won the approval of the Chamber of Deputies to erect the July Column at the Place de la Bastille without a contest, the society drafted a petition to the Chamber of Peers and formed a delegation to carry their protest to the king himself.[15] This action was to no avail as shortly afterward the peers also approved funds for the monument and negated the idea of a contest for it.[16]

Charles de Farcy and Guyot de Féré, two of the most active members of this organization and instigators of the petition, were also editors of the *Journal des Artistes*, one of the few periodicals that gave serious attention to details of administration of the arts in France. The theme of contests reappeared continually in the pages of the journal. In the analysis of the second contest for the Chamber of Deputies, de Farcy, as reviewer, concluded that although the results were generally feeble, the fault lay not with the policy of the government but with the obdurate refusal of certain first-rate artists to enter into the lists.[17]

The discourse of those opposed to public competitions for works of art had, in like manner, both practical and overtly political aspects. Possibly the most serious and intelligent critique of the practice of public concours was that of Raoul-Rochette, the secrétaire perpétuel of the Institut, written while the contests for the decoration of the Chambers were in progress.[18] The distinguished archaeologist began his exposition by quoting Pliny's revealed truth that artists are the only ones qualified to pronounce on the merits of the works of other artists, and then proceeded to explain why this invalidated the very *idea* of contests. According to his peculiar logic, it followed from the first proposition that the best artists were the best judges of artistic merit; that being the case, they must be the contest judges and not the contestants themselves. The inevitable consequence of this state of affairs was that the winning entries in any contest would be by artists of the second rank. He continued his argument by setting forth what he perceived to be another major impediment: the fact that the act of judging in artistic matters, as in courts of law, presumes the existence of an objective and accepted set of principles that can be applied to individual cases. Unfortunately, in aesthetic matters all was governed by the "empire du goût," and no such founding rules exist. That he had earlier proclaimed that certain artists were superior to others, an assertion that would seem to cut the ground out from under this argument, does not seem to have troubled him. Yet another obstacle was that the very idea of a contest implied a certain equality among the competitors when it was a well-established fact that there existed a hierarchy of merit in the artistic realm. He believed this presumed equality would prevent superior artists from competing with their inferiors and with their own students. Furthermore, in an open contest the best artists stood to lose the most in that their reputations suffered if they did not win, while obscure individuals had nothing to lose and everything to gain. This catalogue of theoretical objections was completed by a list of practical ones, such as the inability to judge from models or sketches how completed works would look.

At roughly the same time the same basic arguments were set forth by E.-J. Délécluze in an article that had a much greater audience. Délécluze was opposed not just to competitions for government projects but also to the practice of organized competitions among students in the confines of the Ecole des Beaux-Arts, the institution of which Raoul-Rochette was a staunch defender. For the influential art critic and former student of David, there were simply no advantages to competitions for public works that could possibly outweigh the general mediocrity he maintained they inevitably produced: "Nothing is more aristocratic than talent. . . . and it is always mediocrity that triumphs in contests."[19]

Similar arguments were made by Eugène Delacroix in a well-known essay he published in an 1831 issue of *L'Artiste*. Though admitting that mediocrity occasionally had the good fortune to invent something ingenuous, he believed that it never had the talent to realize its project. His strongest objection was that impartial judgment had become impossible since "the great discovery of the classic and the romantic." In his cover letter to the editor of *L'Artiste*, he went even further, claiming that the "soi-disant classiques" were the party most in favor of contests because they were in a position to determine the results (an assertion denied, of course, by the opinions of Raoul-Rochette and Délécluze, who were both ardent defenders of the classical tradition). For him the issue could be reduced to a power struggle between opposed artistic ideologies. Landscape painter Paul Huet, a friend of Delacroix, recapitulated the various arguments against the practice in the same issue of the journal, concluding that it was preferable that the minister of the interior make his choices himself, after consulting "la publicité."[20]

The minister of the interior at the time was François Guizot, who conceived the program of paintings for the Salle des Séances at the Chambers. Guizot set down his thoughts on the issue of contests in his memoirs. While he wished to choose three eminent history painters to execute the monumental paintings at the Chambers, "the democratic spirit was opposed and imperiously demanded a contest." Finally, according to Guizot, who had undisguised contempt for the notion of democratic rule of the masses, the contestants were charged with electing part of the jury themselves "in an excess of democratic fantasy," a practice he deemed absurd.[21]

Thus, more than a debate over the efficacy of contests as a means of awarding commissions, a political subtext was immediately implicated in the various proposals, whether individuals such as Délécluze or Delacroix wished there to be or not. The issue of contests, then, raised the question of whether rule in France as a whole was to be autocratic or democratic, two alternatives between which the government of Louis-Philippe was attempting to find a middle ground. The discourse and counterdiscourse provoked by this issue, which to simplify matters might be categorized as the "aristocratic/autocratic" and the "democratic/free enterprise" models, also raised the larger political-philosophical question of *where* decision-making power ultimately resided in the new system of constitutional monarchy.

Once again, after the announcement of the return of the emperor, the Société libre des Beaux-Arts found itself in the vanguard of those demanding that his monument be put to a competition. A little more than a month after the announcement of the retour it was proposed at a group meeting that a petition in its name demanding an open competition be submitted to the interior minister. Following this proposal, a committee was formed to study the question.[22] Then, at a meeting on 1 September 1840, Adrien de La Fage, secretary of the committee, announced that he had written a brochure summarizing both his ideas and those of many members of the group on the contest. Less than two weeks later this tract was republished anonymously in the *Journal des Artistes*, whose enthusiastic endorsement it received.[23]

In support of his call for a contest La Fage invoked the argument that a competition, particularly one for a monument of such importance, was both a stimulus to the creative imaginations of artists and a means of discovering new talents. Furthermore, a contest would encourage proposals from individuals who were not practicing artists and whose thoughts were not conditioned by conventions, received ideas, and the discourse of the contemporary art world. Even if the contest produced many mediocre projects, he argued, worthwhile ideas might be found in the worst, which might then be developed by individuals with greater artistic talent. Finally, he declared that if this monument was to be truly national, the nation ought to be heard. But La Fage did not stop with the demand for a public competition; the decree that the tomb was to be erected at the Invalides also came under attack, and in conclusion he expressed the wish that a separate monument be erected, preferably on the hill at Chaillot.

Shortly after the appearance of these personal views, the Société libre des Beaux-Arts published its own position paper.[24] It was in basic agreement with all the points brought up in La Fage's brochure but put more stress on the democratic values expressed by contests, likening them to the election of public officials, who had to place themselves in open competition before their peers. This report called further attention to the fact that the group had argued for the necessity to hold contests for national monuments as early as 1831. In conclusion, it urged even more strongly that a separate monument be built at Chaillot. But the activities of the group did not stop with an official report; its members conducted a collateral lobbying campaign, traces of which remain in its archives, in the form of letters and petitions addressed to legislators and the interior minister.[25]

Among those making the earliest demands for a public contest was the *Journal des Beaux-Arts*, which, less than five days after the announcement of the return of Napoleon's remains, issued a call for a contest and, at the same time, denigrated the work of architect Jacques-Ignace Hittorff, whom it was rumored had received the commission by administrative decree.[26] This attack on Hittorff, who appears never to have had any involvement with the project at all and who was among those advocating contests for public monuments at the very beginning of the July Monarchy, demonstrates that the demand for an open competition was so strong that anyone given the commission without one was sure to encounter the critical animus of the press, regardless of the merits of his project. This must be one factor that reduced the group of potential artists and architects from which the State was able to choose. [27] *L'Artiste* led the chorus of demands for a contest and the condemnation of the government for its dictatorial dispensation of patronage. In all its criticism of Marochetti's project, the journal made patently clear that it was condemning both the design and the arbitrary manner in which the decision was made to award him the commission. Therefore, given the tone of its editorial remarks about the monument, it undoubtedly surprised many of its readers to find an unofficial notice in its columns in the spring of 1841 containing both an announcement that a contest was to be held as well as an enthusiastic eulogy to the minister of the interior for his wise decision. But the journal also qualified its use of the term *concours* to describe the competition, stating that the contest would neither be general nor absolute. However, it declared that the difference was not great and that the principle of a contest was preserved in the plan of the government.

This article continued by outlining the difficulties that a "concours absolu" entailed, such as the fact that it might be won by a painter, who would not possess enough knowledge of the principles of architecture to realize the project after it was confided to him. Another obstacle to the adoption of an absolute contest was that a large, well-defined jury was required to examine the various projects; at the time the only such cohesive body in France was the reactionary Academy. For this reason it lauded the State's decision to make the choice itself, after independent consultation with the leading painters, sculptors, and architects of the day. Also defended was the decision not to provide a written program. This, it assured its readers, was not a serious detriment, since at least three possible locations and types of tombs had already been considered by the government and were still viable possibilities. Instead of being an obstacle imposed by the State, this lack of a program, it argued, could be conceived as an encouragement to artistic freedom and creativity. [28]

The official announcement that a contest was to be held was made in the Chamber of Deputies on 13 April, when a bill came under consideration for an appropriation of five hundred thousand francs to construct the tomb and to pay off the deficit that the translation ceremony had incurred. This bill was introduced by Duchâtel, who stated that the tomb would be a monument "of severe and imposing simplicity," and would be worthy of the name engraved upon it. To achieve this end, he declared that "we will make an appeal to all artists whose proven talents offered to the Administration guarantees of good execution."[29] As usual, a committee was formed to examine the *projet de loi*; in this case it was propitiously headed by Louis Vitet, who made a report to the Chambers a month later, recommending the passage of the law and elaborating to some degree upon the nature of the contest to be held. After expressing his regret that the tomb was to be constructed at the Invalides, Vitet proceeded to defend Duchâtel's decision to hold a "limited" contest, or a competition among only those artists it considered capable of actually executing the work if their designs were chosen. This expedient, according to the influential deputy and man of letters, was much preferable to an open contest—the kind that had never produced anything but unhappy results—since masters were extremely reluctant to enter into competition with their students or those who were manifestly their inferiors.[30]

Vitet's most important part in the process may have been in persuading Duchâtel, his close friend, to relent and hold a contest for the controversial monument. According to Rémusat, it was Vitet who persuaded the minister of the interior to take this step, and this assertion stands to reason in that Vitet was a personal advisor of Duchâtel on aesthetic matters.[31] However, rather than reflecting Vitet's belated conversion to the democratic principle of open competitions, it may have been conceived as a way of encouraging the administration to rethink or reopen the question of the location of the tomb, as well as the means of selecting its design.

For the next six weeks following the announcement of the contest, Duchâtel pursued a policy of strategic ambiguity. Instead of announcing the contest in the daily newspapers with large circulations, the government inserted a short notice in the *Moniteur universel* that escaped the attention of most potential entrants.[32] Thus, information about the contest circulated primarily by word of mouth in the art community of Paris. In addition, no information was forthcoming from the fine arts bureaucracy as to the rules of the contest, who was eligible to enter, or even how the projects submitted were to be selected and exhibited. Since no statement was issued concerning the important question of which projects would be displayed to the public, or under what circumstances, it soon came to be widely believed that the contest was open to everyone and that all projects would be exhibited. The State did nothing to counter this belief, and it became fact almost by default as the date of the contest approached. The deadline for submission of projects proved equally flexible, as it was first set for 1 September, and then, after being changed on several occasions, was finally established as 15 October, that is, nine days before the exhibition was scheduled to open at the Ecole des Beaux-Arts. Even more irritating to many was the fact that no jury was appointed and no method whereby the best projects would be selected was announced. Finally, no program or written statement concerning the dimensions, the materials, or the type of tomb desired was forthcoming.

As the deadline for submission of projects approached, predictable protests arose. Typical of the reaction to the contest's administration was the attack that appeared in *Journal des Artistes* on 15 August, which contained two accusations soon to be commonplace. The first charge was favoritism: "The administration opened a muted contest, with such secrecy that only its favorites could have known about it." And secondly, the whole affair was a sham: "We ask: what is the program of this contest? If someone does not respond to this question, we have the right to conclude that this contest is a simple pleasantry, or a pretext . . . ." The same charges were made in the revue on 24 October, the day of the preview of the projects by selected government officials: "It is unfortunate, as we have said a thousand times, that the choice seems to have been made in advance." Equally condemnatory was an article entitled "Prétendu concours pour le monument de Napoléon I" that appeared in *Journal des Beaux-Arts* on 10 August and in which the competition was called, among other epithets, a "species of clandestine contest," an "illusory contest" and a "veritable deception."[33]

The belief that the competition was rigged was probably the reason many prominent figures failed to submit projects and certainly the cause of the prominent withdrawal of two submissions. The first was by Charles-Joseph Toussaint, an architect who had served the government during the First Empire and who was a prolific writer on architectural matters. In a letter to the editor of *Journal des Artistes*, published on 10 October, he announced that he was withdrawing his project in protest against the "trap" that had been set by the government. Instead of visiting the "official" exhibition to see his plans for the monument, he invited the public to see them at his own studio. He further revealed that he had fruitlessly petitioned the Chamber of Deputies to intercede and to guarantee that some minimal recognition of the basic principles of public competitions be followed. One of his suggestions for making the contest more equitable was that a jury of twelve architects, twelve sculptors, and twelve painters be drawn by lot to judge the entries.[34]

The second withdrawal was that of Antoine Allier, both a practicing artist and a member of the Chamber of Deputies at the time. Not only was Allier a prolific portrait sculptor, who had represented some of the most important personages in France, he had also been a soldier in the Grande Armée. His letter of withdrawal, likewise published in the *Journal des Artistes*, gave as his reason the fact that although only a few days remained before the opening of the contest, the minister of the interior still refused to state whether the contest would be serious, or even how a jury would be selected to judge the entries. One complaint that the sculptor-politician was not able to make, however, is that he had not been given enough time to develop his ideas adequately, for he had already executed a print of his project the previous April.[35]

From this lithograph it is easy to see that had the three-dimensional model for his project actually been exhibited, it would probably have ranked among the simplest and most elegant of the competition (fig. 44). Eschewing complex allegory and symbolism, his conception placed the nude, expiring figure of Napoleon in the arms of France, and both figures atop a stark pedestal carved in such a way as to recall the notorious rock of Saint Helena, upon which he suffered his martyrdom. It appears that since the dual aspects of Napoleon's career were so well known, Allier believed that their recitation was otiose; all that was necessary to suggest them were a simple scroll with the words *code civil* inscribed on it and his unsheathed sword.

In face of the deluge of criticism, the Interior Ministry changed the deadline for the submission of projects, ultimately fixing it at 15 October, or a little more than a week before the

Fig. 44
Antoine Allier, *Project for a Tomb
of Napoleon*. Lithograph by
E. Lassalle, 1841. Photo courtesy
of the Bibliothèque Nationale, Département des Estampes.

exhibition opened. However, it steadfastly refused to select a
jury, in the manner of those that decided which entries were to be
exhibited at the Salon, for example, and refused to indicate how
or when the various projects were to be judged. When the exhibition of entries was finally opened to the Parisian public on 27
October, the subsequent reviews were almost unanimous in their
criticism of the high-handed manner in which the competition
had been conducted. The most impassioned attack came from
the pen of César Daly. Attempting to give his views wider circu-
lation before the contest closed, he published his criticism not
only in his own journal but also in *La France littéraire* and *La
Phalange*, the Fourierist daily.[36] Even though it was drawing to a
close, he argued, there was still time to create an impartial jury
and rectify the scandalous course the contest had taken. As his
solution to the difficult problem of how a fair and impartial jury

might be chosen, he set forth a plan whereby the contestants would themselves select the best project after the more mediocre ones had been eliminated by a secret vote of the entrants.

The direct relationship between the demand for contests and the author's politics is clearly seen in the career of this architect, journalist, and entrepreneur, who from the early thirties had been enchanted by the utopian ideals of Fourierism and Saint-Simonianism. These romantic social theories had in common their stress on the idea that a just social order was one in which social position was a function of merit, rather than birth or privilege. Daly was not opposed to a social hierarchy per se but believed that the social pyramid must be founded on individual worth. One means of attaining this just hierarchy of merit was by means of concours open to all members of society. The central position of this idea in his political belief system is seen in numerous contexts but was made concrete in the "profession de foi" he published in April 1848 to support his candidacy for the Assemblée Nationale. Among the principles he avowed, many of which stress his concern for the welfare of the working class, was the duty of the State to hold open competitions for public works of art: "I have always demanded that the principle of public contests be generalized."[37]

While the preponderance of critical opinion may have been in agreement with Daly on the necessity for contests, there were dissenting views, an example of which is the review in *La France*, a newspaper whose subtitle, *Journal des intérêts monarchiques et religieux de l'Europe*, provides an accurate description of its editorial policy. Instead of criticizing the political implications contained in the concept of a public contest, the reviewer of the exhibition summarized the history of failed and inconclusive competitions of this sort during the previous sixty years and enumerated the many practical difficulties in conducting one. In this particular contest he perceived that sculptors, architects, and painters were in competition with one another to make the essential features of their preferred medium prevail in the design, rather than being concerned with harmonizing the different aspects of the project, as they would be if the principle of authority were respected. It is more difficult to tie the review of E.-J. Délécluze to any such well-defined political or social position, but the rhetoric of his dissenting opinion was far harsher than that

LE CONCOURS POUR LE TOMBEAU de NAPOLÉON.

Vois-tu Grimgalet tous ces farceurs là ont trop de génie !.... c'est embarrassant !.... pour choisir le meilleur projet on sera forcé de les casser les uns contre les autres ! et le dernier qui restera ......adjugé !...

Fig. 45
Clément Pruche, *The Contest for the Tomb of Napoleon*. Lithograph, 1841. Photo courtesy of the Bibliothèque Nationale, Département des Estampes.

of the monarchical journal, attaining a pitch of near hysteria at points: "I recommend to all observers of our time, and in particular to the doctors of the insane, to go to the Palais des Beaux-Arts and judge . . . the degree of exaggeration, of insanity and bad taste to which the collective mind of our time has come."[38]

From this brief overview of the reception of the contest, it can be seen that a drawing by Clément Pruche, published in *La Caricature*, would have received an appreciative laugh from both opponents and proponents of the contest (fig. 45).[39] Standing amidst the models on display, one member of the Parisian artistic bohemia proclaims that the only way one could choose a winner from the group would be to smash them all together; the last to survive would be awarded the prize. This sarcastic joke thus corresponds to the opinions of both those who attributed the low quality of the works on display to the disgraceful manner in which the pseudocontest had been run and those who believed that by their very nature open contests of this variety were bound to produce such mediocre results.

In addition to all the accusations of bad faith and ineptitude on the part of the administration, a more serious charge became a leitmotif of the criticism: that certain contestants had been given inside information by those in power. An instance of this kind of accusation being made by someone hostile to the idea of contests is seen in the review previously cited of the legitimist paper *La France*, where it was alleged that "certain listeners at the door" had access to privileged information that gave their projects a distinct family resemblance and set them apart from all the others. The same charge of State favoritism, which made a mockery of the contest, was leveled by Daly in his first article on the event: "The majority of artists have the conviction, a moral certitude, right or wrong . . . that the work has been given in advance to M. Visconti." Needless to add, the final outcome of the selection process only confirmed these suspicions.[40]

One striking symbol of favoritism and special administrative privilege was unfortunately apparent at the exhibition hall door. An unofficial project executed by the architect Jean-Baptiste Dédéban was hung just outside the official exhibition space.[41] Dédéban had long been concerned with the idea of a tomb for the emperor, an instance of his preoccupation being the drawing he executed in 1836 in which a colossal replica of Canova's statue of Napoleon was placed upon a fantastical mausoleum presumably intended for the hill at Chaillot (fig. 46).[42] This image and others like it executed by the architect at roughly the same time hardly seem to predict that his project of 1841, submitted after the deadline, would deserve the special consideration accorded to it. Although his drawing is not available for judgment, the determining factor in the special treatment it received was probably not so much its quality as the privileged relationship that Dédéban had with Hygin-Auguste Cavé, the Directeur des Beaux-Arts, or someone in a position of power in the administration. The project of Dédéban would have been seen by many as a signboard announcing that the primacy of social position over merit presided at the contest.

Fig. 46
Jean-Baptiste Débéban, *Project for a Monument to Napoleon*. Drawing, 1836. Collection: The Louvre, Cabinet des Dessins. Photo courtesy of the Réunion des Musées Nationaux.

When the exhibition of contest entries finally opened its doors to the public, visitors were greeted by eighty-one projects that ran the gamut of style and type for commemorative or funeral monuments. Several individuals submitted more than one project—there apparently being no limit on the number one might enter in the sweepstakes—but others collaborated on projects, making the total of different names that appear on the list of contestants equal to the total number of entries. Not unexpectedly, half the entrants were architects, and 37 percent of the total were sculptors. However, six entries were from individuals who appear to have occupied positions in neither artistic nor architectural professions, or were amateurs at best.[43]

Of all the proposals in the contest, the one that was undoubtedly the most imaginative and departed the furthest from convention was by a career soldier, one Captain Théophile Bidon (entry no. 33). The critic for the *Journal des Artistes* summarized the opinion of many viewers: "One person only, Monsieur Bidon, has had a new and original idea, but unfortunately, it is too far beyond our customs to be adopted." Bidon himself, in the lengthy written program which accompanied his project, stressed that an unprecedented tomb was required for the "most extraordinary man of modern times."[44] To realize this goal he submitted a model that suspended a gigantic bronze eagle from the dome of the church, holding in its claws Napoleon's coffin, having just

Fig. 47
Alexandre Colin, *Nocturnal Convoy*. Lithograph after his drawing by Rigo brothers, 1840. Photo courtesy of the Bibliothèque Nationale, Département des Estampes.

snatched it from the ground. Bidon also offered two variants on this theme, one of which would have had the eagle suspended by cables from the dome, and the other in which the wings of an eagle, with a span of twenty-five meters, were affixed to each edge of the cupola.[45] Although he confessed that he had no training in the visual arts, he revealed in his cover letter that he had received advice and support from several sculptors, one being David d'Angers.

While Bidon's proposal for a tomb may have had no precedents, the image it presented did have sources in popular prints that perpetuated the mystique of Napoleon. The inspiration for his tomb may well have been, for example, a lithograph executed in 1840 by Alexandre Colin, representing the same act occurring amidst a phalanx of spectral troops of the Grande Armée (fig. 47). In this image bonapartism and romanticism are inseparably joined as they were in many of the similar images by Auguste Raffet. What this points up is that a large number of designs seem to have been inspired by popular imagery surrounding and elaborating the myth of Napoleon, rather than precedents in the history of art or the principles and realities of architectural practice.

Another project by a nonprofessional entrant (no. 49), a drawing of an enormous crystal ball through which the coffin of Napoleon would have been visible at the center, apparently embarrassed Cavé to the extent that he attempted to have it suppressed.[46] This transparent globe was supported by several boulders that were apparently meant to suggest the island of Saint Helena. The author of this idea, Achille Allevy, was an inventor of sorts and a member of one of the more eccentric families of the period. His principal invention was a system of numbers and letters that could serve as a mnemonic strategy for remembering historical dates. The "Levier intellectuel Allevy" was published in several different editions during the July Monarchy and assured its namesake a transitory niche in the annals of popular culture. In the case of Allevy, the director probably wished to remove the project on the grounds that it risked making a joke of a contest already the subject of ridicule.

The government likewise attempted to suppress another one of the more unusual projects in the contest (no. 56): a proposal to construct a bronze sarcophagus to house the remains of the emperor containing a mechanism that would continuously unroll the story of his life around the exterior. This perpetually moving picture show consisted of a clockwork apparatus driving a series of rollers, which kept in motion a continuous canvas support. Upon this moving pictorial field would have been painted the history of the great man. In his written program the inventor made a claim similar to that of Bidon—that it was necessary to create a monument that had no precedent in order to be in accord with the person it commemorated—but he also appealed to the imperatives of modernity, claiming that movement was an essential and defining feature of the modern world. The author of this moving-picture tomb, an obscure decorative painter and inventor named Geslin, simply adopted one of his latest inventions for the contest. In August 1840 he had received a patent for a device called

Fig. 48
P. F. Geslin, *The Historical Clock.* Drawing, 1840. Collection: Patent Office, Paris. Photo: the author.

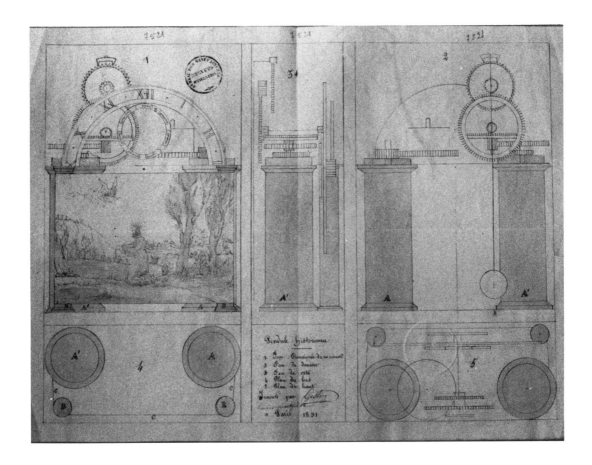

a *pendule historienne*. In his advertisement for the invention, he announced that one of the historical sequences that could be driven by his pendule was the "Tombeau de Napoléon," which would depict the principal events in the fabled career from the schooldays at Brienne to the return of his remains in 1840. An idea of what his project looked like can be gained from his drawing that accompanied his patent application (fig. 48).[47] In this drawing, dated nine years before he applied for his patent, the life of Christ is depicted, but it could just as well have been the torment of Napoleon.

It is obvious that Geslin considered the contest to be an excellent opportunity to gain free publicity for his recently patented product, and he probably entertained no illusions that it would be adopted. Cavé, who also seemed to realize that self-promotion was at the root of this entry, issued an order to have it removed from consideration. But when Geslin reminded him that he had been awarded a patent for his invention by the State, Cavé was forced to relent.[48] However minor this incident, it did point up one liability of open contests: self-promotion is often a stronger motive for competing than any real interest in the subject of the competition.

While most critics of the contest declined comment on Geslin's publicity stunt, César Daly, the author of the most thoughtful critique of the entries, concluded his review with it, declaring that it represented a sterling example of a deleterious tendency than ran through many of the projects. For Daly, Geslin's clockwork tomb demonstrated a general predilection for "reducing monuments to tablets for inscriptions." Contrary to this false practice, he held that "a work of plastic art ought to be an *expression* and not a *description*." This mechanical project was the ultimate projection and epitome of the principles underlying the latter category, or "an appropriate consequence of a false principle we have so often fought."[49]

In making this distinction, Daly was attempting either to establish categorical divisions between the arts or else restrict them to the domains of their own intrinsic competence. Expression, not description, which was simply prose or a genre of literature, was for him the true goal and area of competence of the art of architecture. It is clear from his comments on other entries that an equivalent term for *expression* in his lexicon was *poetry*. By this he meant feeling states that were engendered by the direct experience of expressive form, not by linguistic means or by narrative structures.[50] This distinction between the different logics of the linguistic and visual arts was, of course, one made in Lessing's famous *Laokoon* (1766), but Daly was providing a new set of terms for his binary opposition. Whereas Lessing had separated the arts in terms of their respective concerns with space and time, Daly perceived the difference to be one between nonverbal expression and linguistic presentation of ideas. This shift in emphasis from Lessing's space/time dichotomy to one of plastic expression/discursive presentation is among the most significant changes in the theoretical infrastructure of nineteenth-century art criticism. Daly's comments suggest one way of classifying the apparently heterogeneous assemblage of projects— that is, by placing them on either side of a narrative/nonnarrative or textual/nontextual axis.

It is interesting that he was able to disregard complex narrative or allegorical schemes entirely, since he believed that the dominant expression of a project lay in the realm of plastic form. Thus, he discussed in some detail the project of Joseph Nicolle (no. 8), which proposed many bas-reliefs recounting events from Napoleon's careers and which included an allegorical parade, rendered in mosaic, of victory figures passing the gates of conquered cities. What was important for the critic was not this proliferation of historical detail but the overall form of the sarcophagus in the "primitive etruscan style [which] is entirely a poem in its silence and its nudity."[51] While the work was filled with two-dimensional detail, it was stripped of unnecessary architectural ornament, which would have obscured or undercut its essential, expressive form. This criticism is valuable in that it provides another formal criterion by which the various entries might be classed: the degree to which they tended toward either the pictorial or architectonic poles.

Contrary to what one might assume, preoccupation with the pictorial was not the exclusive prerogative of nonarchitects. An example of hyperpictorialism is seen in the proposal of Auguste Rougevin (no. 9), the architect in charge of maintenance of the entire Hôtel des Invalides complex. For the tomb, he envisioned a circular basin filled with water, in the middle of which would have been placed a sarcophagus on a base meant to simulate the solitary island where Napoleon expired. The source of his imagery seems to be the numerous prints depicting the lonely grave on Saint Helena, such as the lithograph made after a painting by Horace Vernet entitled the *Apotheosis of Napoleon* in which two of Napoleon's generals on the small island grieve over his rough grave upon which is placed his hat and sword (fig. 49).[52]

Another project by an unknown contestant was even more literal in evoking or reconstructing the island, recreating in his model the simple tumulus that covered Napoleon's first burial site. On the stone was placed an imperial eagle crying out in sorrow.[53] Pierre Gauthier, a sculptor and member of the Académie des Beaux-Arts, evoked this place of final exile in yet another manner, placing in his aedicular structure a figure of Napoleon sitting on a boulder—a metonymy for the place of his death (no. 26). For

Fig. 49
The Apotheosis of Napoleon. Lithograph after Horace Vernet's painting of 1821. A. S. K. Brown Collection. Photo: the author.

François Sagaret, author of the most extended critique of the entries in the contest, this kind of literalism raised the fundamental question of what message, from the large range of possibilities, should be expressed by the tomb. In his view this lamentable final episode should not detract from the grandeur of the achievements of Napoleon and therefore should be remembered by nothing more than an inscription with the name of the island.[54]

Pictorialism inserted itself into the contest in other ways as well. Several contestants designed projects in which sculptural groups functioned as *tableaux* representing historical events. Such was the conception in the model exhibited by the architect François Duquesney (no. 55). The *pièce de résistance* of this complex project was a sculptural group in the center of an aedicular structure that represented soldiers of the Grande-Armée shouldering Napoleon's coffin.[55] As in the case of Bidon, when conceiving his tableau Duquesney may have had in mind a popular lithograph like that executed by Aimé Lemud to commemorate the retour des cendres (fig. 22).

Charles-Frédéric Chassériau, architect and cousin of the painter Théodore Chassériau, was likewise taken more with the pictorial possibilities of the project than the architectonic ones. His conception (no. 5) featured very coarse enemy soldiers struggling to support a globe upon which a triumphant equestrian group, with Napoleon in the center, was placed. This project provoked the scornful and predictable comment from Huard in the *Journal des Artistes* that he had created a painting rather than a monument. According to him, Chassériau, like many others in the contest, had followed Horace's precept of *ut pictura poesis* and forgotten that narrative poetry and architecture were different genres.[56] But the most curious of these projects adhering to the pictorial pole was possibly that of the minor painter Fanelli-Semah (no. 54). A critic for *L'Artiste* described it in some detail apparently because of its bizarre character:

> Mr. Fanelli has strewn on a platform, crowned by a joyful apotheosis of Napoleon, a world composed of Frenchmen, Turks, Chinese, Indians, soldiers, Italians, incredible personages, with grimacing physionomies, with grotesque appearances, who chat peacefully among themselves, read the newspaper, meditate gravely, or give themselves up to fantastical laughter. All that is lacking to this comic scene is an explanatory text.[57]

If Fanelli-Semah left the master idea informing his production opaque, others went to just the other extreme in establishing hyperdidactic programs that spelled out in minute detail the various aspects of Napoleon's biography and career. This suggests that another means of classifying the projects might be to place them on a scale of didactic intent. Using this criterion, one would probably have to assign the maximum number of points to the project submitted by Totain and Vigreux (no. 40), whose complex program of allegory and emblematic references required three full pages for Sagaret to summarize. Under this classificatory system, the design of the sculptor Pierre Guersant (no. 75) would also score very high. The critic for *L'Artiste* characterized it as "simply a geography lesson of the most knowledgeable and

Fig. 50
Louis Auvray, *Project for a Tomb of Napoleon*. Engraving by J. Huguenet, from *Revue générale de l'architecture*, 1841. Photo: the author.

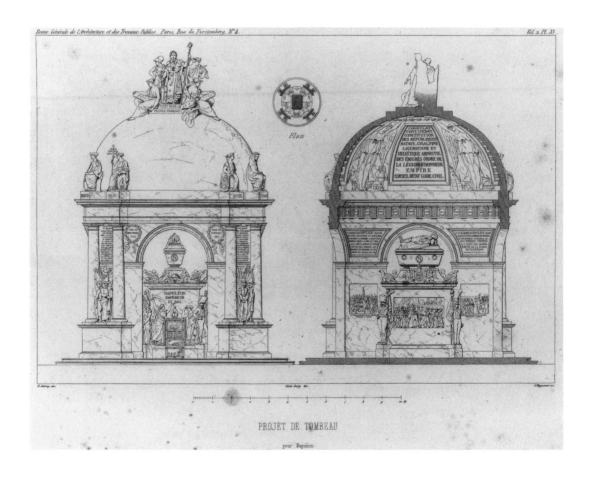

complicated sort."[58] In his representation of Napoleon's world-historical significance, Guersant filled his composition with references to all parts of the world where the glory of Napoleon had presumably penetrated, however faintly.

We possess the most complete documentation for the didactic project of the sculptor and writer Louis Auvray (no. 51). Not only was it discussed at length by critics, but César Daly also reproduced an engraving of it in his critique of the contest (fig. 50). Auvray proposed a tomb of the aedicular type, with a sarcophagus in the center resting on a mausoleumlike structure. On top of the sarcophagus was to be placed a gisant figure of Napoleon in military costume. The circular structure enclosing the sarcophagus, or "Temple de Gloire" as his program described it, would have supported a monumental statue of Napoleon enthroned in imperial regalia. The surfaces of this temple would have been covered, inside and out, with a plethora of depictions of historical

Fig. 51
Louis Auvray, *Maquette for a Tomb of Napoleon*. Plaster. Photo after lost original. Collection: Bibliothèque Municipale, Valenciennes. Photo: the author.

events and inscriptions recounting the details of Napoleon's life, a conception of a monument-as-classroom that demanded a reading stance from a beholder with enough patience to follow the lesson. A theatrical dimension was given to the conception by the proposal of a mortuary chapel accessible through the door in the base supporting the sarcophagus. Upon entering the door and descending the stairwell, one would have found a space decorated to resemble the cabin of the *Belle Poule* and illuminated by a large lamp in the form of an eagle through whose eyes light would have been diffused. Auvray was obviously convinced of the high quality of his project in that he exhibited it again at the Salon of 1852 and published the original program and photographs of his maquette twenty years later. The photograph of his lost model for the sarcophagus in the interior of his structure is valuable in that it provides some idea of the degree of finish possessed by most of the projects (fig. 51).[59]

An aedicular structure was favored by other entrants such as the architect Jules Bouchet, who was to soon become the *inspecteur* of the project and chief assistant to Visconti. Bouchet made his tomb much more of an architectural monument than many of the other projects and also proposed a rich and complex system of relief sculpture and written inscriptions (fig. 52). In designing a monument with an effigy of Napoleon as a gisant inside the open structure and a freestanding figure of immortality above it, his conception was similar to that of Auvray. Bouchet's monument might also be placed in another category, among those projects in which all the figures and allegorical elements are in the classical mode and any reference to the nineteenth century by means of dress is excluded. Sagaret was the only critic to discuss the conception of Bouchet, but his remarks are worth citing since they demonstrate that in the act of perceiving and judging these projects gender distinctions played a part. After making a number of formal observations and opining that the pilasters supporting the canopy over the gisant figure were too feeble, he concluded that "the richness and delicacy of this tomb makes it suitable for a queen."[60]

In this classification scheme, a separate group would be composed of the small number that adhered to César Daly's belief that expressive architectural form should be privileged over both discursive detail and decorative embellishment. This design

Fig. 52
Jules Bouchet, *Project for a Tomb of Napoleon*. Drawing, 1841. Photo courtesy of the Musée Vivenel, Compiègne.

priority was defended emphatically by Emile Seurre, the sculptor who executed the statue of Napoleon for the Vendôme Column. In the written part of his entry (no. 52), he emphasized that he wished to reduce or eliminate narrative content and literary detail in the sculptural program and focus on constructing his monument from a few fundamental geometrical forms. Félix Duban, probably the most prestigious architect who entered the contest, likewise reduced allegory and discursive content to a minimum, stressing simplicity of design in his submission (no. 24). His blocklike sarcophagus rested on a simple base around which were disposed eighteen figures symbolizing different aspects of Napoleon's career (fig. 53). Unlike many other projects that envisioned the use of a variety of rich materials, Duban's would have been composed only of white marble. Daly, a former student of Duban, expressed his admiration for the simplicity of Duban's design and reproduced an engraving of his project, but he wished that the architect had gone further and eliminated the inscriptions above the figures and made a clean break between architecture and literature.[61]

Fig. 53
Félix Duban, *Project for a Tomb of Napoleon*. From *Revue générale de l'architecture*, 1841. Photo: the author.

Revue Générale de l'Architecture et des Travaux Publics. Paris, Rue de Furstemberg, N°4.   Vol. 2. Pl. 32.

Another project that tended toward the architectonic pole, though it included a sculptural group, was the monument conceived by the sculptor and member of the Academy, Louis Petitot (no. 58, fig. 54). His tomb would have been constructed with simple rectilinear units that established an implied pyramid. Four allegorical figures and a seated effigy of Napoleon in imperial dress were placed in a configuration that repeated that of the geo-

Fig. 54
Louis Petitot, *Project for a Monument to Napoleon*, 1841. Lithograph by A. Leloir, from *L'Artiste*, 1841. Photo: the author.

metrical components. In his accompanying written description, Petitot stressed that reliefs of four eagles were the only signs necessary to signify the individual honored by the tomb.[62] It might be noted, however, that in 1836 Petitot had been given a commission for the figure of Louis XIV to be placed on Cartellier's unfinished equestrian monument, now in the central courtyard at Versailles; in that instance he refused to give the Sun King antique dress, as was requested. After taking his demand to execute the work in modern dress to Louis-Philippe himself, he finally had his way.[63] Since he gave his figure of Napoleon antique dress in his project, it seems he believed that modern dress for his sepulchral monument would add an anecdotal or discursive element that would undercut its architectonic qualities.

Among the compositions that fell somewhere in between the poles of architectonic reductionism and didactic elaboration are those such as the proposal (no. 18, fig. 55) of Louis Moreau. Like Duban's, Moreau's design has the appearance of a simple sarcophagus, but it is in fact a mausoleum, the interior of which is accessible from a door in one end. The qualities that distinguish his conception are absolute clarity of structure and additive construction of simple geometric units. Although it displays several historical reliefs and inscriptions, severity of design, recalling the Empire style and the austerity of military life, is the most salient feature. This severity of form is also stressed by a historical reference: the figure of Napoleon reclines in the manner of figures on Etruscan sarcophagi, then thought to be paradigmatic of primitivism in European art.

While the structural clarity of Moreau's project can be considered an attempt to evoke the personal qualities of its namesake, it should also be seen in relation to the architect's own social views. Louis Moreau—the father of the symbolist painter Gustave Moreau—was a committed republican and confirmed anticlerical, opinions that emerge forcefully in a tract he published in 1831 in which he discussed the uses and abuses of the arts by theocratic governments. According to Moreau, the

Fig. 56
Henri de Triqueti, *Model for a Tomb of Napoleon*. Mixed media, 1840–41. Collection: Musée Girodet, Montargis. Photo courtesy of the Courtauld Institute, London.

Fig. 57
Henri de Triqueti, *Project for a Tomb of Napoleon*. Drawing, 1840. Photo courtesy of the Musée des Arts décoratifs, Paris.

fine arts were a primary instrument of social domination in the first monarchies:

> It is they [the rulers] who prepared the mysteries; without them there would have been none; they dressed the idols, placed them in obscure cellas of temples, imposing by the richness of their beautiful disposition, by their sculpture, by their symbolic painting; the music they produced announced in lugubrious and sharp tones, the anger of the clemency of the divinity.[64]

He went on to add in a footnote that the interdependence of art, religion, and autocratic rule, had manifested itself once again in the First Empire and the Restoration. Thus, it seems that an ethical and ideological imperative is encoded in Moreau's design; its euclidean clarity appears to be an antidote to aesthetic mystification and the consequences that follow from it. His tomb might be seen as an attempt to honor but at the same time demystify its occupant.

Of all the projects in the contest executed by sculptors, the most widely remarked upon was that of Henri de Triqueti (no. 73). His contribution was a model constructed of wood, wax, and plaster and a drawing that proffered a variant on it (figs. 56, 57). Although we cannot be sure that they were the ones actually in the contest, a model and drawings for the project survive that provide a very clear idea of what he was proposing.[65] Since his drawing is signed and dated 1840, it appears that he, like others in the exhibition, had been meditating upon the project long before the contest was announced. His proposal consisted of a reclining figure of Napoleon expiring atop a sarcophagus and a base decorated with a program of bas-reliefs (figs. 58, 59).[66] Rather than the semirecumbent figure of Napoleon, the part of the project that attracted the most attention was the bas-relief that ran around the sides of the base. Renowned at the time for his bas-reliefs on the bronze doors of the Church of the Madeleine in Paris, the sculptor appears to have given the greater part of his creative energies to this part of the work.[67] Although Triqueti seems not to have submitted separate drawings of the frieze, those that survive enable one to follow the narrative sequence that was to have been composed of life-size allegorical figures in rhythmical poses and classical dress, with emblematic devices, attributes, and inscriptions serving to comment on their actions. This eurhythmic procession wending its way around the base recounted the significant events in Napoleon's life, from the first Italian campaign to the retour des cendres. In terms of typology, this tomb should be included among those in which narrative plays a major role; however, it evaded the pedantry exhibited by the majority occupying this category.

In Triqueti's relief, the story is suggested and implied, rather than told or illustrated. One must already be familiar with the details of Napoleon's career to make any sense of it. Rather than adopting a reading stance before it, the beholder is invited first of all to appreciate the lyrical movement and countermovement of the figures. This is to say that viewing precedes intellectualization. Of course, this choice was to leave the artist open to charges by some critics that this work was deficient in narrative clarity. However, César Daly leveled just the opposite criticism, declaring that the work, however finely rendered, was a prime example of the conflation of genres, or confusion of "la poésie plastique" and "la poésie écrite." In fairness Daly applied the same critique to another project he admired, that of Antoine Etex (fig. 38), which, as we have seen, featured a statue of Napoleon on horseback on a symbolic globe. In his description, the sculptor indicated that on the bronze globe "the shoes of his horse remain

imprinted" after his passage, a literary image Daly thought should be rigorously excluded from an architectural monument.[68]

Well aware that his project received much critical acclaim, Triqueti attempted to use this praise to win the commission after the contest had concluded. In an undated letter written to

Fig. 58
Henri de Triqueti, *Project for a Bas-relief Running around the Sarcophagus of the Tomb of Napoleon.* Drawing, left half, 1840–41. Photo courtesy of the Musée des Arts décoratifs, Paris.

Rémusat, who had left his position as minister of the interior, the sculptor solicited his aid and expressed both chagrin and bitterness that the result of the contest had apparently been determined in advance, even though his own proposal was the most favorably received of all those submitted by sculptors. He further argued that the commission ought to be given to a sculptor who actually *participated* in the contest and not to Marochetti, who abstained.[69]

Given the original attempts to create a tomb in the form of an equestrian monument and the continued discussions as to how one might be incorporated, it is no surprise to learn that horses have a prominent place in many of the designs in the contest. After the proposal of Etex, the most flamboyant of the various equestrian projects must be that of the painter Achille Devéria and the sculptor Hippolyte Maindron (no. 7 or 72) (fig. 60).[70]

Fig. 59
Henri de Triqueti, *Project for a Bas-relief Running around the Sarcophagus of the Tomb of Napoleon.* Drawing, right half.

Although the body of Napoleon was intended to be encased in the globe on top of which his equestrian figure is precariously perched, little recalls the supposed funereal function of the monument. The impression that movement or kinetic potential is the subject being celebrated here is reinforced by the written description that accompanied the project: "The Emperor launches his eagle from the globe he dominates, and around which all the glories are in agitated motion; the noise they make awakens and an-

Fig. 60
Achille Devéria and Hippolyte
Maindron, *Project for a Tomb of Napoleon*. Lithograph, 1841.
Photo courtesy of the Bibliothèque
Nationale, Département des
Estampes.

imates in diverse ways all the peoples of which the base is composed." Perhaps because of the status of the two artists responsible for this project most critics refrained from comment, but the reviewer for *Journal des Artistes* was less kind, recommending that two well-known circus owners use it as inspiration for one of their future acts.[71]

The collaborative effort (no. 67) of the sculptor Raymond Gayrard and the Corsican architect Louis de Ligny likewise had as a centerpiece an equestrian statue of Napoleon, but in their rendition he was dressed in imperial regalia and placed in a static pose on top of a simple sarcophagus with a rectangular base.[72] Their tomb was intended to be located under the cupola of Hardouin-Mansart's church, but others conceived of the tomb as a two-part undertaking and placed the equestrian component outside. This arrangement appears in the proposal (no. 59) of the elder Antoine Dantan, whose design consisted of a rectangular granite mausoleum with very little decoration or ornament in the interior and an equestrian monument in the inner courtyard. The only link between the two parts would have been conceptual.

The most unusual and complex of the proposals for a tomb with an equestrian statue as part of the design was submitted by the architect Philippe Cannissié (no. 12). It attracted much critical comment in that it departed from the idea of placing the tomb directly under the cupola of the church. Instead, Cannissié proposed to leave the center of the dome unobstructed and place the tomb against the wall of the south portal.[73] As the visitor entered the church through this door, he would have passed through a triumphal arch, on the top of which was situated a monumental sarcophagus in an aedicular structure surmounted by an equestrian statue of Napoleon in his military uniform, placed parallel to the wall. This effigy of the emperor would have been only one of a panoply of sculpted figures, including life-size statues of Mars and Minerva, representing aspects of his civil and military careers.[74] Here Cannissié seems simply to have taken the Renaissance prototype of the tomb of Louis de Brézé in France or the Colleoni tomb in Bergamo, placed a door in its lower tier, and blown it up to truly Napoleonic proportions.

It is unclear what kind of project the architect François Thiollet entered in the contest, but a petition he addressed to the Chamber of Deputies committee charged with studying the

Fig. 61
François Thiollet, *Floor Plan for a Tomb of Napoleon at the Invalides.* Lithograph, 1843. Photo courtesy of the Bibliothèque Nationale.

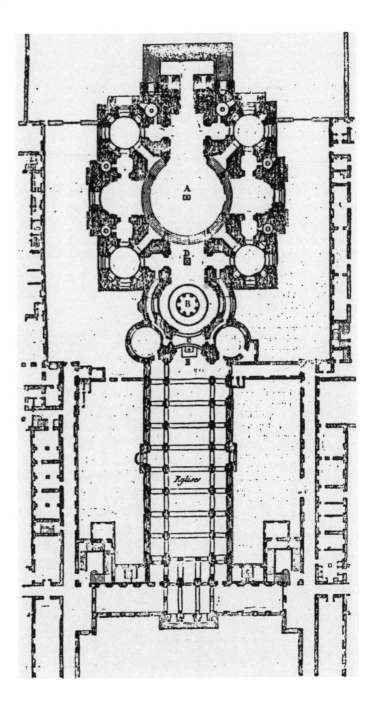

allocation of funds for the tomb complex shows that he also was aware of the difficulty of placing the tomb directly under the dome.[75] His solution to the problem is, from an architectural point of view, one of the most satisfactory to be found either in the contest or in the debate and criticism it engendered. Thiollet accompanied his description with a floor plan, which shows that he desired the monument, topped by a standing effigy of Napoleon, to occupy the circular space between the main altar in Mansart's dome and the basilican-plan church of Bruant (fig. 61). Access to the tomb would have been through doors on either side of the tomb area, a feature that resolved the problem of access, which was one of the principal difficulties created by the decision to install the tomb at the Invalides. This plan also entailed moving the main altar and baldachin to the space directly under the cupola, which was a more logical placement given the special kind of ceremonies conducted there. But most important, his

Projet d'un Monument à Napoléon.
par M.M. Lévêque et Buhot.

Fig. 62
Edmond Lévêque and Louis Buhot, *Project for a Monument to Napoleon*. Lithograph after their drawing by Lerous, from *L'Artiste*, 1841. Photo: the author.

design would have resolved the awkward problem of the transition between the two churches built in different architectural modalities and given the complex a tripartite structure.

Another category in which one might place entries in the contest is the mausoleum. Rather than attempting to integrate their tombs into the architectural fabric of the designated location, many proposed simply to construct a building within a building or a structure that could just as easily be placed, as an autonomous unit, in any cemetery. One such project is the collaborative effort of the sculptors Edmond Lévêque and Louis Buhot (no. 71), which *L'Artiste* preserved for posterity in a lithograph (fig. 62). The distinguishing feature of this design is the contrast established between the blocklike forms of the mausoleum and the scene of apotheosis above, which occurs in some transcendental space. Other submissions combined the features of mausoleum and commemorative monument. Hector Horeau's entry (no. 62) was of this type. Though his plaster model has not survived, we know that it only modified a design after which he made an engraving in October 1840 (fig. 63).[76] According to Daly, who thought it among the best in the exhibition, the revised design projected a structure sixteen meters high, a decrease of five meters from the original drawing, and had a square base, rather than the original octagonal one seen in the print. The effect of reducing the structure to a four-sided pyramidal form was to give it greater simplicity and stasis. In marked contrast to the reductive design of Horeau's mausoleum, others followed the "wedding cake" principle of decorative accretion, an example being the one designed by the painter Antoine Rivoulon (no. 32, fig. 64).[77] On top of a central cube are piled a profusion of decorative detail and allegorical figures, capped by a figure of Napoleon in imperial dress, reminiscent of many in the contest.

A man with a fertile imagination, Antoine Etex was not content to submit only one project for the tomb. After he had had his equestrian tomb accepted, he attempted to put three alternative conceptions in the contest as well but was denied the opportunity, ostensibly because the deadline had passed. However, they became an unofficial part of the contest when Daly, who used this administrative decision as another occasion to criticize the manner in which the contest was conducted, published Etex's description of them.[78] The most finished of Etex's nonexhibited

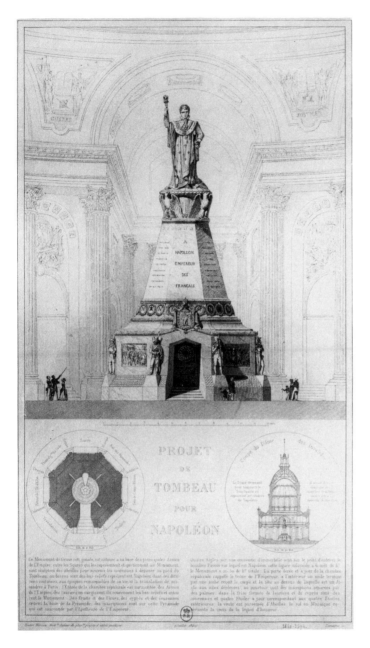

Fig. 63
Hector Horeau, *Project for a Tomb of Napoleon*. Lithograph, 1840. Photo courtesy of the Bibliothèque Nationale, Département des Estampes.

Fig. 64
Antoine Rivoulon, *Project for a
Monument to Napoleon*. Lithograph by Perret after his drawing,
1841, from *L'Artiste*, 1841. Photo:
the author.

drawings presents a dramatic reversal of his earlier depiction of
Napoleon astride a fiery stallion. The emperor in full regalia is
hieratically enthroned on a mausoleumlike structure whose static
forms are in keeping with those of the imperial effigy (fig. 65).
The program for this design states that the feats of Napoleon
would be inscribed on the bronze panels that close the niches of
the structure, but on the anniversary of his death each year they
would be opened, thereby converting it for a brief period into an
aedicular tomb. But another of his nonexhibited designs is more
interesting in that it portends to some degree what many at the
conclusion of the contest came to believe was the State's hidden
agenda. In his plan of 1840 Etex had not intended that the body
of Napoleon be placed in either the bronze sphere or the marble

base, but instead in a crypt underneath the monument that would have been accessible by a stairway at its base.[79] His second nonexhibited project of 1841 retained the ideas of an equestrian monument; a sunken crypt, marked only by a bronze plaque with his name, would have been located at the center of the dome. This last project of Etex, then, might be assigned to another category that was delineated by most critics of the contest: a sunken crypt, either open or closed to the architectural space above.

In terms of its break with precedents, the most daring of the projects falling under the rubric of "crypt" is probably that of Henri Labrouste (no. 3). César Daly, who reproduced an engraving after Labrouste's drawing, pronounced it to be "a truly modern and original creation," and another commentator stated unequivocally that it was "the most original of the contest."[80] One of the most finished architectural drawings to have survived, it both illustrates Labrouste's conception from different points of view and provides a written text describing it (fig. 66). His inno-

Fig. 66
Henri Labrouste, *Project for a Tomb of Napoleon*. Drawing, 1841. Collection: The Louvre, Cabinet des dessins. Photo courtesy of the Réunion des Musées Nationaux.

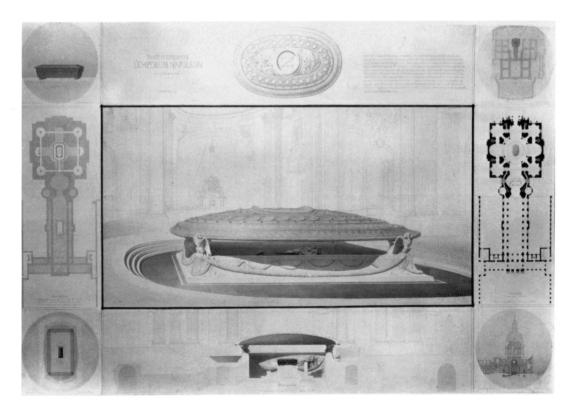

vation was to give the cover of his crypt a form appropriate to the individual whose remains would rest underneath: an oval-shaped shield fabricated in bronze. This shield covered a rectangular opening and was raised above it in such a way that one could gain a partial view of the crypt below from the ground level of the church. On either end of the shield were bas-reliefs representing Napoleon's death and the triumphal return of his remains in 1840. The entryway to the crypt was located in one of the side chapels. Thus, the central space of the dome would have been

Fig. 67
Théodore Labrouste, *Project for a Tomb of Napoleon.* Drawing, 1841. Collection: the Ecole des Beaux-Arts, Paris. Photo courtesy of Bulloz.

unobstructed, but a gigantic metonomy for the person being honored would have been inescapably present. What sets this design apart from the ones already discussed is that it was a fundamentally *architectural* solution to a problem: he did not attempt to add his tomb to an existing structure or simply harmonize it with its architectural frame but tried to make it an integral part of Mansart's building. A shrewd professional, Labrouste also made provision for the much-desired equestrian statue, including a small plan of the site in the upper-right-hand corner of his drawing that illustrated three possible locations for this monument.

Unlike Labrouste's semi-open crypt, most of the projects that employed a crypt in their design (approximately eight) closed it completely to the space above. Even in the project of his brother Théodore (no. 19), the crypt would have been closed. Théodore Labrouste, in his proposal, hedged his bets and chose to include a huge statue of Napoleon, which would have been placed under the cupola and above the closed crypt (figs. 67, 68). At the base of this colossal image, which would have been a highly obtrusive presence in the church that blocked any continuous view along the two principal axes, was a semicircular staircase that led to the

Fig. 68
Théodore Labrouste, *Statue of Napoleon for Tomb Project*. Drawing, 1841. Collection: the Ecole des Beaux-Arts, Paris. Photo courtesy of Bulloz.

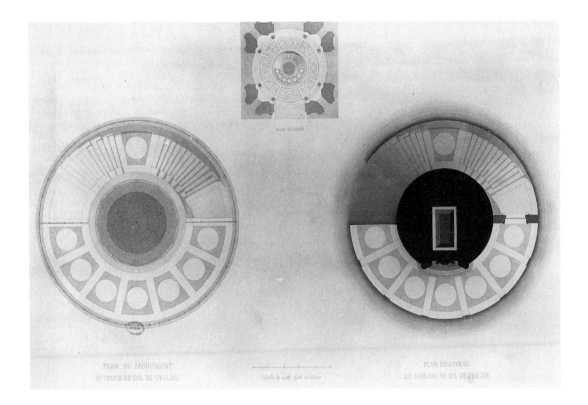

cavern underground (fig. 69). Apart from inscriptions and the ever-present emblematic eagle, there would have been no other sculptural decoration. Labrouste's formula of colossus above/ crypt below was also adopted by architect Victor Lemaire, who imagined a statue of Napoleon thirteen meters high in the same position. And the team of architect Théodore Charpentier and sculptor Jean-Baptiste (Jules) Klagmann, eschewing the representation of the emperor in his human form, projected a fearsome statue of an eagle on roughly the same scale, which would have served as a sentinel for the closed crypt below.[81]

Finally, we should consider three projects that included crypts in their designs but also had certain features in common, which caused them to be grouped together in a distinct subclass in the criticism: all proposed an equestrian statue for the cour d'honneur and an underground crypt in the center of Mansart's dome, the two parts being connected by a subterranean passageway running the length of Bruant's church. The first of these cognate

Fig. 69
Théodore Labrouste, *Floor Plan for Tomb Project*. Drawing, 1841. Collection: the Ecole des Beaux-Arts, Paris. Photo courtesy of Bulloz.

projects sprang from the drafting board of the architect Edouard Isabelle. Although Isabelle's drawing is unavailable for inspection, we do possess a brochure, published at the time of the exhibition, which describes it in detail.[82] His written explanation and defense of his proposal begins by providing philosophical justification and historical precedents for the long tunnel that would have provided the only access to his crypt. In a well-designed mortuary edifice, he argues, there should be enough distance between the main entrance and the actual tomb of the defunct to allow a space of meditation and reflection on the transiency of life as one approaches the sarcophagus. As an example of a monument serving this function, he cites an Egyptian prototype identified as the tomb of Osymandias. More than just a long corridor, however, he conceives of his underground passageway as a military pantheon or place where the tombs of France's most illustrious soldiers would be placed.

But this accounts for only half his project. Like Théodore Labrouste, he also proposed to erect a triumphal monument in the dome over a crypt. This would have consisted of a pyramidal tumulus bearing a statue of Napoleon expiring and would have been decorated by a great assemblage of foreign flags or trophies won in battle by French armies. Recognizing the potential conflict between the monument and the altar as competing visual foci, or between two different functions of the building, he proposed an innovative solution. Arguing that Hardouin-Mansart's church was originally intended to serve as "un monument triomphale" rather than a church where the normal liturgical functions were carried out, he proposed to make this distinction more concrete by relegating the religious function entirely to Bruant's church and converting the dome to a strictly commemorative and triumphal monument, one dedicated to the memory of Napoleon.

The basic components of Isabelle's design were also found in that executed by Victor Baltard, a young architect soon to gain considerable prominence in France and the son of an important member of the Academy. His project differed significantly in one respect, however. While Isabelle's plan called for two entryways on either side of the facade of Bruant's church, Baltard's entry to the underground corridor would have been through a bronze door in the base of the equestrian statue in the courtyard. Another significant difference is that instead of the monumental statue in

Mansart's church, which was part of Isabelle's plan, Baltard proposed a simple cenotaph with a gisant figure of Napoleon.

A noteworthy part of Baltard's submission is the written text that accompanied his drawing and was in part an apology for it, which might be considered his personal criticism of the way the contest was managed. In it he asserted that if he had had more time for reflection, he would have made his project even simpler, replacing the cenotaph under the cupola with a simple plaque with the name "Napoleon" inscribed on it, and eliminated the allegorical figures he originally planned to have executed in mosaic tile in the vault of his closed crypt.[83] He added a further note of apology for the unfinished quality of his drawings, which might be attributed to the circumstance that he, like the other contestants, had completed the work within the original deadlines and had not benefited from the extensions or uncertainty that had marked the organization of the competition. His implied accusations of misrule were followed by a challenge: "but let a serious contest be promulgated, and one will see whether I and the other contestants are ready to make serious efforts."

Baltard refrained from actually naming those who had benefited from the arbitrary extensions of the submission deadline,

Fig. 70
Louis Visconti, *Project for the Tomb of Napoleon*. Tracing after lost drawing, 1841. Photo courtesy of the Archives Nationales.

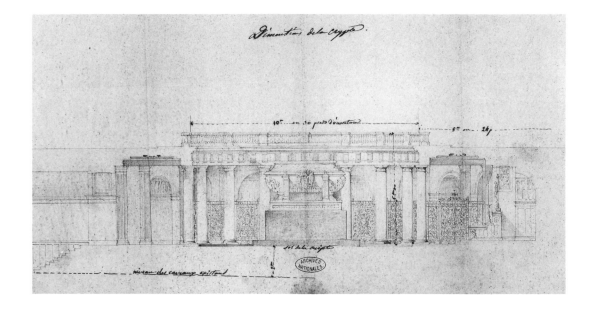

but everyone *au courant* of the gossip surrounding this event knew that the referent of his accusation, or the reputed beneficiary of the government's actions, was Louis Visconti. Whereas one of these two architects may have received preferential treatment, there were certain similarities in their designs. Like Baltard, Visconti proposed an equestrian statue in the courtyard with a door in its base that would give access to an underground passageway leading to a crypt containing the sarcophagus. His innovation, however, was to propose an "open crypt" or cryptlike space that would be open to the interior space of Mansart's church above. This feature made his plan unique in the concours in that he was the only person to advocate such a design. Although his original drawing has disappeared, a tracing of the longitudinal section of the crypt has survived, enabling one to match his written description with it (fig. 70).[84]

In what was surely the most carefully drafted program in the exhibition, Visconti began with a display of his classical erudition, stating that his equestrian figure of Napoleon would be dressed in a *Paludamentum*. He then proceeded to describe his underground corridor that was to serve as a military pantheon, the nature of which can be imagined by modifying an eighteenth-century longitudinal section of the two churches (fig. 71). This passageway would have been decorated with bronze tablets, sepulchers of France's military heroes, and marble bas-reliefs recalling the *fastes* of the Empire and the benefits that devolved from Napoleon's reign. Finally, after walking eighty meters in this tunnel one would have reached the crypt and the granite sarcophagus of the emperor in the center. In this space, whose opening to the cupola above was projected to be ten meters across, there was to be little sculptural decoration except for the statues of Napoleon's generals, which would occupy the niches in the wall of the peristyle surrounding the sarcophagus. In addition, on the side opposite the entry door a hemicycle or small chapel with an unobtrusive altar was to be constructed. Visconti's description concluded by explaining the rationale underlying his plan, stating that this was the only solution that would not alter the *physionomie* of Hardouin-Mansart's justly famous edifice. In answer to the obvious question of why an open rather than a closed crypt was preferable, he was less convincing. His reason was that this arrangement would make "clear to the eyes of everyone that

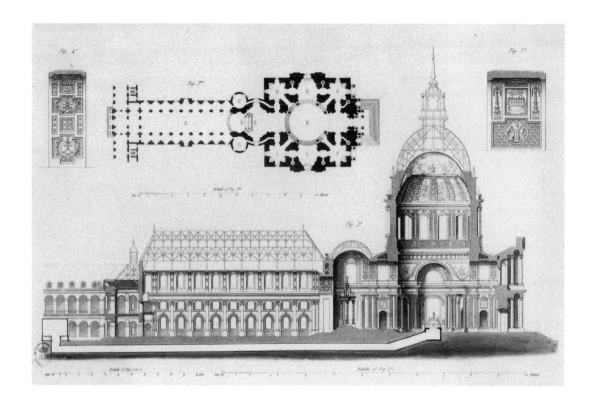

Napoleon rested under the cupola of the Invalides," therefore giving immediate ocular proof that the pledge of the king and the will of the chambers had been realized. What passed unsaid in this program was that with this kind of design, one that struck a juste-milieu between monument and crypt, or mediated conflicting conceptions as to the type of structure required.

The severest critic of Visconti's design was César Daly, who devoted almost as many words to it as to the other projects combined. Despite Daly's avowed preference for structures that placed expressive architectural form above pictorial description, his verdict on the effort of Visconti was resolutely negative. Pulling out all the stops in his attack, he declared that this project represented the confused views of the administration and proceeded to ridicule the idea of an open crypt, claiming that it was a contradiction in terms and that regardless of Visconti's disclaimer, it certainly did alter Hardouin-Mansart's venerable building. During this torrent of critical abuse he further likened

Fig. 71
Longitudinal Section of the Invalides. Plan modified to show Visconti's proposed passageway. Photo: the author.

the crypt to the sunken pits at the Jardin des Plantes where the bears were kept and implied that the crowd leaning over Visconti's balustrade would perform the same sort of act as the visitors to this popular zoological garden. Switching similes, he also declared that if a fountain were to replace the sarcophagus, one would "believe oneself transported to the gardens of the Alhambra."[85]

It is perhaps significant that Daly began his critique not with a discussion of the formal defects in Visconti's conception but with an *ad hominem* attack on the architect himself. Rather than being a creator, he pictured Visconti as a network man, a "véritable *officier commandant*" who supervised a large number of skilled assistants but had no individual artistic vision himself. In short, he was a large cog in the wheels of the administrative machine. At stake, then, in his implication that the plan was the collective product of an administrative process was the romantic concept of creative vision, individual expression, and authorial presence as the source of aesthetic value. One might also see these comments as indicative of the widening gulf between the concepts of public and private art.

CHAPTER 4

The Process

Despite the tergiversations of the government, the decision to open a public contest for the tomb of Napoleon must have been easier than the one about how to close it. Completely in accord with his ambivalent stance toward this contest (or quasi-contest), Duchâtel refused to divulge how—if at all—the entries were to be judged until two days after the end of the exhibition. Then, on 23 November, it was announced that a commission had been formed to write a report and comment on the merits of the individual projects. As was usually the case with these kinds of governmental committees, most of Duchâtel's appointees to the commission were members or former members of the State's administrative machine, but Ingres, David d'Angers, and Pierre Fontaine were included as representatives of both the Institut and the disciplines of painting, sculpture, and architecture. The representative of the world of letters and person charged with drafting the report was Théophile Gautier.

At its first *séance* the group reduced the list of projects to be considered to twenty-three.[1] Another cut was made at the following session, leaving ten projects that were believed to merit further study. In arriving at the final group, each member of the committee drew up his own list of the ten best projects, and a rank order was established based on the frequency with which the names appeared on these lists. The completed tally showed that Victor Baltard and Louis Visconti were the only names appearing on all the lists, with Louis Duc failing to obtain a consensus by only one vote.[2] But in the final analysis, the commission held that none of the projects was completely satisfactory and declined to name a specific winner of the competition, thereby leaving the decision up to Duchâtel, the official who had shown so little enthusiasm for the contest to begin with. While the commission refused to declare any one project clearly superior, its members did present their views on the *kind* of tomb that ought to be constructed, and in doing so indirectly selected the winning entry.

The basic issue in the discussion was whether the structure was to be constructed above or below the floor level of Hardouin-Mansart's dome, and if the latter were adopted, whether it should be in an open or a closed crypt. The primary argument of those in favor of a tomb below ground was that it would be impossible to harmonize a monument above floor level with the architecture of Hardouin-Mansart. Furthermore, it was argued, if a monument were erected in the center of the church, it would of necessity obscure the view of the baldachin and altar from the main doorway. Conversely, if the primary entryway were to be through the church of Bruant, the altar would obscure the view of the tomb upon entering the dome. In response to these objections, the five members of the group advocating a monument above ground level maintained that the dimensions of the church were surely vast enough to accommodate any monument, and, although it presented a challenge, a tomb compatible with the architecture could be designed, even if it was not executed in the same style.

It appears that these arguments only summarized those thrashed about in administrative circles during the previous months. As early as 1840, for example, Prosper Mérimée wrote a friend that the architect Huyot had advised the administration that a closed crypt was the appropriate type of tomb for the dome. Mérimée himself, however, was opposed to a crypt of this sort because he believed it incompatible with Mansart's architecture, and, more importantly, because this kind of structure was traditionally reserved for saints and "Napoleon has not yet been canonized."[3] In another letter dating from February 1841, he revealed that he had discussed the problem of the tomb with Duchâtel, recommending a simple sarcophagus with gisant figure that would be designed by Ingres and executed by Pradier.[4]

But more than just a division of opinion on formal grounds as to how the tomb would relate to its architectural surround, there was a deeper split in the debate of the commission over the meanings the design would express or encode. Those supporting a tomb that rose above floor level argued, according to the official report, that "The ideas of strength and victory, which the memory of Napoleon awaken, demand an ascendant figure. . . . Enthusiasm tends to rise toward the heavens; despondancy and despair, alone, seek obscure and subterranean forms." Countering arguments that a tomb commemorating a secular figure would compete or interfere with the liturgical function of the church, they replied, "Art, which has celebrated God, could also easily celebrate Napoleon." In brief, their position was that the most appropriate structure would be at one and the same time "an expiatory and a triumphal monument," celebrating the dynamism of the Napoleonic myth, rather than laying it to rest. On the other hand, supporters of a tomb below the ground level argued that

> It is not a triumphal monument that one should raise to Napoleon. It is a tomb on the banks of the Seine, so that his wish can be fulfilled. Therefore, the idea of a crypt, a cavern, a subterranean chapel, by the mystery that subdued light and architectural severity can bring to it, promotes this pious destination marvelously. [5]

In addition to the claim that mystery was the most desirable quality in the design, advocates of a sunken tomb held that this was the best formal solution to the difficult architectural problem of integrating the nineteenth-century monument and the seventeenth-century church.

This problem of meaning had already been addressed by César Daly, who declared in his second article on the contest that what was at stake was a dichotomy between conceptions that celebrated either active or passive principles. The active element, in his personal semiotic system, signified wakefulness and was represented by vertical structures, while sleep and death were best represented by passive, horizontal lines. Reason dictated that the finality of death should be signified by horizontality. Inasmuch as death was the great leveler of men, it was furthermore rational that they be buried beneath the soil. But, on the other hand, Daly was a firm believer in the hierarchy of merit or achievement, and under this aspect Napoleon clearly rose above the common run of mankind; secondly, his myth was still very much alive in the collective mind of France. For these reasons he was opposed to a crypt and strongly supported a triumphal monument that would rise dramatically above the earth. However, since the architecture of Hardouin-Mansart's church was not able to accommodate such a monument, he proposed that another site be chosen.[6]

When the question of whether the monument was to be above or below ground came down to a vote of the committee, advocates of the latter alternative had a majority of seven to five. Having decided that this was the preferable design, the next question was whether it was to be an open or a closed crypt. An open-crypt design was decided to be the more desirable, thus becoming the formal recommendation of the commission.[7] It was further recommended that no ornament, statues, architectural elements, or allegories be employed that would interfere with the contemplation of the sarcophagus, which should be the exclusive center of attention. Given that the container for the imperial body was to be the central focus, it followed that it should be "visible at all hours, and while remaining visible to the beholder, should be at a distance from the crowd in such a manner that facility of access did not diminish its venerable and religious character." As for the problem of the equestrian monument, the commission recommended that it be placed outside the church but still be considered part of the tomb complex. The report continued with a further stipulation as to the character of this statue: "Napoleon should be represented in imperial costume so that one might see that it is not only a warrior that one glorifies, but also a ruler and a legislator."

For the sake of clarity the terms in the debate might be put in the form of a table that applies not only to the division of opinion within the commission but also in the discussion of the project external to its deliberations, both before and after the contest.

Terms of the Debate	Above Ground	Below Ground
Visibility	High	Low
Character	Active	Passive
Expression	Celebration	Mystery
Temporal Order	The Present	Eternity
Typology	Monument	Sepulcher
Architectural Form	Vertical	Horizontal
Relation to Existing Architecture	Independence	Subservience

What is perhaps most significant about this schematic representation is that one can clearly see that the final recommendation of the commission mediated these sets of oppositions; it partially reconciled opposed demands for a monument and for a sunken tomb. It established a compromise between those wishing to create a highly visible monument to the glory of Napoleon and those who desired to bury him or to place him in the conditions of eternity. This is to say that the sunken crypt with a monumental sarcophagus centered in an open space and raised dramatically above the floor of the crypt, but at the same time below the main-floor level of the church, partially satisfied the conditions of both a triumphal monument and a subterranean tomb, and mediated the division of opinion on the fundamental issue of whether it was a tomb or a monument that should be constructed. It was a solution appropriate to a government that consciously pursued the juste milieu as a matter of political philosophy.

Therefore, although the report refused to declare a winner of the competition, the basic thrust was to advocate that Louis Visconti be awarded the commission for the monument. Visconti was the only one in the contest to combine an open crypt and an equestrian statue and at the same time satisfy the less specific suggestions as to the decoration. The committee in essence both described and prescribed the project of Visconti. In so doing it also voted indirectly for the person whom critics of the administration had long claimed had been given the project in advance. In his autobiography Visconti emphatically denied that he had informally been awarded the commission before the contest but confirmed the fact that "[mine] being the *only* project that met their recommendations, it named me."[8]

No direct record survives as to how the various members voted on these questions, but other evidence exists from which to make some conjectures. Rémusat, who was the president of the commission, states in his memoirs that he was originally opposed to a tomb below ground. After the initial vote had approved this kind of design, however, he agreed that Visconti's plan fulfilled the prerequisites better than any other. More revealing is his comment that Louis Vitet considered Visconti to be his protégé and promoted his plan in the meetings of the committee. Indeed a close relationship had existed between Vitet and Visconti since at least 1839, when the former wrote a report on the Molière

Fountain—a project for which Visconti had already been given the commission—urging the Chamber of Deputies to allocate funds necessary for its construction.[9] In his autobiographical sketch Visconti expressed his debt of gratitude to Vitet and declared that at this time he learned how fortunate one was "to encounter men of such great erudition and perfect tact." And in the same document Visconti stated that after receiving the commission for the tomb he greatly profited from Vitet's advice. Even after Visconti's death Vitet remained a staunch supporter, as is seen in an article he published in *Revue des Deux Mondes* in 1866 where he vigorously defended Visconti's design for the Nouveau Louvre and opposed the changes of the architect Lefuel.[10]

But Vitet's role may have been even more decisive in the design of the monument than in promoting the plan of Visconti: he may well be, at least to some degree, the author of this symbolic mediation. Circumstantial evidence suggests that he was the individual who proposed the open-crypt design to Visconti. In his article on Marochetti's initial tomb project, Vitet, while opposed to the erection of the monument at the Invalides, nonetheless offered a solution to the problem of how to integrate it with the dome of Mansart, if it had to be built there:

> One can employ another expedient: change nothing of the size of the monument, but diminish its apparent height by lowering its base into a recess below the level of the spectator. . . . The tomb placed at the bottom would lose nothing of its real height, but its relative height would be decreased by the depth of its recession.[11]

After making this suggestion, he discounted it because the space would also require a stairway down into it; that would create problems inasmuch as the area under the dome was not large enough to accommodate both an open crypt and the requisite means of access. With Visconti's plan allowing access behind the main altar, however, that problem was solved. Thus, there should be little question as to the line of argument taken by Vitet in the committee's discussions. He not only promoted Visconti's design, he also argued for a concept that he himself probably had a large share in developing.

There is no need to conjecture about Ingres's ideas about the tomb either; he made them explicit in a letter he wrote to

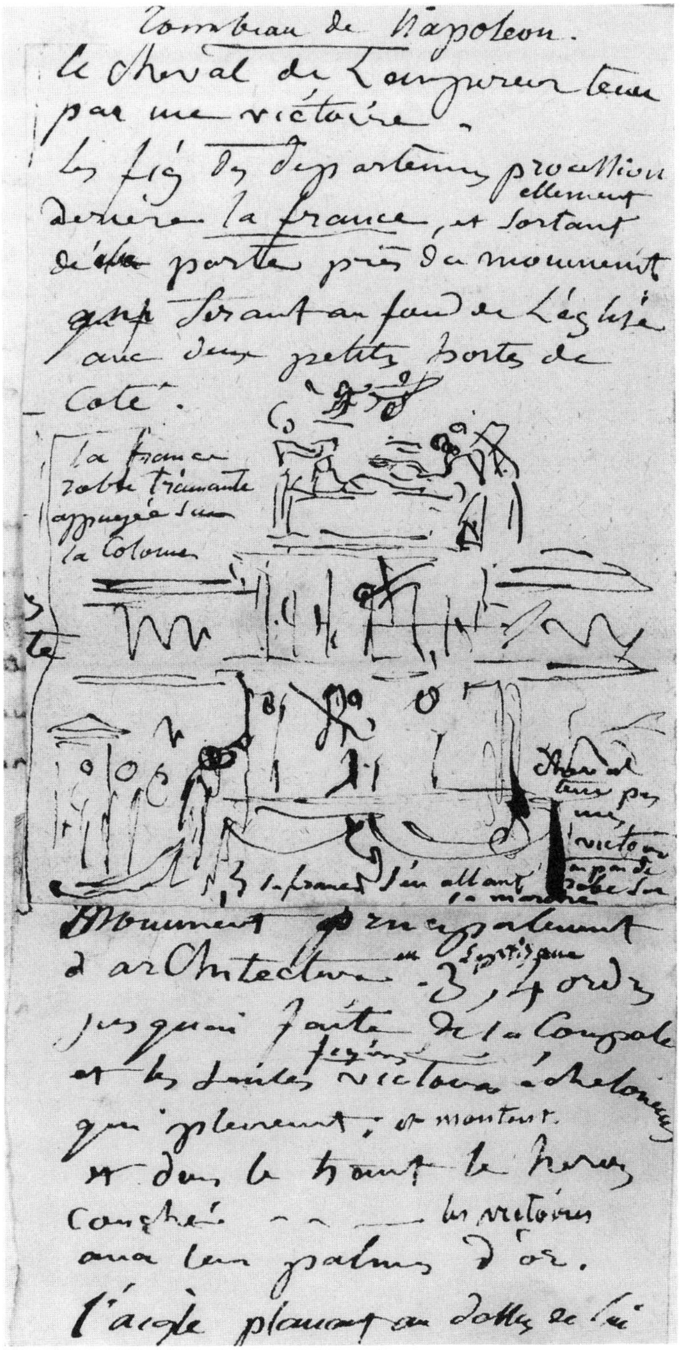

Fig. 72
J.-A.-D. Ingres, *Sketch of a Tomb for Napoleon*. Drawing, 1840–41. Photo courtesy of the Musée Ingres, Montauban.

Visconti in 1848, stating that while he had vigorously opposed his design as a member of the commission, he was profoundly impressed by its "grand and mysterious character" after seeing the monument in its state of near completion. A quick sketch by Ingres, setting down his own conception of the proper tomb for Napoleon, also survives (fig 72).[12] His complex design called for a monument, composed of three or four different architectural orders, that would rise "just to the pinnacle of the cupola." It would have been loaded with pictorial detail and allegorical figures, including a statue of Napoleon's horse held by a victory figure that might be considered Ingres's response to the demands for an equestrian tomb. Thus, Ingres's project would have been decidedly a monument, not a tomb, and would have dominated the space in which it was located. It is a conception that left no doubt that it was the active or dynamic aspect of the Napoleonic myth being celebrated. Obviously, establishing a harmony between this monument and Mansart's architectural surround held a low priority for Ingres.

David d'Angers is another member of the commission who in all likelihood cast a negative vote for a sunken tomb. But he acted from different motivations than Ingres and had a much more problematic relationship to the persona and myth of Napoleon. Either shortly before or after the report of the commission was published, he recorded his own thoughts on the tomb and the concept of a crypt design:

> The great Napoleon, regardless of all his glory, has not been able to choose his own tomb . . . after conquering the great warrior, they nailed him to a rock at Saint Helena, in the middle of the ocean, and it required a little man, very little [Thiers] and the Tartuffe Louis-Philippe to bring him back . . . to confine him in a little hole at the Invalides, under blocks of marble unworthy of modern art; and all this with a cheap political idea in mind.[13]

In his opposition to the July Monarchy he was evidently willing to put aside his own objections to Napoleon and view the crypt design as a part of a political strategy by the government. Thus, his vote against the crypt might be considered another expression of his opposition to the politics of Louis-Philippe. However, from another passage in his notebooks, dating a few years earlier, one can surmise that he endorsed the recommendation that the equestrian statue of Napoleon be clothed in imperial dress. Writing in 1838 on Seurre's statue of Napoleon commissioned by the July Monarchy to crown the Vendôme Column, he recorded his belief that the choice of military costume for the statue had a political motivation behind it:

> They wished to remove all idea of grandeur [from it]. An apotheosis of the Emperor would have elevated him above the earth. . . . it was a political act. They wished to represent only the general. The costume of his apotheosis would have represented the great man, and this would have moved the soul of the people. . . . [14]

As a consequence, he expressed his view that a simple tomb with only his name as decoration was the most appropriate. This idea, of course, was part of the final recommendations of the committee. In any event, from his views on Napoleon and the July Monarchy, it seems that simply serving on the commission must have posed a serious ethical and political quandary for the sculptor.

No record exists to document the opinion of Pierre Fontaine, the only architect on the committee, as to the most appropriate design for the tomb.[15] However, the views of the principal *literatus* of the commission, written prior to his service on it, do survive. Before receiving the call from the administration, Théophile Gautier had drafted an article on the contest that for obvious reasons was never published. Gautier's first move in his unpublished review was to rehearse the arguments for and against the various proposed sites for the tomb. Of all the possible locations, he expressed his strong preference not for the Invalides but the Panthéon. Hardouin-Mansart's church was a "supremely poor choice," in his opinion, because the imprint of Louis XIV was inescapable, and its function as a Catholic church was in conflict with its use to celebrate a secular hero. If, of necessity, the monument had to be placed in a church, a simple sarcophagus with a gisant figure on top was the least obtrusive solution to this conflict of functions.[16] Whatever his reservations about the site before he was invited to write the commission's report, he quickly changed his tune after accepting the charge.

For his meritorious service on this commission Gautier was awarded the medal of the *Légion d'honneur* on 17 January 1842 the day following the publication of his report.[17] A predictable consequence of this official honor was that he soon became the butt of ridicule in the opposition press, and he, not Rémusat, who served as its president, was commonly credited as being the person who imposed the will of the administration upon the body. From all available evidence, it appears that these charges were not far from the mark. That Gautier received this position and the honors that followed from it was due primarily to the lobbying efforts of his protector, one Joseph Lingay, a journalist, minor author, and personal secretary of Montalivet, the director of the *Liste Civile,* or to the funds that were available for the exclusive use of the royal house for patronage purposes. At the end of 1840 Lingay began sending a series of letters to Rémusat, reminding him of an unpaid political debt and urging that he use his influence as a former minister to gain the Légion d'honneur for his protégé.[18] In one of these letters, written during the spring of 1841, he made it explicit that Gautier was more than willing to perform whatever service was necessary to win this mark of distinction: "The government, will it remain in arrears on a commitment it has made? Has it already too many talented individuals, favorably disposed to those in power?"[19] On the day that Gautier was named as *rapporteur* for the commission, Lingay wrote once again to Rémusat, expressing his gratitude for the favor.[20] Thus, this appointment of a secretary for the commission, charged with singling out merit, was a patent example of the principle of favoritism or administrative privilege that advocates of a public contest were combating.

Far from taking the commission's refusal to select a winner at face value, most of those writing for the opposition press were convinced that its report was in reality a roundabout endorsement of Visconti as the architect for the tomb and Marochetti as the sculptor for the equestrian statue, just as they had predicted throughout the contest. The architect and the sculptor, in addition to Gautier, became objects of critical scorn in the months that followed. Shortly after the exhibition closed, Eugène Pelletan, writing in the Saint-Simonian *La Revue indépendante,* stated flatly that Duchâtel had informed only Visconti of the conditions of the program and given his approval to his project in advance. And in the third installment of his review of the contest, César Daly made this charge even more emphatically, declaring

that the postponement of the contest was a maneuver to benefit
Visconti, who in reality had not even begun his project by the
original deadline.[21] Visconti's response to Daly's accusations was
to obtain a letter from Cavé stating that this was false and, furthermore, that the delay had been granted at the request of another architect. The threat of a lawsuit for defamation of
character—a threat Visconti was to use more than once as the
project progressed—forced Daly to publish Cavé's letter in the
Revue générale de l'architecture. When Daly did print the letters
of Visconti and Cavé, he added a long commentary on the affair
and issued a challenge: if Visconti were to be awarded the commission, as certain critics believed he already had been unoffi-
cially, and declined to accept it on the grounds that such
decisions ought to be determined by a fair contest and not an administrative decision, Daly would make a public retraction of all
his accusations.[22] This, of course, was a disavowal he was never
forced to make.

Fig. 73
Honoré Daumier, *Future Monu-
ment of Napoleon at the Invalides*.
Lithograph, 1842. Photo courtesy
of the Bibliothèque Nationale,
Département des Estampes.

Not only the opposition newspapers but the satirical press as well joined in the ridicule of the report. Eight days after its conclusions were made public, *Le Charivari* published a biting satire entitled "Renfoncement donné à Napoléon," in which the idea of the sunken crypt was lampooned as adhering to the rule that "the less one sees of a funerary monument, the greater is its effect." With this rule in mind the satirist made a proposal that followed logically from it and would, at the same time, greatly reduce the cost of the tomb. One could simply place Napoleon's body in one of the wells recently sunk at Grenelle by the engineer named Mulot: "I vote for the crypt-Mulot, and even though my idea is ingenious, I won't demand the Légion d'honneur for it."[23]

The campaign of ridicule of both the report and the commission continued the following month with another satirical article accompanied by a caricature by Daumier (fig. 73).[24] In his projection of what the tomb was going to look like, a one-legged guard lifts a manhole cover so that a bourgeois family can strain their eyes in an attempt to catch sight of the tomb far below. The guard explains that the rationale behind the design is an exemplification of the general rule that "the less one sees of a monument, the more beautiful it is." *Journal des Artistes*, the periodical that had been the most adamant in demanding a contest, joined in heaping ridicule on Gautier for selling out for a simple medal. After describing the poet-critic as "professor-demonstrator of the language of the cottage and of the figures

Fig. 74
Louis Visconti, *Longitudinal Section for the Tomb of Napoleon*. Drawing, 1842. Collection: Archives of the Assemblée Nationale, Paris. Photo courtesy of Studio Littré.

of the cancan, expert on culinary language," it continued with an explication of the subtext of the report. What it said to critics of authority was "this will teach you to demand a contest next time."[25]

On 22 March 1842, the State officially bestowed the commission for the tomb upon Visconti and charged Marochetti with executing the model for the equestrian statue. In so doing it confirmed once and for all the allegations and suspicions of its critics.[26] At the beginning of December Visconti obtained approval for his revisions to the original plan, and a bill increasing the appropriation for its construction was drafted. As can be seen in his revised longitudinal section, the design for the crypt was essentially the same as his contest entry, but the most significant difference was the elimination of the underground passageway connecting the courtyard and crypt (fig. 74).[27] Also the Doric columns were replaced by simple, unadorned pilasters and architectural detail was reduced, giving the structure the appearance of greater simplicity and severity. Corresponding to this increased austerity, the sarcophagus was made more blocklike and given a look of greater solidity. The same process of simplification was pursued in an accompanying large drawing of the revised entryway into the crypt behind the main altar and baldachin (fig. 75). Here a strong contrast was established between the severely architectonic entryway to the tomb, appropriate to the soldier being honored, and the gilded, baroque baldachin that is more in keeping with Hardouin-Mansart's church and the original baldachin. Two bronze caryatid figures stand on either side of the door and a large bronze eagle perches above, providing the only figurative sculpture for the monument.

As was customary, after the Chamber of Deputies received the request for funds, a committee was appointed to study the proposition, and its report was forthcoming the following spring. The report of this group, designated as the Sapey Commission after the deputy who served as the chair, put its stamp of approval on the request for an additional 1,500,000 francs. It also made several significant recommendations: it proposed that the troublesome equestrian statue, once again included in the project by the architect, be removed from the courtyard entirely and placed on the esplanade outside the walls of the Invalides, and that there be no other decoration in the crypt than Napoleon's name on the

Fig. 75
Louis Visconti, *Elevation of the Entry to the crypt, the dome of the Invalides*. Drawing, 1842. Archives of the Assemblée Nationale, Paris. Photo courtesy of Studio Littré.

sarcophagus.[28] The bill appropriating the funds was then passed in both legislative chambers.

In recommending the relocation of the equestrian statue, the Sapey Commission pointed out that this was the desire of Maréchal Soult, who was both minister of war and director of the Hôtel des Invalides. In a letter to the minister of the interior written in December, Soult had demanded not only that it be removed to this large parade ground but also that the effigy of Napoleon be clothed in his military uniform. This latter

Fig. 76
Charles Marochetti, *Project for the Equestrian Statue of Napoleon.* Tracing after lost drawing, 1844. Photo courtesy of the Archives Nationales.

request was denied in the Sapey Report, which declared that the Emperor Napoleon should be dressed "with the attributes of sovereignty." The stricture was also contrary to the wishes of Visconti, who a month before the report had submitted his estimate of the cost of the monument and recommended that Napoleon be represented in military dress.[29]

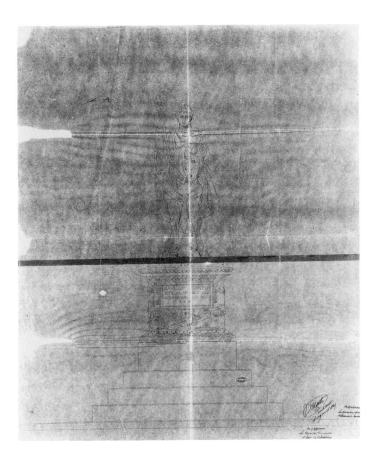

Fig. 77
Louis Visconti, *Project for the Pedestal for the Equestrian Statue of Napoleon, Frontal View.* Tracing after lost drawing, 1845. Photo courtesy of the Archives Nationales.

In conformity with the wishes of the Chambers, Visconti submitted Marochetti's drawing of the proposed statue for approval in June 1844 (fig. 76).[30] In the rigidly hieratic pose of both horse and rider, the sculptor was simply repeating the form of his failed tomb project of 1840 (fig. 36). There was a significant difference, however, in the costumes of the two figures. The first dressed the emperor in the classical toga of a roman ruler, while in the latter he was given full coronation regalia. Louis-Philippe's reception of the remains of Napoleon the day of their return was to be represented on one bas-relief on the pedestal supporting this immobile figure. The other relief would have depicted the exhumation of Napoleon's body on the island of Saint Helena.

Not satisfied with the costume of Napoleon in Marochetti's drawing, Visconti used a new study for the pedestal he was de-

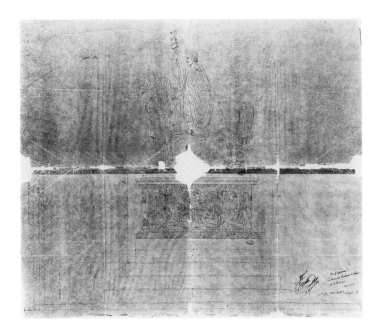

Fig. 78
Louis Visconti, *Project for the Pedestal for the Equestrian Statue of Napoleon, Profile View.* Tracing after lost drawing, 1845. Photo courtesy of the Archives Nationales.

signing as an occasion several months later to convey to the minister of the interior his belief that "it was very essential" that a classical toga be employed instead of the imperial robe.[31] To illustrate his argument he included his own drawing of an equestrian figure of Napoleon in such a costume, astride a horse that struck a pose much closer to that of the famous Roman statue of Marcus Aurelius than Marochetti's flatfooted depiction.[32] The following year Visconti obtained official approval for this mode of dress when he submitted two new drawings of the equestrian monument as the final studies for the work (figs. 77, 78).[33] In keeping with the universal character given to Napoleon, the two historical reliefs on either side of the pedestal were replaced with conglomerations of military emblems. In choosing to remove Napoleon from his historical context by representing him neither as a soldier nor as a ruler during a specific historical epoch, Visconti mediated opposed conceptions of what Napoleon really signified for his time. This solution was, of course, directly in accord with the strategy of mediation implicit in the design of his tomb.

Although the monument by Marochetti was included in the appropriation bill, the elaborate decorative scheme which Visconti began to develop soon after its passage clearly was not.

In the middle of August 1843 he presented to Duchâtel his ideas for this program and the names of sculptors to execute it. It was divided into three parts. The first concerned the entryway to the crypt, which was to have two giant figures in bronze bearing imperial insignia. He named Francisque Duret as the sculptor best qualified to execute this work. In the crypt itself he envisioned twelve winged-victory figures, placed against the pillars of the crypt and facing the sarcophagus, which would be executed in marble by James Pradier. Finally, he proposed that a mosaic composition, narrating the principal events in the life of Napoleon, be used to decorate the inner wall of the peristyle. For this ambitious task he recommended Henri de Triqueti, who had had "the happy idea" of basing this work on the mosaics of Siena. What Visconti was most emphatic about, however, was that in the interest of harmony the commission for the models of the victory figures be given to one sculptor *only*, since in a program where several artists were working in competition with one another "the ensemble will lose [as a whole] what it gains in detail."[34]

In conformity with the architect's wishes, Pradier was soon given the commission for the victory figures, an act destined to be the first step in a struggle for hegemony lasting nine years.[35] For this task the artist, a native of Switzerland who occupied a prominent position in the French Academy, was to be given the princely sum of 240,000 francs but in turn was expected to pay the salaries of assistants required to execute the statues. Probably both to save money and to avoid conflict with other authorial egos, he soon decided to hire simple *metteurs à point* to copy and enlarge his plaster models, rather than more highly skilled and better paid *practiciens*.

This decision was soon to provoke much acrimony in the Parisian artistic community, an example of which is found in the caustic attack the *Journal des Artistes* directed at Pradier at the end of 1845. The article had much praise for the skilled practiciens who had assisted on Pradier's other projects but condemned his actions unequivocally, classifying him among "those men who recognize only blind and brutal egotism." Furthermore, he was a "foreigner" who was depriving native Frenchmen of their daily bread. Similar charges were frequently leveled against Marochetti, an example of which is an 1843 article in an art journal directed by the radical republican Théophile Thoré.

According to the critic, Marochetti received the commission because he was very wealthy and had influential friends, but even worse was the fact that while it was claimed that the only thing his practiciens did was enlarge his model, in reality "it is the practiciens who do everything."[36] Ultimately at stake were the issues of social class and whether funds allocated to public monuments were to go to many or to the privileged few who received the State's largesse by administrative decree. Once again, the very nature of the social order and its locus of authority were being called into question.

If one can believe the remarks in his autobiography concerning the difficulties he had with Pradier on an earlier project, it is strange that Visconti should have recommended him as a sculptor for the tomb at all. Pradier had provided two of the full-length female figures for Visconti's Molière Fountain, inaugurated in 1842; according to the architect, he proved a very difficult collaborator, resisting suggestions that he modify his figures to conform to the style of the monument. According to Visconti: "Despite all the efforts that I expended, Pradier made small sketches of women entirely nude. I told the Prefect that this did not satisfy my ideas and that I would refuse them. Pradier then sent me sketches with a veil above. I protested again and pleaded with the Prefect to name a committee that would reject these sketches and demand clothed figures."[37] There appears to be no other documentation to corroborate this dispute, but if one assumes that Visconti's account is true, then it might follow that the architect, rather than simply recommending those he felt best suited for task, was told by the administration whom to nominate.

From the very start of the project, the relationship between Visconti and Pradier was less than cordial, as can be inferred from the coldly formal letter, co-signed by the minister of the interior, that the architect wrote to the sculptor in November 1844. This official communiqué carefully specified the stylistic characteristics the figures were to have:

> The twelve figures . . . will conform in their dimensions to the model provided by the architect and will be executed in the most elevated, most general and most grave style . . . inspired by the Greek caryatids at the Temple of the Erechtheon. . . . here will be a very great conformity of lines between them, so that the eye is not

distracted by any broken or contorted form that would detract from the architectonic character they should have. These figures should differ from one another only in expression, arrangement of drapery and in their attributes. . . . Finally, one should avoid too much finish.[38]

Well aware of Pradier's predilection for sensual depictions of the female body, the architect apparently wished to warn him against any such indulgence on this project. One sheet of Pradier's sketches for these figures might well illustrate the difference between the kind of image that the architect desired and that for which Pradier was generally known. On one side of his paper he sketched three heraldic and columnar figures, but on the other side we find a semi-draped, full-bodied nude in a relaxed pose with head turned casually to one side—the kind of figure and pose Visconti intended his letter to proscribe.[39]

Although it is doubtful that Visconti was as concerned as the *Journal des Artistes* about the use of state funds to support the multitude of sculptors in the Parisian art community, he nonetheless soon attempted to force Pradier to discharge his metteurs à point and employ sculptors for the task of enlarging his models and carving the marble statues themselves. He also was greatly disturbed by Pradier's cavalier decision to let unskilled individuals work from models that were loosely finished and only one-third the size of execution. Hence, in the spring of 1847 he asked the minister of the interior to intervene on this issue. At this point the administration apparently attempted to enlist David d'Angers to undertake the project. The sculptor recorded in his journal that he declined on the principle that if one did not like a government, one should not accept its favors.[40] Other sculptors may have also been approached, but nothing was resolved before the February Revolution of 1848 toppled the July Monarchy.

The matter remained dormant until August 1851, when Pradier attempted to secure final payment for the statues, claiming that they were finished. Visconti disagreed strongly, stating that they had not been completed to his satisfaction. A three-member commission was appointed to examine them and pronounce on the question. In response Pradier wrote to the minister, invoking his reputation as a member of the academy and stating flatly that "nothing can make me change an IOTA of them."[41] This commission issued a report vaguely favorable to

Pradier's claims but was dissolved with the inauguration of the Second Empire; no action was taken on its recommendations. Finally, early in 1852, an inspecteur des beaux-arts was sent to study the works again and definitively settle the matter. Regarding the question of author's rights in mid–nineteenth-century France, this report is highly interesting. First of all, he defends the execution of the works, judging them to be superior, but then he makes a statement of general principle:

His [Pradier's] practical experience makes him the sovereign judge in these kinds of difficulties. . . . I am of the opinion that when an artist of great renown is called upon to execute a work, one should let him (within the limits and of the demands of the architecture) freely

Fig. 79
James Pradier, *Victory Figure: The Italian Campaign*. Marble. Completed 1853 by assistants. Photo courtesy of Lauros-Giraudon.

develop his thoughts. . . . The tomb of Napoleon is a durable, eternal work. Mr. Pradier, in associating his name and reputation to it, offers the administration a sufficient guarantee.

In sum, the sculptor-author's reputation took precedence over considerations of whether he was cooperative, in tune with the larger collective aims of the project or truly putting his heart into the work.[42]

Notwithstanding this favorable judgment, Pradier had the misfortune to die several months later, removing a major obstacle to the modifications Visconti wished to make. Shortly after the sculptor's demise Visconti began negotiations with Eugène Lequesne, Pradier's chief assistant, to make the desired retouches; an agreement was reached at the end of the year. The following June these reworkings had been completed to Visconti's satisfaction, and the sculpture was pronounced finished, greater longevity having given the victory to the architect.[43] Therefore, when one examines the sculpture as it exists today, it is very difficult to determine whose hand is most evident in the finished appearance, or how much of the finished product can be attributed to Pradier himself (fig. 79, 80). Nonetheless, the figures are perfectly adapted to the character of the structure they decorate.

Roughly contemporaneous with Pradier's commission was one awarded to Henri de Triqueti for his mosaic. Of the two, Triqueti's work was by far more adventuresome, there being no precedent in France for such an ambitious mosaic program, which would have been seventy meters in length. No atelier in France specialized in the manufacture of this kind of decoration, so after receiving the charge for his project, the sculptor travelled to Siena to study the mosaic pavements there and experimented with the medium for almost a year. His efforts were to little avail, however, due to the decision that this kind of endeavor was not suitable for the location.[44] All that survives of this project today is one finished drawing of a section of the crypt, illustrating the proposed decorative scheme.[45] Had the work been executed, a sort of mosaic panathenaic procession would have encircled the walls of the crypt with the figures dressed in classical garments and assuming poses very similar to those in the drawings for Napoleon's tomb that Triqueti submitted to the 1841 contest.

In recompense for this lost commission, Triqueti was subsequently awarded the marble statue of Christ on the cross for the

Fig. 80
James Pradier, *Victory Figure: The
First Austrian Campaign*. Marble.
Completed 1853 by assistants.
Photo courtesy of Lauros-
Giraudon.

main altar of the dome. Visconti's letter to the administration
proposing the sculptor for the project asked that he be paid twenty
thousand francs, which was admittedly high for a sculpture of this
kind, but the excess should be considered additional payment for
the work he had already done on the cancelled mosaic project.
Several years after Triqueti finished this marble statue, Visconti
had it put in place above the main altar. However, he decided
that it was not only too small for its location but also that it
was composed of the wrong materials (fig. 81). This marble figure, a *tour de force* of anatomical realism, was then replaced by
another statue cast in bronze from a new model by Triqueti, and
the marble work was installed in the nave of Bruant's church

Fig. 81
Henri de Triqueti, *Christ on the Cross*. Marble. Bruant's Church, The Invalides. Photo courtesy of the Caisse Nationale des Monuments Historiques © 1992 ARS, New York/SPADEM, Paris.

where it is found today. A similar reworking of Duret's models for the bronze caryatid figures at the entry door, originally intended to be rendered in marble, was required when Visconti had the full-scale models put in place and found they were not the right proportions for the location.[46] Unlike Pradier, neither Triqueti nor Duret seems to have registered any resistance to Visconti's decisions; they accepted the fact that the heuristic process of trial and error was a part of the modus operandi of this project from the very beginning.

Shortly before the cancellation of Triqueti's mosaic experiment, Visconti had requested that in lieu of this means of decoration, a series of ten marble bas-reliefs be adopted.[47] Exactly a year later, he presented to the minister of the interior a list of ten sculptors to execute these bas-reliefs. In drawing up this list, he must have bowed to administrative pressure inasmuch as the idea of giving the bas-relief project to a series of different artists is completely contrary to his plea two years earlier that only one sculptor execute the victory figures in the crypt. Triqueti's name was among the ten, but the most favored sculptor on the list was Pierre-Charles Simart, who was recommended to execute personally one relief and to create the models for all of them.[48] In effect this made the other sculptors, all of whom enjoyed at least some repute in the profession and several who were highly regarded, little more than mere practiciens for Simart, the author-creator of the cycle.[49] Thus, this division of labor can be seen as a strategic move to avoid some of the controversy generated by Pradier's commission and assuage the demand from many artists and their supporters for a share in the action.[50] The same letter added yet another new element to the decoration: it proposed that Simart be commissioned to execute both the model and the finished statue of the freestanding figure of Napoleon in the chamber adjoining the central space of the crypt, a move that reinforced Simart's dominant position in the project.

Rather than immediately attempting to enlist the services of the designated sculptors for the marble reliefs, the government awarded a commission to Simart for plaster sketches.[51] By the following March, Simart's sketches were complete, and the delicate matter of awarding the contracts for their execution in marble became unavoidable. As the administration hesitated, Ingres, both a former teacher and friend of Simart, wrote the directeur des beaux-arts urging that Simart alone be given the contract to execute the marbles. According to Ingres, to turn his sketches into finished works he would need only several "useful practiciens, useful machines, but intelligent and naive, to enlarge them, in all their truth until the master came to give them their final perfection with his own chisel."[52]

Ingres's harsh comments indicate that a major dispute, or even rebellion, was brewing between Simart and the various sculptors who were to be chosen as assistants. This seems confirmed by a letter that Visconti wrote to the director the following month, in which he stated that "I am menaced and under siege. However, one must not compromise this monument in order to oblige these gentlemen. One must have the courage to give the commission to Simart and tell him to take as collaborators only those who will consent to his benevolent direction." Shortly thereafter, the administration gave the commission for the execution of all the marbles to Simart but did not accept Ingres's view of the efficiency of docile and "useful machines." Instead Simart was asked to recommend five sculptors who were former recipients of the Prix de Rome and willing to serve as his assistants.[53] But even this decision to let Simart choose his assistants from former students at the Ecole des Beaux-Arts, where he was a professor, was not enough to avoid the ensuing charges of callous disregard for the community of sculptors in France.

It was another prominent sculptor, Théodore Bra, who, in a series of articles he published in 1847, led the attack against both the decision to give the commission to one sculptor and the style of the reliefs. He argued that in the past the State had been able to distribute work to a large number of individuals and at the same time maintain the principle of decorative harmony, and that one should return to this system. To do otherwise would be to turn the government into "a cruel executioner," since it had expended great resources to multiply the members of the artistic profession but was effectively abandoning them to misery. In sum, although the principle of democratic distribution of patronage took precedence over that of decorative unity, Bra did not think them incompatible. In the ensuing articles he attacked the style in which the works were done, claiming that they were totally opposed to the "génie de vitalité" represented by Napoleon.[54] One senses from his remarks that he considered the hieratic symmetry of the reliefs, which he had seen only in the form of plaster sketches, to be symbolic of the authoritarian, antidemocratic mindset in control of State patronage in France as a whole.

The *Journal des Artistes*, which published the articles by Bra, carried on the attack in even stronger terms. In one article in the July issue, the editor began by claiming that it was because Countess Duchâtel favored Simart that he received this commission, which took bread from the mouths of ten sculptors. He continued with an attack on the classical mode chosen for the reliefs, claiming that it was as "unFrench" as the individuals in charge of the project.[55] Similarly caustic criticism appeared at the same time in the pages of *L'Artiste*. Arsène Houssaye, editor of the journal and a staunch republican, condemned Simart's reliefs as "hieroglyphs" designed to please members of the Institut and woefully forgetful of their true audience, le peuple, who would only jeer in derision at them. The criticism continued a week later in another article in which the style of Ingres, which the reliefs were seen to celebrate, was equated with authoritarianism: "Public opinion does not wish a tomb covered with superannuated allegories. . . . For a long time Mr. Ingres has wished, in his blind absolutism, to restrict French art to his narrow horizon. But art is free like the imperial eagle and it will victoriously break free of the restraints of Mr. Ingres." Joining this chorus of discontent was the respected scholar Paul Lacroix, sometimes known as the

Fig. 82
Charles Simart, *The Civil Code*. Bas-relief, marble. Completed 1853. Photo courtesy of the Musée de l'Armée.

"Bibliophile Jacob," who charged that this project, which should have been executed by twenty artists, had "been confiscated by Mr. Simart" at a time when sculptors were dying of hunger. He continued by making a charge that left him open to legal action: "The funeral of the emperor has been celebrated in the ancient manner: they have distributed the kick-backs ('pots-de-vin') on his tomb."[56] Under the threat of a lawsuit for defamation, the author quickly issued a retraction to these insinuations of official corruption, but it certainly did not remove the spector from the minds of many who followed the project's progress.

It was to be almost two years—a delay partly the result of the fall of the July Monarchy in 1848—before Simart's choices of assistants were approved by the government and the actual execution of the sculptures could begin. Simart's struggle with the individuals he himself had chosen began shortly thereafter. His first clash was with Louis Chambard, who was charged with executing the relief entitled *Le Code civil* (fig. 82).[57] In September 1850, Chambard wrote to the directeur des beaux-arts charging that Simart and Visconti had provided him with an unheated and unsuitable studio to execute his full-scale clay model; as a result of these conditions, the model had frozen and been ruined.[58] He demanded recompense from the government for his lost time and materials. This request was denied, and the young sculptor was reminded that he was working for Simart and should resolve the matter with him. Chambard's complaint is symptomatic of the relationship that Simart was to have with the other artists on the project. His next clash was with Victor Vilain, winner of the Prix de Rome in 1838. This time Simart wrote Visconti asking him to take the matter to the directeur des beaux-arts, and reported that when he paid a visit to the studio of Vilain to check on his work on the bas-relief, he found that

> [the artist] was no longer disposed to accept my direction, and after some observations that I made concerning the execution of the bas-relief, he forbade me to enter his studio again and told me in violent terms that this relief was his own work, that the minister had confided it to him and that he did not recognize my right to judge it. Being responsible for this work, I cannot accept this, and my relationship with Mr. Vilain can no longer exist. I have ordered him to cease work on this bas-relief.[59]

At the same time he formally requested that he be no longer required to use sculptors merely because they had won the Prix de Rome. Implicit in this request and the dispute was the belief that rather than making these elite members of the sculptural profession good collaborators on a project, the system of organized competitions at the Ecole des Beaux-Arts did just the opposite.[60]

Following this encounter, Simart had similar problems with Auguste Ottin, who was awarded a contract to execute the relief entitled *L'Administration française*. After a dispute with Simart in September 1851, Ottin refused to return to his studio and continue work on his relief. In an attempt to resolve the matter, an inspector was sent by the directeur des beaux-arts to interview the two sculptors and report on the nature of the affair. He recommended that Ottin be encouraged to return to work since the unfinished nature of his full-scale model would make it very difficult for a simple praticien to continue the process of enlarging Simart's model.[61] No record exists of how Ottin was persuaded to continue, but he did eventually complete his relief.

The end result of the turmoil over the reliefs is that when they were finally finished in 1853, three of the ten works were co-signed, with Simart bearing the title of "inventor" and another artist given the honorific of "sculptor." The three sculptors who were given the authorial privilege of signing them were Ottin, Lanno, and Petit. Their names are inconspicuous and little noted by visitors to the monument, but the troubled history of the entire project might be symbolized by them.

One final index of the struggle for authorial recognition, or the prominence of ego investment in all aspects of the project, might be found in a biographical notice written in 1860 by the architect and architectural writer Adolphe Lance. It concerned the career of architect Jules Bouchet, the first inspector of the work on Napoleon's tomb in 1842 and a principal assistant to Visconti until his death, at which point he became the official architect of the Invalides. Strangely enough, in the praise-filled essay written shortly after Bouchet's death, Lance made a particular point of denying him any authorial contribution to the project:

> It is wrong to attribute to him any part in the design and composition of this fastidious mausoleum. We know from a good source that he

was not part of the study for the project, and that his role, entirely secondary, was limited to the inspection and surveillance of the work. If we insist on this point, it is because he [Bouchet] always claimed, and sometimes with a certain vivacity, to have collaborated to some degree in the study and preparation of the plans and details of the tomb at the Invalides.[62]

While we have no documentation with which to decide what contribution, if any, Bouchet made to the design of the tomb, it may be that, like the sculptural practiciens who executed the bas-reliefs after Simart's models, he considered his close involvement with the project, which at the very least included making drawings for many of the details, to be tantamount to participating in the creative process. He may even have been strengthened in this belief by seeing just how difficult it was to pin down any specific and unique contribution Visconti himself made to the project.

Constantly beset by conflicts of one sort or another during the five years following the approval of Visconti's plans by the Chamber of Deputies, work on the tomb nevertheless proceeded apace until the February Revolution of 1848. But with the advent of the Second Republic the decoration came to a halt, and the monument became the object of intense scrutiny and debate. Almost as soon as he assumed the position of minister of the interior, Ledru-Rollin appointed a committee of thirteen members to investigate the project, among whom were David d'Angers and Henri Labrouste.[63] On 29 May the report of the commission was completed and sent to Ledru-Rollin. While it had praise for certain aspects of the project, it severely condemned the actions of Visconti, Duchâtel, and the administration of the arts during the regime of Louis-Philippe.

The first charge—levied against the architect and the minister of the interior, who awarded him the commission—was that the plans for the original project submitted to and approved by the Chambers in 1843 had been ignored and that an extravagant and costly decorative scheme had been undertaken without the consent of the legislature. This was considered symptomatic of the general autocratic or antidemocratic attitudes of the former administration: "If Mr. Duchâtel were Louis XIV, if Mr. Visconti were named Mansart, things would be very simple and it would not be worth the trouble to bring the matter up; but in a representative government, the amount voted by the Chambers cannot be exceeded without the architect and the minister incurring severe blame."[64] Autocratic disregard for the general will is, of course, the charge that had been leveled against the project since its undertaking was first announced: the installation of a government supposedly based on republican principles made the tomb a symbol of the policies of the July Monarchy and all that to which it was opposed. It is against the background of the spurious 1841 contest that one must understand the promptness with which the provisional government of the Second Republic inaugurated open competitions in various media for the image of the new republic. On 14 March 1848 Ledru-Rollin officially announced that these contests were to be held; two weeks later he published a precise and detailed program of the sort that the previous government had autocratically disdained.[65]

The report of the commission appointed by Ledru-Rollin, the only publication of which appeared in the Fourierist journal *Démocratie pacifique*, criticized the ways that funds had been spent (or misappropriated), commented on the quality of the sculpture, and made recommendations as to items and expenses that could be eliminated to reduce the fiscal deficit it had incurred.[66] Its severest criticism was directed toward the twelve victory figures in the crypt, which the committee unanimously concluded "were not the work of Mr. Pradier" and were not worthy of his name in their present state, and that Pradier had not lived up to the terms of his contract by providing the type of models specified and the degree of finish necessary to turn them into finished works without considerable intervention on the part of praticiens. This was, of course, a verdict that only confirmed complaints already registered by Visconti. The commission found much more merit in the reliefs of Simart and recommended clothing the figures in classical dress rather than contemporary costume despite certain reservations about the appropriateness of the practice in the modern era. Likewise, it gave its guarded approval to the use of imperial costume for the equestrian statue by Marochetti, which was to be erected in the esplanade of the Invalides; however, it severely criticized the execution of his model and the general lack of elevation in the figure. Equally lacking in elevation was the marble figure of the crucified Christ that Triqueti had executed for the main altar. It was declared to lack the severity appropriate to a figure of its dimensions destined for a central location, which is to say that it was too naturalistic in relation to the idealization in the remainder of the program.

The most important modifications in the sculptural program it proposed were the elimination of Simart's cult statue of Napoleon for the Chambre de l'épée (fig. 12) and the two reliefs at the bottom of the entry staircase by Dumont and Jouffroy. Ideology, more than finance, of course, accounts for these decisions inasmuch as Simart's statue was entirely out of keeping with the republican values that were being celebrated across France. Also, the reliefs were reminders that the return of Napoleon's body was the work of the deposed citizen-king (figs. 13, 14). With these cuts and others on decorative details and materials, the commission found that the project could be completed with the expenditure of one-third less than Visconti had estimated.[67]

Ironically, charges of undemocratic ideas and conduct leveled against the administration of the project by the Ledru-Rollin commission were in turn brought against it by one of the commission's own members. Hippolyte Delaunay, the director of *Journal des Artistes*, submitted his letter of resignation before the report was written because of the autocratic ideas of its members. Among these undemocratic notions were the ideas that an equestrian statue of Napoleon in imperial dress was acceptable, that the representation of Napoleon's accomplishments could be framed in the allegorical mode, and, finally, that it was better to have the bas-reliefs executed by one artist rather than ten. In charging this commission with betraying republican values, Delaunay was repeating the sort of charges brought against Ledru-Rollin shortly after he took office—that he was only following practices characteristic of the previous regime. These accusations began when, on his own authority, the minister of the interior awarded the commission for a monumental decorative cycle in the Panthéon to Paul Chenavard. Objectively, his decree differed little from those of Rémusat and Duchâtel on the tomb of Napoleon. For this autocratic act he was roundly chastised in the pages of *L'Artiste*: "It is not appropriate for a minister of the Republic, after three successive revolutions, made in the name of the democratic principle, to disdain this democratic principle, to disdain a contest judged by an elected jury."[68]

Possibly the most serious criticism that the Ledru-Rollin commission advanced against the project, one that suggested corruption as well as poor judgment, concerned the acquisition of the marble for the tomb complex and the red porphyry for the sarcophagus. The Sapey Report of 1843, recommending that additional funds be allocated for the construction of the tomb, had been quite specific about the need to employ only French materials for this national monument, and had suggested that either granite or porphyry from Corsica be used for the sarcophagus. But efforts to find a suitable stone were to no avail, and the government had commissioned Léouzon-le-Duc, an entrepreneur and man of letters with a knowledge of Russian, to travel to Finland to search for and choose the porphyry for the sarcophagus, and another individual to deliver the blocks of the precious material to France.[69] Their expenses, one section of which included a suspect item entitled "Dépenses secrètes," were considered to be grossly exorbitant and to reflect the total lack of concern for expenditure of public funds typical of its administration as a whole. Although this report provoked rumors concerning the misuse of funds, only a daily newspaper in Bastia, Corsica, had the temerity or bad judgment to make accusations of malfeasance concerning the acquisition of porphyry from Finland. Visconti's response to its article was to begin defamation proceedings against the newspaper, a suit he won in January 1849.[70]

The landslide victory of Louis Bonaparte in the presidential elections of 10 December 1848 and the flight of Ledru-Rollin into exile after republican demonstrations in June 1849 assured that this report would be put aside and yet another committee formed to study the affair. This commission headed by Alfred de Luynes—the wealthy patron of the arts, amateur archaeologist, and militant legitimist—began another study of the massive documentation for the project on 21 July, the date an appropriation bill for the tomb was presented to the Chamber of Deputies. Its findings were published on 15 December. Known as the de Luynes Report, it was even more severe in its criticism of Visconti and the administration of the July Monarchy than the previous commission, dominated by ardent republicans, had been. It concluded by making three recommendations: that Visconti should receive no further honoraria for his work in completing the project; that the fine arts administration should maintain an active surveillance over the project; and that no further funding for the project should be granted until a revised plan was formulated for its completion.[71] How much this recommendation may have been due to genuine indignation over mismanagement by the July Monarchy and how much to the growing presence of bonapartism in the political arena in the person of Louis Bonaparte one can only guess. In any event, the proposed law allocating funds for the completion of the tomb was withdrawn after the report was made.

As everyone knew it would be, the effect of this failure to pass an appropriation bill was simply to necessitate yet another committee to study the project. Five weeks later the minister of the interior introduced a new bill and appointed a new commission to report on it. Headed by Henri de la Rochejaquelein, a fervent legitimist from a family famous for its activity during the Vendean wars, the composition of this committee was of a different nature than the previous ones.[72] While the Duc de Luynes was again a member, the committee also included Louis Vitet, who was without doubt the most knowledgeable and accomplished member of the commission and an individual who had been closely involved with the project from its inception. He also just happened to be close friends of both Duchâtel, the former minister of the interior whose actions were under scrutiny, and Louis Visconti. The secretary of this commission and the individual charged with writing the report was Hippolyte Fortoul, a prolific author who was destined to be the minister of education and religion in the Second Empire. Unlike the previous reports, this one exonerated Duchâtel and Visconti of any serious or criminal wrongdoing, attributing their neglect to stay within the budget and the strictures of the 1843 appropriation bill to their desire to create the most impressive monument possible. As for the statues of Pradier, the report refrained from passing judgment on them, given their unfinished state, but recommended that the sculptor be paid in full only when they had been approved by the minister of the interior. In addition, it was recommended that the two bas-reliefs of Jouffroy and Dumont at the entry of the crypt be retained. Likewise, it urged that the cult statue of Simart and the Chambre de l'épée in which it was to be installed be included in the project. Its most controversial recommendation was that the equestrian statue on the esplanade be eliminated in order to reduce the expenditure on this monument, which was already laboring under a huge deficit. On 4 June 1850 the report of the

LE MONUMENT DE L'EMPEREUR.

— Ah! ça! tas de paresseux, vous déciderez-vous enfin à me terminer mon tombeau!

Fig. 83
Cham, *The Monument of the Emperor.* Lithograph, 1850. Photo courtesy of the Bibliothèque Nationale, Département des Estampes.

committee was presented to the Assemblée Nationale, and a vote approving the bill took place eight days later.[73]

The entanglement of the tomb in the legislative rhetoric and politics of the Second Republic did not escape the attention of the satirical press. On 15 March 1850, *La Caricature* published a drawing by Cham that summarized the impatience of many over the delays in completion of this project (fig. 83). Wearing his famous greatcoat and trademark hat, Napoleon suddenly appears under Hardouin-Mansart's dome amid a group of laborers, chiding them for their laziness and demanding, "[w]hen will you decide finally to finish my tomb[?]" The humor, as any viewer would have been aware, lies in the ironical displacement of the cause of the problem from the nation's legislators to the humble stonemasons, who were entirely powerless to speed up the process. Visconti is one individual involved with the project, however, who should not be accused of laziness. Throughout the Second Republic he attempted to exert pressure on various government officials to continue work on the tomb and shrewdly tailored his entreaties to fit the prevailing political climate of the moment. Thus, in what can be interpreted as an attempt to preserve the equestrian statue of Napoleon from annulment by the newly inaugurated republic, he wrote Charles Blanc, the directeur des beaux-arts, shortly after the February Revolution and suggested that it "would be more rational to put Napoleon in a uniform such as the one he wore on the battlefield." He undoubtedly knew that Napoleon as the *petit caporal* stood a much better chance of surviving the policies of the new regime than Napoleon the Emperor. In another letter to Ledru-Rollin, he proposed that the State bypass the contractor and directly employ the craftsmen necessary to complete the floor mosaic in order to keep work on the tomb moving. He undoubtedly believed this act would be favorably received in that it would be in harmony with both the minister's and Louis Blanc's socialist theories, which underpinned the great experiment with the national workshops in the early months of the new government. And in August he wrote a similar message to the minister of the interior, urging that the State intervene to expedite the bronze-casting operations for the ornament on the structure. In support of his plea he included a letter from Edouard Vittoz, the owner of a large bronze-casting studio, who described the profound state of economic depression of the tradespeople, and stated that there were three hundred foundry workers in his employ who might soon be without a livelihood unless the State proceeded with the execution of public works such as the tomb of Napoleon. Playing upon the National Workshop theme, he further proposed that his own studio be made a State workshop and a school for bronze casters, if that would induce the government to provide more funds for public monuments.[74]

With the aid of the additional appropriation voted on 12 June 1850, Visconti continued to press to get the tomb completed satisfactorily; at long last, in October 1853, he was able to announce that all work had been finished, except the permanent placement of the cover on the sarcophagus.[75] Shortly after this announcement, on 29 December 1853, Visconti died unexpectedly. Although he saw the monument completed to his satisfaction, he was not destined to see it inaugurated. To witness this event he would have had to live eight more years.

The only item to provoke any parliamentary discussion before the passage of the new appropriation bill in June 1850 was the suppression of the equestrian statue. This suggestion produced a heated exchange between Rochejaquelein, the head of the committee who reported on the bill, and several former soldiers in the legislature who believed that this was an insult not only to Napoleon but to France's national honor, as well. Supporters of the bill insisted, on the contrary, that the purpose of the provision was to separate the tomb from the equestrian monument in order that the former could be completed, and argued that a vote for the bill did not necessarily entail that the latter was to be definitively canceled; additional funds could be approved separately to finance the completion of this part of the original project. When a vote was taken, however, the bill with its provision to eliminate the equestrian statue carried by a vote of more than two to one, with 443 for and 166 against.

The decision concerning the equestrian statue occurred while Marochetti was in London busy with other projects. His plaster model, however, still remained in his studio at Vaux-sur-Seine. In his absence, the government took possession of this model and put it in storage in a warehouse to await further disposition. In March 1852, with Louis Napoleon installed in the office of President of the Republic for a renewable term of ten years, the project was revived and the new minister of the interior, Victor Failin, duc de Persigny, wrote to Marochetti informing him that another installment on the amount he had been awarded for the commission was now at his disposal in Paris, but that the subjects of the bas-reliefs for the pedestal had been changed. Marochetti's exasperated response was simply to ignore this latest communication regarding his ill-fated project. More than a year passed before Charles Gaudin, a functionary of the French Embassy in London, was assigned the task of securing a definitive response from the sculptor as to whether he would return to his project and complete it according to the new program. To this inquiry Marochetti finally responded with a long list of recriminations and charges that the successive administrations had done everything possible to produce a monument *manqué* and declared that he would have to have the unequivocal assurance of the government that he would henceforth have complete control over the statue, reliefs, and decoration of the pedestal before he would once again begin work on it.[76] In December it was finally decided that the conditions laid down by the sculptor were unacceptable and that for a variety of reasons the project should remain unfinished. On 10 December 1853, the commission was officially annulled, leaving the capital without the much-desired equestrian statue of Napoleon in either civilian or military dress.[77]

Marochetti's experience and performance were to be repeated in the last major commission he was awarded: the seated effigy of Prince Albert for the Albert Memorial in London. He received the commissioning letter in July 1864 and worked on the project until his death on 29 December 1867. His relationship with the architect of this monument, George Gilbert Scott, and the officials administering the project proved to be as strained as that with Visconti and the others employed on the tomb of Napoleon. At one point in the process of developing his figure Marochetti declared that an equestrian statue was preferable to a seated image of the Prince Consort, probably hoping to use at long last his many studies for the monument to Napoleon. This suggestion met with an unenthusiastic response, and Marochetti was destined never to have any statue completed for the monument.[78]

The final irony in Marochetti's failed attempt to create an equestrian monument in conjunction with the tomb of Napoleon is that the most ambitious equestrian tomb to be executed during the century was for the remains of Napoleon's arch-nemesis, the Duke of Wellington, commander of the allied forces at the fateful Battle of Waterloo. This is the colossal aedicular tomb structure in Saint Paul's Cathedral in London executed by Alfred Stevens, who received the commission in 1856. When a worldwide competition was held for the monument, the first prize was awarded to William Calder Marshall, but as the result of a web of circumstances as complicated as those surrounding the contest for the tomb of Napoleon, the commission was finally awarded to Stevens. The freestanding structure consists of a massive marble canopy supported by Corinthian columns that enclose a bronze gisant figure of the duke. On top of this canopy stands a bronze equestrian statue of the soldier in a military uniform with his arm outstretched in a gesture of command.[79]

Marochetti's statue was not the only part of the sculptural program for the tomb of Napoleon that was destined not to be inaugurated, at least in the nineteenth century. The two bas-reliefs of Dumont and Jouffroy, which had been approved by the Rochejaquelein report in June 1850, were actually completed and briefly installed at the entry to the crypt, but their Orleanist iconography made it inevitable that they would be quickly removed and put in storage along with Marochetti's plaster model. On 8 December 1851, six days after the coup d'état of Louis Napoleon, Jouffroy's relief representing Louis-Philippe receiving the remains of Napoleon at the Invalides was mounted in its niche; the companion relief by Dumont, depicting the Prince de Joinville at Saint Helena, followed on 17 January 1852. The fact that these two works were put in place so quickly after Louis Napoleon's seizure of power may stem from Visconti's realization that if they were ever going to be installed, it had to be before the new government was organized enough to inspect—and suppress—the project. But the inspecteur des beaux-arts set the removal process in motion by writing to the personal physician and confidant of Louis Napoleon shortly after their installation and asking him to sound out the ruler on the matter. "If he decides to remove these sculptures, this could be done in an instant without anyone knowing," he declared. And with the requisite stealth, the two bas-reliefs were removed and placed in permanent storage on 18 June 1852.[80]

Naturally, this was not the end of the matter. Three days after the removal of the two politically unwelcome reliefs, a subordinate of Prince Jérôme Bonaparte, president of the Senate and governor of the Invalides, wrote to Visconti relaying the prince's desire that two new bas-reliefs with different subjects be commissioned to replace them. Instead of Dumont and Jouffroy, sculptor Jean-Louis Brian was recommended as the person to execute them. The reason given for the choice of Brian was one that directly relates to the struggle of authorial egos, which had plagued the project and must have been well known in administrative circles: "Mr. Brian is a modest artist, who never demands anything and who, for this reason ought to attract the attention of a man as eminent as Mr. Visconti." Visconti then dutifully wrote to the minister of the interior singing the praises of Brian and proposing two new themes for the reliefs. This was to no avail, however, as it was soon decided that the empty niches would be covered up with marble plaques.[81] This solution to the problem was to remain in place until 1910, when the bas-reliefs were restored to their original destination, where they are found today.

Why it required such an extraordinary length of time to move the body of Napoleon from its temporary resting place in one of the side chapels a few yards away to the sarcophagus in the crypt once the project was completed is one of the mysteries of the Second Empire. Equally puzzling is the dearth of comment on this strange delay in the press and in the numerous descriptions of the tomb published after 1852. Typical of the strategies of avoidance when discussing the project during the Second Empire is the description of the tomb and the dome of Invalides in the most ambitious guide book published during the reign of Napoleon III, Emile de Labédollière's extremely detailed and richly illustrated *Le Nouveau Paris* (1860). The author provides a guided tour through the monument, describing the sculptural program and identifying the artists responsible for each part, and describes the sarcophagus in such a way as to imply that Napoleon's remains were housed in it. The only reference to the delay in inaugurating the monument is found in one terse comment: "Deposed in the Chapel of Saint-Jerome, the body of Napoleon occupied the magnificent mausoleum built on the plans of Visconti a long time afterwards."[82] But the refusal of authors to discuss this strange delay likewise continued in the numerous histories of the Second Empire written after its fall, hence the need to examine the question here.

Ample documentation exists to show that the work was near completion early in the year 1853 and could have been finished in the spring if the government had desired to do so.[83] In fact, Visconti prepared a set of drawings and plans to be displayed for the inaugural ceremony planned for 5 May 1853, the anniversary of Napoleon's death. And Eugène Oudiné dutifully executed the commemorative medallion commissioned for the projected event, which bore the inscription "La France et Napoléon III inaugurent le tombeau de l'Empereur Napoléon I . . . MDCCCLIII," and exhibited it at the Salon of 1852.[84] Although there is no evidence that an official announcement was made, it was commonly believed that the monument would be inaugurated sometime in the middle of 1853. Acting on this assumption, the 1852 *Almanach de Napoléon* gave a detailed description of the tomb complex and confidently proclaimed that its inauguration would be held on 5 May of the following year.[85]

Fig. 84
Edouard Hollier, *Saint Napoleon, Patron of Warriors*. Lithograph, 1852. Photo courtesy of Bibliothèque Nationale, Département des Estampes.

S. N A P O L E O N,
Patron des Guerriers.

Many in France anticipated that the inauguration would be held in conjunction with the great celebration scheduled for 15 August, the birthday of Napoleon and the feast day of Saint Napoleon. The year before Louis Napoleon, who was shortly to become Emperor Napoleon III, had reestablished this feast day for the roman warrior-saint, who had been invented in 1806 by Cardinal Caprara at the behest of Napoleon I, and had arranged a grand festival and *feux d'artifice* on the appointed date. The total conflation of the fictive roman saint and the warrior who suffered his martyrdom on Saint Helena is apparent in the profusion of doggerel verse honoring the occasion and in prints such as that of Hollier in which the subject of adoration wears a strange mixture of costumes but bears the visage of Napoleon Bonaparte (fig. 84). Therefore, many came to believe that this was but a prelude to the inauguration ceremony. Indeed a great pageant was held on the esplanade of the Invalides with many colossal, temporary constructions designed by Visconti, including an enormous plaster statue of Napoleon, adding a further note of unreality to the event.[86]

Why then did Napoleon III obstinately continue to honor his uncle, yet refuse him his final resting place? An answer might be that he simply did not like the design or the location of the

Fig. 85
Antoine Etex, *The Tomb of Vauban*. The Dome of the Invalides. Completed 1852. Photo courtesy of the Caisse Nationale des Musées Nationaux © 1992 ARS, New York/SPADEM, Paris.

tomb. Although the anecdotes of Etex are not to be trusted very far, this is the thrust of the conversation that the sculptor purportedly had with the new emperor in June 1853, during which Napoleon III commented that "this large hole invites one to spit into it."[87] According to Etex, the subject was then dropped after the emperor agreed with Etex's suggestion that the only way to improve the monument would be to cover the crypt. When reading this account, one must bear in mind the fact that Etex had an enormously inflated sense of his own self-worth and would probably have welcomed a revision of the design that would have removed the sarcophagus as the center of attention in the dome and given more prominence to his own tomb of Vauban, which is located in the east crossing (fig. 85). This monument was commissioned in 1843 as a corollary to the tomb of Turenne in the west crossing and was apparently considered as a peripheral part of the decoration for the tomb of Napoleon. A further indication that Napoleon III disliked the open-crypt design is found in a letter written on 10 May 1858 by Jules Bouchet, the architect in charge of the Hôtel des Invalides and its two churches at the time and former assistant of Visconti on the project. He began his letter to the minister of the interior by stating that Napoleon III had conveyed to him, in one of his visits "already distant," that he regretted that the tomb did not "present an aspect as severe and religious" as others he had seen in France and Italy.[88] To remedy this state of affairs Bouchet proposed that the opening of the crypt be covered and that the original floor paving be replaced. In the center of this repaved area would be placed Simart's standing statue of Napoleon turned toward the altar. The architect concluded by expressing his hope that the sarcophagus would not continue to remain empty much longer.

While it may be true that Napoleon III did not appreciate Visconti's design, there is little evidence that he tried to alter it, and it seems improbable that simple dissatisfaction could have accounted for the extraordinary delay in inaugurating the tomb. A more plausible explanation is that he decided that Napoleon should be remembered primarily not as a soldier or as a saint, but as the founder of a dynasty. To attain this end another location was necessary: the Basilica of Saint-Denis, a traditional burial site for royalty and the location Napoleon I had himself chosen for his dynastic tomb complex.

Even more than Napoleon III, the individual preoccupied with founding this fourth dynasty was duc de Persigny, who became minister of the interior in January 1852. A militant bonapartist since 1833, de Persigny had helped plan Louis Napoleon's attempted putsch at Strasbourg in 1836 and that at Boulogne in 1840, and was one of the primary architects of the empire's restoration during the Second Republic. His idea of the legacy of Napoleon was made patently clear as early as 1834 in the first pages of a newspaper he founded:

> For us the napoleonic idea! In this imperial idea resides the tradition that has been searched for so much in the eighteenth and nineteenth centuries, the true law of the modern world. . . . The time has come to proclaim this imperial gospel all over Europe. . . . The time has come to raise the old flag of the Emperor, not only the standard of Marengo and Austerlitz, but the one of Burgos and Moscow. The Emperor! All for the Emperor![89]

In his memoirs he further elaborated his theory of the fourth dynasty and explained why it was necessary for Napoleon III to give his rule the appropriate physical and ceremonial trappings:

> I argued that to bring back the throne of Napoleon was to complete the Revolution, and as one might say, to crown the Republic; that this also entailed the restoration of monarchical ideas and a continuation of the old royalty of France by a fourth dynasty; that consequently the fourth dynasty ought not to be placed in conditions of splendor, grandeur and power inferior to the older ones; that to create a monarchy at a discount was certainly not in accord with the desires of the masses, who had acclaimed the Empire. . . . that this distinction was especially necessary to make in France where the people love the splendor, pomp and magnificence of public ceremonies.[90]

He then made explicit his idea that the purpose of the *liste civile*, or funds allocated for patronage of the arts by the head of State, was to contribute to this grandeur. Bluntly put, the function of art, when commissioned by the State, was propagandistic. Although we appear to have no explicit statement on the matter, it is probable that de Persigny would have considered a tomb at Saint-Denis to satisfy his political agenda better than one at the Invalides.

That de Persigny's conception of an appropriate burial site for
the emperor was not shared by other members of the government
might be inferred from the way a petition from the Municipal
Council of Saint-Denis was handled by one of his subordinates.
On 3 February 1852 this group unanimously approved a resolu-
tion to have the body of Napoleon transferred to the basilica of
Saint-Denis and forwarded it to the directeur des beaux-arts.
More than five months later this functionary transmitted it to de
Persigny with the advice that it be disapproved.[91] It may be that
this rejection was at least partly the result of the debate that took
place during a meeting held in April 1853, at which Napoleon III
presided, to draw up a program for the inauguration. Our only
source of information about this meeting is the generally reliable
Revue des Beaux-Arts, a major art journal whose editor must
have been informed about it by someone in the government. According to this account, General Sauboul proposed that to commemorate Napoleon's status as a monarch his heart be removed
and transferred to Saint-Denis, while his body remain at the
Invalides. In response, Jérôme Bonaparte, Napoleon's youngest
brother and governor of the Invalides, indignantly declared that
this would never happen while he was alive. As a consequence
of this exchange, Napoleon III allegedly adjourned the meeting
and postponed the inauguration of the tomb until the following
year. Had the issue come up again later, it is likely that Jérôme
Bonaparte, still among the living, but age sixty-nine, would have
continued to reject the idea. Instead, this recalcitrant brother
lived until 1860, apparently posing an obstacle to this strategy
until his death.[92]

Viollet-le-Duc, as the most favored architect of Napoleon III,
may have been asked for his opinion on the matter, or he may
have simply proffered it uninvited, but a proposal in his hand-
writing survives, which sheds more light on the matter of the
suggested transfer of Napoleon's remains to Saint-Denis. In this
communication dated 8 April 1853, which had no addressee, the
architect began with a description of the kind of tomb he considered appropriate for Napoleon at the Basilica of Saint-Denis.
The design consisted of a simple sarcophagus raised above the
floor of the choir, supported by four porphyry columns and covered with enameled and gilded copper plate. He then continued
by outlining a plan whereby Napoleon's body could be, either

Fig. 86
E. E. Viollet-le-Duc, *Floor Plan for Restoration of Saint-Denis*. Drawing, 1859. Collection: Musée des Monuments français, Paris. Photo courtesy of the Caisse Nationale des Musées Nationaux © 1992 ARS, New York/ SPADEM, Paris.

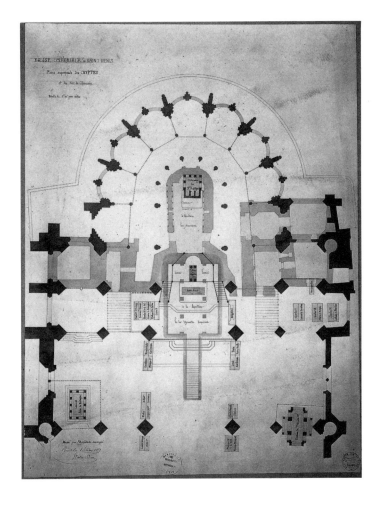

surreptitiously or clandestinely, transferred to Saint-Denis; according to this plan, the event would occur on 15 August at six in the morning. The government would let it be known that Napoleon's heart was to be surgically removed on the previous night and transferred to Saint-Denis. However, in reality, the heart would be left behind at the Invalides and the body taken to the basilica accompanied by a small funeral cortege led by Napoleon III. In Viollet's estimate, the deed would be a *fait accompli* by ten o'clock, as the imperial body would already be safely sealed in its new sarcophagus in the most prominent position in the venerable church.[93]

Fig. 87
E. E. Viollet-le-Duc, *Plan for Restoration of Saint-Denis.* Drawing, 1859. Collection: Musée des Monuments français, Paris. Photo courtesy of the Caisse Nationale des Musées Nationaux © 1992 ARS, New York/SPADEM, Paris.

It appears that Napoleon III and de Persigny, no matter how much they may have been in sympathy with the plan, feared to carry it out; at the same time, they declined to reject it outright. Hence, the project remained in limbo until 1858, when Viollet-le-Duc was asked, as part of the restoration he was supervising at Saint-Denis, to construct a crypt under the main altar for the Napoleonic dynasty. Naturally the architect complied, and on 1 March 1859 he signed the drawings he had executed for the project over which he had meditated for six years (figs. 86, 87). The plan shows that the entry to the imperial crypt would have been by a stairway in front of the main altar, a feature that clearly established the hegemony of the Napoleonic dynasty over the other three royal dynasties represented in the church. The longitudinal and transverse sections clearly show that the type of sarcophagus he had envisioned in 1853 would have dominated the altar and provided the visual focal point for beholders in the nave.

Although Viollet-le-Duc constructed the imperial crypt more or less as indicated in the drawings, it was never used for the burial of Napoleon III or members of his family, and the sarcophagus for Napoleon I was never executed for it was decided sometime in 1860 or early 1861 that the Invalides was a suitable site after all.[94] At two o'clock in the afternoon of 2 April 1861

Fig. 88
Anonymous, *Translation of the Remains of Napoleon Ier*. Illustration from *Le Monde illustré*, 1861. Photo: the author.

Napoleon's body was finally installed in the porphyry sarcophagus of Visconti at the Invalides in a private ceremony attended only by the imperial family, ministers of State, and the highest ranking generals in the military.[95] All that the public learned of the ceremony, which paled into insignificance in comparison to that which was staged for the retour des cendres twenty-one years before, derived from a few brief descriptions in the daily newspapers and a few popular images in the illustrated press (fig. 88). That this operation was so low-key at a time when the Second Empire was noted for the splendor of its public spectacles, and that it was held on neither 5 May nor 15 August—dates charged with special significance for the cult of Napoleon—can only lead to the conclusion that the reigning emperor was profoundly embarrassed by the event, on one hand, and, on the other, did not wish to call attention to the abandoned political strategy to which the body of his uncle had been held hostage. But what motivated this about-face?

The most plausible explanation for the decision to abandon plans to create a dynastic tomb at Saint-Denis is the major shift in the political agenda of Napoleon III that occurred shortly before, a shift from the so-called authoritarian phase of the Second Empire to what was referred to as the Liberal Empire. On 24 November 1860, Napoleon III issued a decree that appeared to encourage greater participation of the Chambers in the affairs of the Empire and be a move toward a constitutional government; among its provisions were the publication of parliamentary reports and debates in the *Moniteur universel* and the opportunity for the Corps législatif to respond to speeches from the throne. From that date followed a series of measures that served to stress that the Empire was responsive to the needs and demands of the larger populace and its elected officials. Given this decision to de-emphasize the authority formerly invested in the person of Napoleon III, it followed that his dynastic aspirations had to likewise be de-emphasized. Thus, the dream of a dynastic funeral monument was at odds with this new political policy.[96]

While Napoleon III may have been compelled to renounce his dynastic ambitions for Saint-Denis, he appears to have conceived another project as recompense, or as a surrogate measure for it. On 9 August 1862 Augustin Dumont—the sculptor who had executed the relief depicting the exhumation of the body of

Napoleon on the island of Saint Helena—was commissioned to execute a monumental statue of Napoleon in the toga of a roman emperor to replace Seurre's effigy of Napoleon in military costume that had stood atop the Vendôme Column since the July Monarchy.[97] The new statue was hoisted to the top of the column in November 1863. This representation of Napoleon as a modern Caesar, or as a conspicuous sign for the power lying behind the imperial throne of Napoleon III, led to a shift in public opinion regarding the Napoleonic legacy and in the political associations inscribed in the Place Vendôme.

In September 1840, when debate over the proper location for the tomb of Napoleon was at its most heated, *Le Charivari*, in a moment of seriousness, cast its vote for the Vendôme Column and made a prediction: "Let us imagine, if ever the soil of France were invaded again, if Paris saw itself again filled with foreign bayonets, it is around this heroic mausoleum that the final remains of its army would conquer or die; and without question, like El Cid of the novelist, the great captain would triumph again after his death."[98] Whether the body of Napoleon had been placed in the base of this column or not, it is doubtful that this prophecy would have been fulfilled during the Franco-Prussian War. It is equally doubtful that it would have been spared its fate, when, on 16 May 1871, during the last days of the Paris Commune, the column and its imperial effigy were toppled to the ground. Thus, history turns in its circle.

With the humiliating defeat of France in the Franco-Prussian War and the fall of the Second Empire, bonapartism as a belief system and the myth of Napoleon experienced a dramatic decline for two decades. However, with the growth of a fervent nationalist movement in the 1890s, Napoleon assumed a renewed place of importance in French culture. Representative of this resurgence of nationalism is Maurice Barrès's novel *Les Déracinés*, published in 1897. One chapter of this *roman à these* is set in the dome of the Invalides, where five young protagonists, in reaction against the decadence of contemporary French culture, have gone to honor Napoleon on the anniversary of his death and discuss his meaning for French history. The tomb complex itself is described as "this well, where architects, who despaired of constructing him a satisfactory throne, let the too heavy body sink." Nonetheless, the tomb was for its beholders

[a] cross-road of all the energies that one names audacity, will power, appetite. The imagination, for a hundred years dispersed everywhere, is concentrated at this point. Cover up with thought this crypt where the sublime is deposited, level history, suppress Napoleon: you will annihilate the condensed imagination of a century. One does not hear here the silence of the dead, but a heroic rumbling; this well under the dome, it is an epic clarion.[99]

This reading of history and the meaning of this monument at the Invalides was, of course, to be revised a number of times in our own century, particularly after two world wars devastated European culture. It is cited here as an example of the truth that funeral monuments live posthumous lives, which are tied to the vagaries of history.

CHAPTER 5

Authorship, Meaning, and Method

My story, as it has developed thus far, has paid relatively scant attention to issues of individual artistic vision, creativity, and originality in the construction of this monument. The primary working hypothesis has been that its form and meaning were transpersonal resolutions of forces and ideas existing in the cultural milieu in which it was produced, and not creative acts of some individual authorial will or presence. But this approach raises questions about whether the architect of our project has any right to be considered its author or a creative artist at all, for that matter, and if so, in what sense?

To explore further the problem of individual authorial creativity, we might begin by turning to a funeral monument inaugurated in 1859, two years before that of Napoleon: the tomb of Louis Visconti himself (fig. 89). Located in the cemetery of Père Lachaise in Paris, this monument pays homage to both the architect and his father. At the rear of the rectangular enclosure, surrounded by trees, stands the funeral stela of the renowned archaeologist. Positioned before it, almost as a counterpoint, is the tomb of the son. The effigy of the architect assumes a semi-recumbent pose of profound meditation and wears the costume of the French Academy. In his hands he holds plans for the completion of the Louvre, and at his side are placed a compass, protractor, and other tools of his exacting art or craft.[1] What a striking contrast exists, then, between this romantic representation of the fictive reverie of a solitary artistic genius, contemplating his work in silence, and the frenetic career of the real architect, who in his many official capacities was continually immersed in bureaucratic detail and administrative brouhaha of

the most mundane and public sort. This effigy provides a dramatic refutation of the judgment of Adolphe Lance and other contemporaries on Visconti's lack of creativity, and a sterling illustration of both the belief in artistic genius and the mythmaking powers of funeral sculpture. [2]

It also serves as a concrete index of the increased social standing of both the Visconti family and of the profession of architecture as a whole during the nineteenth century. This upward mobility is evidenced by the displacement of the tomb of Visconti's father. [3] When Ennius Quirnius Visconti died in 1818, he was buried in a modest site in the thirteenth division of the cemetery; his funereal monument was appropriately humble, consisting of a classical stela capped by a copy of a portrait head of the defunct peering out from his niche in hieratic frontality. [4] In 1854, shortly after the death of the architect, a public subscription was begun to raise money for a monument to him at Père Lachaise. Funds were quickly gathered for the construction of the tomb, but the subscription committee's effort to induce the city of Paris to

Fig. 89
Tomb of Louis Visconti. Cemetery of Père Lachaise, Paris. Le Harivel-Durocher, sculptor, 1855–59. Photo: the author.

donate a larger plot in the cemetery met with failure. Thereupon, the Visconti family purchased a new plot for the dual tomb in the prestigious fourth division of the cemetery and on one of its most important axes, symbolically placing their name among those of the monied or cultural elite of France.[5] Again, there is a sharp contrast between the social reality underlying the placement and prominence of this tomb and the isolated image of creative meditation it presents. There is also a certain irony at the origin of the public subscription for this monument. Two individuals primarily responsible for initiating its fund-raising campaign were the architects Théodore Lejeune and Félix Pigeory, both members of the Société libre des Beaux-Arts. The subscription was actively promoted by the *Revue des Beaux-Arts*, which was closely tied to this organization. It will be remembered that this society of artists and architects had actively supported an open contest for the project and was adamantly opposed to the manner in which the government conferred the commission on Visconti.[6] Therefore, in a space of little more than ten years, the position of the architect among the members of the organization shifted from obloquy to celebration of genius.

Pierre-Charles Simart, the sculptor originally chosen by the committee for the monument, was one of the few artists to maintain a cordial relationship with Visconti throughout the construction of Napoleon's tomb.[7] In 1856 Simart agreed to execute the effigy without a fee, asking reimbursement only for the wages of his praticien and for the materials used. Unfortunately, Simart died the following year without having completed his studies for the figure. The commission was then given to the relatively little-known sculptor Victor Le Harivel-Durocher, who accepted the same terms as Simart for the work. Because he realized that his successful execution of this monument would greatly enhance his reputation and serve as a conspicuous advertisement for his talents as a sculptor, he declined compensation for his creative labors.

After completion of this project, Le Harivel-Durocher's name became known to the public more due to a legal battle between himself and Félix Ravaisson, a prominent philosopher and curator at the Louvre, than for his creative endeavors. Ravaisson was concerned with an archaeological question being debated by scholars across Europe: whether the statue of the Venus de Milo, located in the Louvre, was originally executed as a single figure or as part of a group. It was Ravaisson's opinion, expressed in an essay he later published, that the figure of Venus was created as part of a sculptural group representing the theme of Mars being disarmed by Venus.[8] In support of his theory in 1871 he commissioned the sculptor to execute this restitution according to his verbal and written instructions. However, a dispute erupted when Ravaisson refused to pay the sculptor. Le Harivel-Durocher then proceeded to sue Ravaisson; the crux of the matter was revealed during the hearing when the sculptor produced a letter from his patron that justified this refusal on the grounds that the project "has become more and more your own personal work, although the theme was provided by me."[9] It can be easily seen that this conflict echoes that which occurred between Visconti and Pradier over the victory figures for the tomb of Napoleon and between Simart and his assistants in the execution of the bas-reliefs. But it also reflects a larger cultural debate over the individual artist's rights in a collaborative effort: how much autonomy was the sculptor to have, and how much control was the architect or patron of the work permitted? There is a rich irony in the fact that an artist who took this issue to a court of law was the same individual who executed the romantic funeral effigy to an architectural genius, whose own endeavors at the Invalides were continually haunted or hampered by this very problem.

The dispute between Ravaisson and Le Harivel-Durocher was given a more popular dimension by the realist art critic and novelist Jules Champfleury. In his novel *Madame Eugenio* (1874), he incorporated details of the case into his narrative as a means of addressing the question of artistic creativity and promoting the idea of individual artistic autonomy, longstanding concerns of his. Although ostensibly a champion of that collective entity known as le peuple, Champfleury was a fervent believer in the uniqueness of individual artistic inspiration. This article of faith is easily seen in a letter that he wrote to George Sand in 1855, on the occasion of Courbet's one-man exhibition in his so-called "Pavilion of Realism." His aim was to convince his fellow novelist of the unconventionality, subversiveness, and uniqueness of Courbet's art:

It is an incredibly audacious act; it is the subversion of all institutions associated with the jury; it is a direct appeal to the public, it is liberty, say some. . . .

I admit, Madame, that I think . . . like all those who demand the most complete liberty under all its manifestations. Juries, academies, contests of all kinds have shown more than once their powerlessness to create men or works. . . . We do not know how many unknown geniuses die who do not know how to comply to the requirements of society, who cannot tame their wildness, and who finally commit suicide in the dungeons of conventionality.[10]

It would be easy to produce other nineteenth-century examples of this kind of rhetoric, but to put the problem of individual creativity in a larger perspective we might turn to a best-selling work of popular fiction, or pop philosophy, written in the middle of the current century, Ayn Rand's *The Fountainhead* (1943). Instead of a painter or sculptor her protagonist is an architect. In what is perhaps modern literature's most emphatic assertion of authorial creativity of the architectural profession, Rand's hero delivers a number of perorations on the authorial independence of the architect:

An architect needs clients, but he does not subordinate his work to their wishes. . . . No work is ever done collectively, by a majority decision. Every creative job is achieved under the guidance of a single individual thought. An architect requires a great many men to erect his building. But he does not ask them to vote on his design. . . . the materials remain just so much steel, glass and concrete until he touches them. What he does with them is his individual product and his individual property. This is the only pattern for proper cooperation among men.[11]

In this prescription (which verges on caricature), the architect possesses the qualities of initiative, invention, originality, authority, and autonomy. These are, of course, properties assigned to the artistic genius by tradition since the romantic era. Most interesting about the discourse in Rand's novel is that these properties are described in almost the same manner in another best-selling work written almost three hundred years earlier. In studying the genealogy of the modern construction of the author, one might begin with a remarkable passage in Thomas Hobbes's famous

Leviathan (1654), where a clear-cut distinction is made between an actor and an author:

> A Person, is he, *whose words or actions are considered, either his own, or as representing the words and actions of another man, or of any other thing, to whom they are attributed, whether truly or in fiction.* . . . When they are considered his own, then is he called a *natural* person: and when they are considered as representing the words and actions of another, then he is a *feigned* or *artificial person.* Of persons artificial, some have their words and actions *owned* by those whom they represent. And then the person is the *actor:* and he that owneth his words and actions, is the AUTHOR: in which case the actor acteth by authority. For that which in speaking of goods and possessions, is called an *owner* . . . is called author. . . . So the right of doing any action, is called *Authority*.[12]

This equation of authorship, authority, and ownership is thus made in both works, the one supplying philosophical justification for the developing free enterprise or capitalist economic system and the other celebrating its triumph.

As a foil to the architect-genius, who exemplifies the virtues of the capitalist system, Rand inserted another character in the plot, a socialist art critic and ideological adversary of the hero, whose thought is summarized in detail:

> He said that architecture was truly the greatest of the arts, because it was anonymous, as all greatness. He said that the world had many famous buildings, but few renowned builders, which was as it should be, since no one man had ever created anything of importance in architecture. . . . A great building is not the private invention of some genius or other. It is merely the condensation of the spirit of the people.[13]

Like the discourse of Rand's hero, this socialist conception of the collective authorship of cultural artifacts can be traced to sources in the last century, if not before. But it received its emphatic expression in the theories of the Constructivist movement after the Russian Revolution. El Lissitzky—the painter, architect, and theorist who principally made its ideas concerning the social basis of art known in Western Europe—published an essay in 1930 that sounds as if it could have been written by Rand's socialist nemesis:

To our minds the work of an artist has no value "in itself," is not an end in itself, has no inherent beauty; all this it acquires only through its relationship with the community. In the creation of any great work the architects' part is manifest, the community's part is latent. The artist, the creative man, discovers nothing which falls from heaven into his lap. Therefore, by "reconstruction" we understand the conquest of the unexplained, of the "mysterious," of the chaotic.[14]

Thus, in Rand's novelistic debate we have a clear representation of the two extremes, or opposed models, between which narratives in architectural history usually position themselves, although most intelligent writers recognize that their mode of interpretation should be to a certain extent contingent upon the type of work being analyzed and the strength of personality of its architect. In any event, these are the contemporary conceptual-ideological parameters confronting any investigator of Napoleon's tomb or any other public work of the nineteenth century, and the reader should be aware of the intellectual topography in which the present work was written.

With these ideas in mind one might examine for the last time the role of Visconti in the project under three aspects that are at the heart of the debate over authorship: invention, ownership, and authority. In terms of invention, we have seen that there is little direct and unequivocal evidence proving or disproving the claim that he invented or discovered the solution to the problem of the tomb by himself. What has been shown is that the project exhibited in 1841 was unique. But much stress has been placed on the various circumstances that might have led him to this solution, such as the fact that he had discussed the problem with many highly placed officials in the government, who undoubtedly made suggestions and offered opinions on the matter. Indeed, it has been shown that some circumstantial evidence points to Louis Vitet as the source for the idea of the open crypt. However, barring any new discoveries, one must accept Visconti's signature on the drawing for the contest as that of the inventor or author, all the while bearing in mind the complex nature of invention and authorship in the architectural profession, and particularly in the creation of public monuments. This signature made Visconti the natural person, to use Hobbes's terminology, and as a consequence his assistants, who must have performed the many practical tasks involved in translating the summary draw-

ings approved by the State into the physical structure at the Invalides, became artificial persons. His relationship with these
assistants was thus similar to that of Simart and the sculptors who
served as his practiciens and who greatly resented being considered artificial persons.

The question of ownership, the logical concomitant of authorship according to Hobbes, is one much easier to answer. It cannot
be said that Visconti *owned* his design or its realization in any
legal sense. His design was never purchased by the State, and the
issue of ownership never arose in any of the negotiations for the
project. He did not sell his plans to the State but instead was
employed to render a specific and well-defined service to it. As
for the issue of authority, there is no question that it was possessed in great quantity by Visconti. But rather than deriving
from ownership, it was delegated by the State. This authority is
manifest in the hundreds of documents and letters he signed dealing with every phase of the project. Despite its physical appearance of unity, order, and coherence, this enterprise was riven by
political, institutional, and personal conflicts from beginning to
end. To bring it to a successful conclusion, a steady hand on the
helm to perform the "author-function" was a necessity.[15] Thus,
Visconti's authority over and responsibility for the project, which
is to say his role as its administrator, is in the final analysis his
strongest claim to being the author of, or the giver of meaning to,
the tomb.

Among the interpretative leaps in the preceding pages is the
argument that the architectural form of Visconti's tomb project
was a symbolic mediation of a variety of conflicting social, political, and aesthetic ideas and aspirations. In reaching this conclusion much documentary evidence was used as a springboard,
but an unacknowledged debt is owed, at least in part, to the theories of structural anthropology. At this point, one might move
further toward the synchronic mode of interpretation preferred by
that discipline and consider the meaning and function of this
monument in larger terms. To this end, we should turn to another major public work upon which Visconti was engaged during the period of most of the construction on the tomb of
Napoleon: the Saint-Sulpice fountain, or the so-called Fountain
of the Four Bishops, located in the large open area directly opposite the Church of Saint-Sulpice. Commissioned in 1842 and

Fig. 90
Louis Visconti, architect, Fountain
of the Four Bishops. Place Saint-
Sulpice, Paris, 1843–49. Photo:
the author.

inaugurated in 1848, it consists of three large basins superim-
posed one above the other, on top of which is placed a square
aedicular structure whose niches house the huge enthroned figures of four famous French bishops (fig. 90).[16] What these prel-
ates had in common, besides their positions in the hierarchy of
the Church, is that all were authors of considerable authority, or
possessors of the word. Upon completion of the monument this

quartier, famous for its seminary and boutiques selling images of piety, was provided with a representation of both clerical authority on a truly intimidating scale and the centrality of the written word in spiritual life.

But this logocentric monument represents authority on a deeper level than its iconography or scale. In its embodiment of pure presence in the center of a large open space, a palpable absence, it forms a structural analogue for the locus of power and authority in the social and cultural life of mid–nineteenth-century France as a whole. Monument and site posit a dialectic of center and periphery, of positive and negative valences, which is structurally relevant to far more than French society. One of the major themes of modern sociology has been the relationship of center and periphery as a structuring principle in cultures across the globe. Among the many prominent social theorists one could quote in this regard is Edward Shils:

> The central zone is not, as such, a spatially located phenomenon. It almost always has a more or less definite location with the bounded territory in which the society lives. Its centrality has, however, nothing to do with geometry and little with geography. . . .

> The center . . . is a phenomenon of the realm of values and beliefs. It is the center of the order of symbols, values, beliefs, which govern the society. It is the center because it is the ultimate and irreducible; and it is felt to be such by many who cannot give explicit articulation to its irreducibility. . . .

> It is central because of its intimate connection with what society holds to be sacred; it is central because it is espoused by the ruling authorities of the society. These two kinds of centrality are vitally related. Each defines and supports the other.[17]

Regardless of Shils's claim that the center, or the locus of social authority, has little to do with geometry or geography, the metropolis of Paris has a complex network of nodal points of irreducibility, homologous to this social centrality, which, like the Saint-Sulpice fountain, were commissioned as public monuments. It would be difficult or impossible to demonstrate that they were specifically commissioned and constructed as representations of the irreducibility of social power, or maps of the desired social order, but this is one function they nonetheless appear to have served.

While Shils was speaking from the theoretical perspective of an academic sociologist, Clifford Geertz, one of America's leading cultural anthropologists who has immersed himself in ethnographic studies of world cultures, has come to a similar conclusion regarding the symbolics of power:

> At the political center of any complexly organized society . . . there is both a governing elite and a set of symbolic forms expressing the fact that it is in truth governing. No matter how democratically the members of the elite are chosen . . . or how deeply divided among themselves they may be, they justify their existence and order their actions in terms of a collection of stories, ceremonies, insignia, formalities, and appurtenances that they have inherited, or in more revolutionary situations, invented. It is these . . . that mark the center as center and give what goes on there its aura of being not merely important but in some odd fashion connected with the way the world is built. [18]

While Geertz finds centers in all sorts of social ceremonies and trappings, the most obvious representations of societal values are found in public monuments; it is to these that one should look for confirmation of his contentions.

Shils's preoccupation with the location of social authority and the problem of center and periphery can, of course, be directly related to his well-known political conservatism, but individuals at the other end of the ideological spectrum have also been deeply concerned with these questions, the most important of whom is Michel Foucault. For Foucault the architectural manifestation of the values of modern society is not its monuments but its prisons, and the relation of center and periphery is addressed most directly by him in a chapter on panopticism in his book on the birth of the modern prison. The term *panopticism* is taken from the plans and descriptions utilitarian philosopher Jeremy Bentham developed from 1787 to 1791 for a panopticon prison, or a carceral environment in which individual cells were to be arranged in a circle or semicircle around a central observation post from which guards would observe continuously the prisoners on the periphery yet remain unseen themselves. For Foucault this sinister plan is a paradigm of a major transformation in western culture that developed in the seventeenth and eighteenth centuries and culminated at the beginning of the nineteenth. It represents the shift from a culture in which the exercise of power depended upon physical display and the exercise of force to one in which control was effected by impersonal mechanisms of surveillance by unseen agents of social authority:

> The celebrated, transparent, circular cage, with its high tower, powerful and knowing may have been for Bentham a project of a perfect disciplinary institution; but he also set out to show how one may "unlock" the disciplines and get them to function in a diffused, multiple, polyvalent way throughout the whole social body. . . . Bentham dreamt of transforming [them] into a network of mechanisms that would be everywhere and always alert, running throughout society without interruption in space or in time. The panoptic arrangement provides the formula for this generalization. It programs, at the level of an elementary and easily transferable mechanism, the basic functioning of a society penetrated through and through with disciplinary mechanisms.[19]

Although Foucault focuses his discussion around the scheme of Bentham, there were numerous panopticon designs developed in France before and after his plan. However, the 1840s saw the greatest interest in the practical application of this idea. The panopticon design was given its highest official sanction on 9 August 1841, when Duchâtel sent his communique, *Instructions et programme pour les constructions de maisons d'arrêt et de justice*, to the prefects of all the departments of France explaining the underlying rationale for this kind of prison and providing a series of exemplary designs by the architects Abel Blouet, Hector Horeau, and Harou-Romain fils. This letter provoked considerable discussion in the architectural community at just the time Visconti was pondering his plan for the tomb of Napoleon; it is reasonable to infer that it may have influenced the project he submitted to the contest several months later.[20] To be sure, Visconti would have intended no reference to incarceration in his design, but the unseen ruler in a sealed sarcophagus in the center of a circular space, at the periphery of which lesser members of society stand in attitudes of reverence, is an arrangement that the panopticon prison and the tomb of Napoleon have in common. And while the Saint-Sulpice fountain cannot be considered a panopticon design, it shares a common conceptual basis in its assertion of center and periphery, presence and absence, power and powerlessness.

That the notions of center and periphery still bear an emotional charge and carry tacit social and political meanings even today might be inferred from the reception of a public monument completed in Paris in May 1986, which might be considered a deconstruction of panopticism as well as the logic informing Visconti's fountain and many similar structures occupying public spaces. This monument and fountain, covering three thousand square meters, was constructed in the cour d'honneur of the eighteenth-century complex of buildings known as the Palais Royal after the plans of Daniel Buren, one of the most important contemporary French artists (fig. 91). The project consists of a gridwork of rhythmically aligned columns clad in vertical black and white marble stripes. These standardized col-

Fig. 91
Daniel Buren, *Column Monument*. Courtyard, Palais Royal, Paris, 1985–86. Photo: the author.

umns are all of the same height but are placed at various distances above and below the ground level in such a way as to give the impression that half the monument lies under one's feet. The fountain, which is created by the intersection of two underground channels visible through a steel grate, is viewed by standing next to a square opening and looking down into a cryptlike space below. This focus of attention is placed near one corner of the grid, rather than in a central position. At night a system of regularly spaced red and blue lights illuminates the space uniformly, avoiding any suggestion that light is being used to give priority to or accentuate any one part of the grid.

This sort of dry description of formal properties certainly belies the critical reception it met in the right-wing press before and after its inauguration. For many it was (and is) a highly visible symbol of the decay of social and cultural life in France and the target of an outpouring of ideological spleen. Having been commissioned by the minister of culture of the Socialist government of François Mitterand and executed by a notable member of the Socialist party, it quickly became known as a Monument to Socialism. A carefully orchestrated campaign of hysteria was led by *Le Figaro*, the major voice of conservatives in France, and in one of its editorials it was labeled with the phrase *AIDS Of The Spirit*. While under construction, the wooden barrier that surrounded it was covered with far more scurrilous comments by irate spectators.[21] Its defenders, on the contrary, tended to argue that it was in complete accord with the colonnade of the peristyle around the court and only underlined the architectural characteristics of the buildings, thereby respecting tradition. Amazingly enough, no one, on either the Right or Left, seems to have thoughtfully analyzed the relation between the formal qualities of the monument and the response from the populace, or what specifically in the form of the monument itself could have produced such an outcry.

The meaning inscribed in the form of this monument becomes visible in the act of comparison. If one places it alongside the Saint-Sulpice fountain, it can clearly be read as an antitype or as a model against which it establishes its difference. On the horizontal plane the most conspicuous difference is its complete dissolution of the relationship of center and periphery, which is the primary carrier of meaning in Visconti's monument. But this deconstruction is pursued on the vertical axis as well. If one considers the ground plane to be the line dividing positive from negative space, or presence from absence, then Visconti's emblem of authority stresses only the former, while Buren's monument gives equal attention to both. Therefore, one can consider the work of Buren to be an emblem of democracy or the democratic alternative to the hierarchical representation of social power inscribed in the Saint-Sulpice fountain. It appears then that the opponents of this monument rightly perceived its meaning on some level of consciousness, even if they were unable to articulate it in this manner. Whether the artist himself conceived of the meaning in this way is something that is unclear from his published statements, but regardless of his personal intentions, his work assumed this meaning the moment it became part of the network of monuments punctuating the public space of the capital.

But to place Buren's conception in a more contemporary context it might be compared to Richard Serra's highly controversial monument, *The Tilted Arc*, erected in New York's Federal Plaza in 1981. Consisting of a giant sheet of welded Corten steel measuring 112 feet in length and 12 feet in height, the structure was designed to divide the open space in which it was located and to play off the facades of the nondescript governmental buildings surrounding it. The protests of the disgruntled officeworkers and bureaucrats against this structure, resulting in a legal battle that occupied the press for months and ended in its removal, were primarily that its massive scale and presence were menacing and that it formed an unpleasant barrier that forced them to make an inconvenient detour when crossing the plaza.[22] On the other hand, the sculptor maintained that its aim was to engage the public in a dialogue concerning its relationship to the empty space and its environment. Yet, despite the seemingly avant-garde nature of Serra's ambitions, if one considers his monument in relation to the Saint-Sulpice fountain of Visconti and the Column Monument of Buren, it clearly has a strong affinity with the former. Like Visconti's monument, it is a visual representation of authority and social control of the populace, over whom power is being exercised in an undisguised fashion. From this example one may conclude that the symbolics of power, or the representation of power and powerlessness in a public monument, is not limited to the literal relationship of center and periphery.

With these alternative representations of the locus of social power in mind, we might consider once again the implications in the tomb of Napoleon. It seems apparent that it occupies a place between these two alternatives. On the horizontal axis it both denies and then reasserts the relationship of center and periphery. When one stands at a certain distance from the open crypt, the sarcophagus is invisible, and other than the relatively inconspicuous balustrade, there is no center. As one approaches the balustrade, the central position of the sarcophagus and the decorative sculpture becomes apparent. But the force of centrality

Fig. 92
George W. Keller, *The James A. Garfield National Memorial*. Lake View Cemetery, Cleveland, Ohio, inaugurated 1890. Photo: the author.

is diminished by the fact that it is located in the negative space below the ground level, which one can easily enter. On the other hand, in relation to the ground level of the crypt and the peristyle, it assumes a dramatic vertical thrust, rendering the distinction of positive and negative space ambiguous. Likewise, the balustrade on the floor level of the dome acts as a physical and psychological barrier distancing the viewer from the tomb, yet at the same time the openness of the expanse it guards imparts a sensation of immediate accessibility, a feeling that one can literally reach down and touch the hallowed and irreducible object in the center. Thus, one of the impressions that we are left with after visiting the dome of the Invalides is a sense of ambiguity about periphery and center, or the prescribed relation between viewer and object. While the design considered abstractly might suggest panopticism, the actual experience of viewing and exploring the monument undermines the concept. And this sensation is perfectly in accord with the fundamental ambivalence in the response that many had, and still have, to the multifarious history, myth, and legend of the person commemorated.

If one were to develop a rudimentary taxonomy of funerary monuments for political leaders and place the tomb of Napoleon within it, a productive point of departure might be those erected to American presidents. While some of these structures are strictly commemorative, others also serve as tombs. An impressive member of the latter category is the huge mausoleum erected to James Garfield in Cleveland, Ohio, from 1885 to 1890 (fig. 92). This monument consists of a 180-foot tower and a rectangular, fortresslike structure at its base. Built in a high Victorian Gothic or Romanesque Revival style, its heavy rustication augments the expression of physical power conveyed by its proportions. When the visitor enters the monument through its underscaled portals, he or she is confronted by a greater than life-size effigy of the assassinated president in the center of the rotunda.[23] Inside this building, one's sense of the presence of centralized power is less than when viewed from the exterior; the symbolics are essentially the same.

The experience one has of this building is of a different order from that dedicated to another American president seven years later. Grant's Tomb, or more properly the Monument to General Ulysses S. Grant, was built on the plans of John H. Duncan and inaugurated on Manhattan Island in April 1897.[24] Its facade is composed of a combination of classical elements adapted from archaeological sources; its dome is a variation on contemporary reconstructions of the Mausoleum at Halicarnassos. The structure, rising 160 feet above the ground and placed on a promontory overlooking the Hudson River, offers a dramatic presence in relation to its site, more imposing even than Visconti's Saint-Sulpice fountain, and emphatically demarcating center and periphery. However, the remoteness of the exterior is transformed when one enters the structure and approaches the tomb of the general. Intentionally modeled on Visconti's design at the Invalides, an open crypt is located under the dome with an austere sarcophagus in the center. As at the Invalides, access to the crypt

Fig. 93
Philip Johnson, *The Kennedy Memorial*. Dallas, Texas, inaugurated 1970. Photo: the author.

is by means of a stairway not visible while beholding the crypt from above. A primary difference between the monument in Paris and this one in America, however, is that the opening of the crypt is considerably smaller in diameter and there is no decorative sculpture to interrupt the contemplation of the sarcophagus. This reduction of scale and disavowal of ornamentation gives the structure greater intimacy and accessibility than its Parisian counterpart and establishes an emphatic dialectic between remoteness and accessibility when viewing it from the outside and the inside.

In contrast to these structures is the Kennedy Memorial in Dallas, Texas, located two blocks from the infamous Texas School Book Depository building. This memorial, inaugurated on 24 June 1970, is the only such structure designed by Philip Johnson, one of the leading architects of our era.[25] When one stands at the edge of the square on which the monument is situated, the structure presents an imposing presence in the center of the space, leaving no doubt as to the location of the periphery (fig. 93). Constructed on a deliberate upgrade and composed of huge vertical sections of unadorned concrete aggregate, which give the impression they are the palisades of a colossal fortress, it distances the viewer with a display of power in a manner that is not too dissimilar from the tomb of Garfield. However, on further inspection the remoteness of this structure is undercut by carefully considered details. In the gap between the bottom of these palisades, which gives it a floating effect, and the ground level, one can clearly discern a black cenotaph, which is obviously the intended destination. Access to the cenotaph is through two openings on opposite ends of the structure. But the concrete sections at either side of these entrances hang cantilevered in the air, unsupported by any posts below. This gives them the appearance of being parts of swinging doors, a suggestion of mobility that is completely at odds with the impregnability of the material constituting the structure. Upon entering the monument, one is immediately confronted with the eight-feet-square cenotaph situated in a slightly recessed square. It bears the only inscription on the monument: JOHN FITZGERALD KENNEDY (fig. 94). The recess containing this black slab is small enough so that one can walk within a few feet of the cenotaph and peer down at it. Thus, when one penetrates the walls of the bastion, a relationship of intimacy is established with the object in the center, the walls

serving as protective shields against the disturbing elements of the
environment. The viewer feels at one with, or part of, the center.
All this is to say that the Kennedy Memorial is much more closely
related to the tomb of Napoleon than is the Garfield mausoleum,
although in different ways both mediate the categories of remoteness and accessibility and of center and periphery. This comparison might demonstrate that the response built into the tomb of
Napoleon can be elicited by structures of another era that at first
sight have only a distant visual resemblance to it.[26]

When the Kennedy Memorial was still at the discussion stage,
one of the primary promoters of the project urged that the city of
Dallas erect a fitting memorial, a monument that might resemble
the Lincoln Memorial.[27] One can well imagine a Doric temple,
such as that designed by Henry Bacon and inaugurated in 1922

Fig. 94
Philip Johnson, *Cenotaph in
The Kennedy Memorial*. Photo:
the author.

Fig. 95
Daniel Chester French, *Lincoln Enthroned*. The Lincoln Memorial, inaugurated 1922, Washington, D.C. Photo: the author.

at the west end of the Washington Mall, as a fitting structure to commemorate this president, who also fell to an assassin's bullet. But it is difficult to believe that anyone in the present era would accept a colossal effigy of John F. Kennedy even remotely resembling Daniel Chester French's awe-inspiring statue of Lincoln, enthroned like the famous lost figure of Jupiter in the temple of Olympia, which is the focal point in the interior of Bacon's shrine (fig. 95).[28] The reasons are that, despite Kennedy's enormous popularity and the aura that surrounded him, his actions did not affect the course of this country to even a remotely similar degree; secondly, simply not enough time had passed. It required more than fifty years for a representation of Lincoln in this manner to become acceptable, a period in which every American child learned the Lincoln legend and in which the image of Honest-Abe-the-Rail-Splitter became both an essential part of American folklore and an emblem of democracy. But the crucial point is that this representation of Lincoln is permissible because it runs *counter* to our shared notion of the man. Because the populist image of Lincoln is so firmly engraved in the American psyche, this enthroned figure is perceived as an agreeable fiction. He could be portrayed this way because we know in our hearts that the sculpture depicts what he was *not*. Another reason why this hieratic effigy is acceptable to the masses who visit the monument is that Lincoln is not dressed as the Jupiter Olympian. Instead, he wears an unbuttoned and rumpled frock coat that suggests a state of relaxed informality and lack of concern for outward appearances. His pose and costume is thus in marked contrast to a famous and controversial marble statue of George Washington executed by Horatio Greenough between 1832 and 1841 for the Capitol Rotunda. More than ten feet in height, Greenough's statue represents the first president in the hieratic seated pose of Jupiter on his throne, wearing classical drapery but nude to the waist. The literalism of the godlike reference and the remoteness of his image made this work completely unacceptable to the public and resulted in its removal from its original destination shortly after its inauguration.[29]

With these comments in mind we might return to the tomb of Napoleon and ask hypothetically whether an effigy on such a scale and in such a pose could have ever been constructed at the Invalides and whether it might have been costumed in the manner of Greenough's *Washington?* Some imagined even more colossal statues of Napoleon for this location, but could any of them have been executed? Likewise, could the image of the enthroned Napoleon in Simart's bas-reliefs (cf. fig. 82), which bears a marked resemblance to Greenough's *Washington*, have been blown up to a huge scale, removed from the semi-obscurity of the peristyle, and placed at a focal point of Mansart's dome? The severe criticism provoked by the style of Simart's reliefs and the decision to represent only Napoleon's civilian career did not address the implications of divinity and supreme power suggested by the pose. Although no one seems to have addressed the issue at the time in this manner, such a depiction of Napoleon would have been impossible because, unlike that of Abraham Lincoln, it would have been a represention of what he *wished* to be. The viewer could not have beheld such a statue and believed that posterity was honoring the man with a posthumous fiction. The fact that at least in part of his career Napoleon assiduously sought absolute power and its trappings could not have escaped any of those in France opposed to his legacy. For the government of Louis-Philippe to have attempted such a representation, even if it wanted to, would have provoked much discontent and placed this monument under the sign of absolutism.

Finally, after all the historical facts have been adduced to explain the meanings of the tomb of Napoleon, we might turn to an ahistorical theory in order to illuminate what may be other latent implications in the project. If we were to adopt a Freudian approach to public monuments and accept claims that on an unconscious level vertical or columnar structures—the Washington Monument on the Mall in Washington, D.C., being a case in point—signify phallic presence, then the sunken crypt might be construed as a sign of castration or absence of the fabled phallic signifier. We might further inscribe the terms *phallic potency* and *phallic absence*, or *male* and *female*, as unstated but implicit terms in the debate over the design of the tomb.[30] Given the value placed on the virility of male heroes in the sociocultural milieu of the nineteenth century, it can be readily understood why many might oppose a design that commemorated one under the sign of absence. These implications may be what make a caricature by Bernard Kliban, entitled "The Nixon Monument," done after the Watergate scandal and the fall of an American president, so maliciously satirical (fig. 96).[31] However, it should also be noted that the humor of Kliban's drawing derives from his manipulation of a cliché or stereotype of popular culture about the meaning of vertical monuments that is itself a caricature of Freudian theory. Therefore, how much our response to gender implications in public monuments is based upon folklore and how much upon subliminal promptings seems to pose an epistemological dilemma for which there is no solution.

A significant difference exists, however, between the Nixon monument and that of Napoleon at the Invalides. Whereas in the former Kliban's beholders peer down into a void, or into pure absence, in the latter their gazes into the excavated space would encounter an impermeable block of stone rising dramatically from

the floor of the excavation, emphatically reasserting presence. But rather than simply signaling the simultaneous presence and absence of the male signifier, one might find deeper gender associations inscribed in Visconti's design, recalling Freud's celebrated and greatly overinterpreted discussion of the "fort/da" game in the beginning of his *Beyond the Pleasure Principle*. The passage concerns a child's apparently obsessive play with the ideas of presence and absence in a game that consisted of throwing a toy from his cot and repeating the word "fort" ("there it goes"), and then the word "da" ("here it is") after it was returned to him. Freud concluded that this repetitive play was a reenactment of the withdrawal of his source of satisfaction, or his mother, and of her reappearance.[32] By means of the phonemes O and A, the child was attempting to master the situation or gain control over this maternal other by symbolic means. Hence, one might liken the experience of beholding the tomb at the Invalides to an architectural fort/da game, or the visual play with the presence and absence of the maternal signifier. The problem here is that

Fig. 96
Bernard Kliban, *The Nixon Monument*. Illustration from *Never Eat Anything Bigger Than Your Head*, 1976. Photo courtesy of Workman Publishing, New York.

there is no evidence that, until now, anyone has ever played a fort/da game with it or ventured an interpretation of the design in this manner. This raises the questions of the temporal and physical locations of this hypothesized meaning, or whether it was in the mind of the architect, is inherent in the plan of the monument, or is a product of psychoanalytic discourse in our own century.[33] And lastly, of course, whether it is only in the mind of the present writer.

With this concluding bit of speculation as to the meaning of the monument, my investigation has traversed the hermeneutic scale. At one end stands the hard, documentary evidence that has been painstakingly gathered in archives and libraries over a number of years and forged into a more or less coherent narrative. At the other end of the interpretative scale can be placed propositions that have been suggested by contemporary theoretical discourse in the humanities and were not the fruit of archival research, such as those concerned with authorship, the interrelation of center and periphery, and the psychosexual implications in the open crypt. Somewhere in between are numerous inductive judgments, such as the structuralist claim that the form of the tomb represents a symbolic mediation of opposed discourses about Napoleon and the nature of the appropriate funeral monument. The truthfulness of the first kind of account can be empirically tested by consulting records in the public domain, whose location I have attempted to provide in scrupulous detail. This is to say that the so-called "correspondence theory of truth"—the belief that close correlation between brute or institutional facts and their linguistic descriptions is a standard for truth—can validate these empiricist assertions.

In adhering to this standard for truth, I am aware that I am at odds with much poststructuralist theory in which truth is relative to the frame of reference that contains it. Among the individuals most responsible for promoting this perspective is Michel Foucault, whose analysis of panopticism has been cited above in relation to the design of the tomb, and whose thought has certainly promoted interpretations of cultural practices and artifacts such as those that form the other pole of my hermeneutic scale. The great irony here is that if one follows Foucault's theory as to the relative and context-determined nature of historical knowledge, then there is little reason to exempt his own work and theories from this judgment.[34] It follows from this relativist position that reinterpretations of the tomb of Napoleon are not foreclosed by my investigation, and that future generations, working in different cultural frames, will discover or constitute new meanings for it. What will stand the test of time, however, is the fundamental body of facts presented here, documentary evidence that should provide the foundation or point of departure for future imaginative interpretations of this complex monument.

Chronology of Significant Events Related to the Tomb

1840

12 MAY   Rémusat announces to the Chamber of Deputies that the body of Napoleon is to be returned to France. He asks for an appropriation of one million francs to pay for the transportation expenses and the ceremony to be held at the Invalides.

23 MAY   The Clauzel Commission reports on the bill, approving the Invalides as the site for the tomb, recommending that a proviso for an equestrian statue on a public place be included, and urging that an additional one million francs be added to the original request.

25 MAY   The architect Duban accepts Rémusat's invitation to design the tomb and provides a plan and estimate.

26 MAY   The Chamber of Deputies votes to grant the original request of one million francs only and disapproves the recommendation for an equestrian monument.

JUNE   Marochetti prepares his first studies for the tomb.

JULY   Construction of full-scale model of tomb by Marochetti in the dome of the Invalides.

15 OCT.   Thiers resigns as prime minister.

29 OCT.   Duchâtel becomes minister of the interior in the new government of Soult and Guizot.

15 DEC.   Napoleon's body is disembarked at Courbevoie and taken in a great funeral procession to the dome of the Invalides.

1841

6 FEB.   Napoleon's body transferred to the Chapel of Saint Jerome in the dome of the Invalides.

13 APR.   Annnouncement made in the Chamber of Deputies that a contest for the design of the tomb is to be held.

1 OCT.   Final deadline for the submission of projects for the contest.

27 OCT.   Exhibition of eighty-one projects opens to the public.

21 NOV.   Exhibition closes.

23 NOV.   Commission appointed to report on the contest.

21 DEC.   The commission submits its report to the minister of the interior.

1842

16 JAN.   The commission's report is published in the *Moniteur universel*.

22 MAR.   Visconti awarded commission for the tomb. Marochetti given the commission for the model for an equestrian monument in the cour d'honneur of the Invalides.

23 NOV.   Visconti informs minister of the interior that trial decoration has begun and that final plans are ready for approval.

31 DEC.   Visconti's final drawings are approved and signed by the minister of the interior.

1843

29 APR.   Report of the Sapey Commission to the Chamber of Deputies approving Visconti's plans and recommending an appropriation of an additional 1,500,000 francs for the project. It recommends that there be no decoration other than Napoleon's name on the sarcophagus, the equestrian statue be located on the esplanade of the Invalides, and Napoleon be dressed in imperial regalia.

18 JUNE   It is announced in the *Journal des Artistes* that the excavation for the crypt is complete and masonry work is about to begin.

| 1 JULY | Law passed in the Chamber of Deputies approving both the findings of the Sapey Commission and the requested allocation. |

1 JULY   Law passed in the Chamber of Deputies approving both the findings of the Sapey Commission and the requested allocation.

16 AUG.   Visconti informs the minister of the interior that his model of the crypt is finished and proposes a program of decoration consisting of two monumental figures for the doorway to the crypt, twelve victory figures in the crypt surrounding the sarcophagus, and a series of mosaics on the wall of the crypt illustrating the principal events in the life of Napoleon. For the commission for these works he recommends Duret, Pradier, and Triqueti.

15 SEPT.   Pradier given commission to execute the twelve victory figures in the crypt.

19 SEPT.   Marochetti given another contract for the models of the equestrian statue and the bas-reliefs for the pedestal, to be located on the esplanade of the Invalides.

1844

JAN.   Visconti proposes to the minister of the interior that a commission be formed to judge the sketches of the artists executing the decoration.

20 FEB.   Francisque Duret given commission for the models for two monumental marble caryatid figures at the doorway to the crypt.

24 MAY   Visconti announces that the first sketches for the decoration leave something to be desired and that modifications in the decorative program will be necessary.

30 NOV.   Visconti provides Pradier with precise stylistic criteria for the victory figures.

6 DEC.   Visconti reports that the experiments have shown the mosaic decoration in the crypt to be inappropriate and thus recommends a series of marble bas-reliefs to replace it.

1845

28 JAN.   Jean-Baptiste Feuchère awarded commission for two groups of children, carved from wood, to be placed on the baldachin.

| 18 SEPT. | Visconti announces that the models for the caryatid figures of Duret are finished. |

| 6 DEC. | Visconti writes to the minister of the interior that the time has come to name the sculptors for the bas-reliefs in the crypt. As requested, he names ten sculptors to execute them but recommends that Simart be assigned with all the models. He further recommends Simart for the standing figure for the cella. |

1846

| 17 MAR. | Simart awarded the commission for the standing figure in imperial regalia for the cella. |

| 31 MAR. | Triqueti given the commission for a marble sculpture of the crucifixion on the main altar. |

| 10 JUNE | Simart is commissioned to execute the sketches for the bas-reliefs. |

1847

| 11 APR. | Visconti writes to the minister of the interior for the first time concerning the "imperfections" in Pradier's victory figures. |

| 27 JULY | Simart given the commission to execute all ten bas-reliefs. It is stipulated that he employ at least five sculptors who had won the Prix de Rome to assist in the actual process. |

| 7 AUG. | Simart given the program for the reliefs. |

1848

| 24 FEB. | First Revolution of 1848 forces Louis-Philippe to abdicate. A provisional government is installed. |

| 18 MAR. | Ledru-Rollin, the new minister of the interior, appoints a committee to investigate the project. |

| 4 MAY | Opening of the new Constituent Assembly after elections of April. |

| 29 MAY | Ledru-Rollin Committee completes report. |

26 JUNE	Second Revolution of 1848 is suppressed.
25 SEPT.	Ledru-Rollin Committee report published in *Democratie pacifique*.
3 NOV.	Visconti informs the minister of the interior that he is bringing a defamation of character suit against the Corsican newspaper *L'Ere nouvelle* for allegations it made based on the Ledru-Rollin Commission Report.
10 DEC.	Louis Napoleon Bonaparte is elected president of the Republic.

1849

25 JAN.	Visconti wins his suit against *L'Ere nouvelle*.
4 JUNE	Charles Blanc, directeur des beaux-arts, approves Simart's choice of five sculptors to execute the bas-reliefs after his models.
13 JUNE	Democratic manifestation lead by Ledru-Rollin is severely repressed.
21 JUNE	Dufaure, the minister of the interior, asks the Legislative Assembly, dominated by the Parti de l'ordre, to approve an additional appropriation to finish the tomb. A committee headed by the Duc de Luynes is appointed to study the request and state of the project.
15 DEC.	Report of the de Luynes Committee to the Assembly recommending that no new appropriation be approved for the tomb.

1850

28 JAN.	Another proposal is made by the minister of the interior to the Assembly to allocate funds to finish the tomb. Committee headed by Rochejaquelin is appointed to study the request and the project.
31 MAY	An electoral law is passed severely reducing the number of individuals eligible to vote.
4 JUNE	Rochejaquelin report presented to the Assembly supports the request for funds to finish the tomb.

| 31 DEC. | Visconti writes to the minister of the interior reporting the difficulties Simart had encountered with the sculptors executing the bas-reliefs after his sketches. |

1851

| 6 OCT. | Visconti writes to the directeur des beaux-arts announcing that the marble crucifixion of Triqueti is not large enough and demanding that another work in bronze be undertaken. |

| 2 DEC. | Coup d'état of Louis-Napoleon. The Assembly is dissolved. Universal suffrage reinstituted. |

| 4 DEC. | The Resistance to the coup d'état in Paris is crushed. |

| 8 DEC. | The bas-relief by Jouffroy installed at the lower entry to the crypt. |

| 20 DEC. | National plebiscite ratifies the coup d'état. |

1852

| 17 JAN. | The bas-relief by Dumont installed at the lower entry to the crypt. |

| 2 APR. | The model for the bronze crucifixion by Triqueti is officially approved. |

| 18 JUNE | The bas-reliefs of Dumont and Jouffroy are removed and placed in storage. |

| 22 NOV. | National plebiscite re-establishes the Empire. |

| 1 DEC. | Proclamation of the Empire. |

| 10 DEC. | Commission given to Eugène Lequesne to make the "retouches" to Pradier's victory figures desired by Visconti. |

1853

| 8 APR. | Viollet-le-Duc drafts proposal for a tomb of Napoleon at Saint-Denis. |

| 20 JUNE | Lequesne paid for having completed the "retouches" of Pradier's figures. |

10 DEC.	Commission for the equestrian monument of Marochetti definitively annulled.
1859	
1 MAR.	Viollet-le-Duc signs his drawings for a tomb of Napoleon at Saint-Denis.
1861	
2 APR.	Napoleon's body transferred to the sarcophagus under the dome of the Invalides.

Sculptural Program for the Tomb

I. Main door to the crypt: Two bronze caryatid figures representing *Civil Force* and *Military Force* by Francisque Duret.

II. Bottom of the corridor to the crypt: Two marble bas-reliefs.

> Left: *Louis-Philippe Receiving the Remains of Napoleon at the Invalides on 15 December 1840* by Augustin Dumont.

> Right: *The Prince de Joinville Exhuming the Body of Napoleon at Saint Helena* by François Jouffroy.

III. Wall of the peristyle of the crypt: Ten marble bas-reliefs after models by Pierre-Charles Simart. Inscriptions taken from de Las Cases's *Mémorial de Sainte-Hélène*.

> Order of subjects running counter-clockwise from the entry to the crypt:

> A. *Creation of the Order of the Legion d'honneur.* Executed by Simart.

> B. *The Great Public Works.* Executed by Simart.

> C. *Protection Accorded to Commerce and Industry.* Executed by Simart.

> D. *Establishment of the Cour des Comptes.* Executed by Jean-Claude Petit.

> E. *Organization of the University.* Executed by François Gaspard Lanno.

> F. *The Concordat.* Executed by Simart.

> G. *The Civil Code.* Executed by Simart.

> H. *Creation of the Conseil d'Etat.* Executed by Simart.

I. *Administrative Centralization.* Executed by Auguste Ottin.

J. *Pacification of Civil Disturbances.* Executed by Simart.

IV. Marble statue in the reliquary or "cella" of the crypt representing Napoleon in imperial regalia. Composed and executed by Simart.

V. Twelve marble statues of Napoleonic victories designed by Pradier. Executed by Pradier and assistants. The sequence runs counter-clockwise from the entry to the crypt.

A. *The Italian Campaign: Montenotte, Millesimo, Lodi, Castiglione, Arcole, Rivoli.*

B. *The Egyptian Campaign: Pyramides, Mount Tabor, Aboukir.*

C. *The Italian Campaign: Passage at Saint Bernard, Montebello, Marengo.*

D. *The First Austrian Campaign: Ulm, Austerlitz.*

E. *The Prussian Campaign: Iena.*

F. *The Polish Campaign: Eylau, Friedland.*

G. *The Spanish Campaign: Madrid.*

H. *The Second Austrian Campaign: Echmülh, Essling, Wagram.*

I. *The Russian Campaign: Moscow.*

J. *The Campaign in Saxony: Lutzen, Bautzen, Dresden, Leipzig, Hanau.*

K. *The French Campaign: Brienne, Champ-Aubert, Montmirail, Nangis, Craonne, Laon.*

L. *The Belgium Campaign: Ligny, Sous, Fleurus.*

VI. Bronze statue of Christ on the cross above the main altar and under the baldachin. Designed and executed by Henri de Triqueti.

List of Official Entries in 1841 Contest

The following list of names derives from the registers of entrants, receipts for the projects, and correspondence in the Archives nationales, A.J.52.493. For the most part only the contestants' last names were recorded in the registers, but often their addresses are to be found on the receipts. In order to identify the various participants, criticism, which often refers to the full name of the contestants, was carefully studied. Wherever possible addresses were checked in professional directories of the period.

CONTEST NO.	NAME	PROFESSION
1	Victor Baltard	Architect
2	Mathieu-Prosper Morey	Architect
3	Henri Labrouste	Architect
4	Antoine-Martin Garnaud	Architect
5	Charles-Fréderic Chassériau	Architect
6	Vincenzo Gajassi	Sculptor
7	Achille Devéria	Painter
	Hippolyte Maindron	Sculptor
8	Joseph Nicolle	Architect
9	Auguste Rougevin	Architect

[1] This entry must be that of architect Léon Danjoy. His project was much discussed in the criticism of the contest, but his name does not appear on the register list in the Archives Nationales, A.J.52.493. On his deposit receipt he gave as the name of the contestant the code-phrase "Je souhaite . . . sur les bords de la Seine" and signed his own name underneath. This act might be considered his declaration in favor of the principle that all entries in contests such as this should be anonymous.

[2] Receipt in A.J.52.493 gives no first name but lists the profession as "Architecte" and the address at 8 rue Fontaine St. Georges. This address is the same as that listed for an architect for the city of Paris with the same last name in the Annuaire des Bâtiments of 1841. This directory provides no first name.

[3] The entrant's receipt gives his full name. The only well-known figure with this name active in Paris at the time was Italian writer, publisher, and typographer Nicolò Bettoni. He is the author of a book, L'Europe ne s'en va pas: lettres à M. Philarete Chasles et à la Revue des Deux mondes, Paris, 1841, in which he discusses the Napoleonic legacy in guarded terms.

[4] Receipt gives name as "Delande", his profession as architect, and an address that corresponds to one listed for an architect in Annuaire des Bâtiments in 1841. No first name appears in this directory.

[5] A note in A.J.52.493 indicates that his collaborator was an architect named A. Sievert, but only the painter was listed as the author in the documentation and criticism.

10	Antoine Lassus	Architect
11	Louis-Joseph Duc	Architect
12	Jean-Baptiste-Philippe Cannissié	Architect
13	Jean-Jacques Feuchère	Sculptor
14	Feuchère (second project)	
15	Edouard Isabelle	Architect
16	Emile-Jacques Gilbert	Architect
17	Antoine-Gaspard Coutel	Painter
18	Louis Moreau	Architect
19	Théodore Labrouste	Architect
20	Louis-Tullis Visconti	Architect
21	Antoine Demeunynck	Architect
22	Anonymous[1]	
23	Victor-Benoit Lenoir	Architect
24	Félix Duban	Architect
25	Victor Lemaire	Architect
26	Martin-Pierre Gauthier	Architect
27	Jules Bouchet	Architect
28	Desplans[2]	Architect
29	Nicolò Bettoni	Uncertain[3]
30	Lucien-Tyrtée Van Cleemputte	Architect
31	Delande[4]	Architect
32	Antoine Rivoulon[5]	Painter
33	Théophile Bidon	Army Officer

34	Bidon (second project)	
35	Chamouillet (identity unknown)	
36	Eugène Lacroix	Architect
37	Martin Laureyssens (identity unknown)	
38	Antoine Coussin	Architect
39	Henri Sirodot	Architect
40	Louis-Anne Totain	Architect
	Louis-Victor Vigreux	Architect
41	Jean-Baptiste Klagmann	Sculptor
	Théodore Charpentier	Architect
42	Dennier (identity unknown)[6]	
43	Alfred Ferot	Architect
44	Alexandre-Jules Frary	Architect
45	François Thiollet	Architect
46	Thiollet (second-project)	
47	Hilaire Garlin	Architect
48	Edouard Marly	Architect
49	Achille Allevy	Teacher, Inventor
50	Pierre-Ephège Mouton	Architect
51	Louis Auvray	Sculptor
52	Emile Seurre	Sculptor
53	Louis Rochet	Sculptor
54	Louis Fanelli-Semah	Painter

[6]It is possible that the name was misspelled in the register and that it should be "Denière," a bronze caster active at the time in Paris.

55	François Duquesney[7]	Architect
56	P. F. Geslin[8]	Painter
57	Michel Dagand	Sculptor
58	Louis Petitot	Sculptor
59	Antoine-Laurent Dantan	Sculptor
60	Eugène-André Oudiné	Sculptor
61	Pierre-Alphonse Fessard	Sculptor
62	Hector Horeau	Architect
63	Gabriel-Joseph Garraud	Sculptor
64	Julien-Jean Gourdel	Sculptor
65	Louis Desprez	Sculptor
66	Auguste-Hyacinthe Debay	Sculptor
	Jean-Baptiste-Joseph Debay	Sculptor
67	Louis-Achille-Valery Hurlupé de Ligny	Architect
	Raymond Gayrard	Sculptor
68	Denis Foyatier	Sculptor
69	Arthur Guillot	Sculptor
70	Georges Jacquot	Sculptor
71	Edmond Lévêque	Sculptor
	Louis Buhot	Sculptor
72	Devéria and Maindron (second project)	
73	Henri de Triqueti	Sculptor
74	Antoine Etex	Sculptor

[7]No first name in register, but receipt gives title as "Architecte du gouvernment" and address is the same as that for this individual in the 1841 *Annuaire des Bâtiments*.

[8]Geslin was a decorative painter by trade who specialized in polychromed interiors, but he also considered himself an inventor and author.

75	Pierre-Sébastien Guersant	Sculptor
76	Auger[9]	Unknown
77	Maindron (third project)	
78	Louis-Joseph Daumas	Sculptor
79	Charles Callet	Architect
80	Louis-Victor Bougron	Sculptor
81	Anonymous[10]	

[9] This is possibly either Adrien-Victor Auger or Charles Auger, both of whom are painters, but there is no further documentation to verify the identity of the entrant.

[10] This must be the entry of sculptor Pierre-Jules Cavelier. Although he is not listed by name in the register, his project was much discussed in the criticism and was ranked tenth in the report of the commission, which judged the contest in 1841.

Notes

PREFACE

1 James Wines, *De-architecture* (New York, 1987), 62. The author is both a prolific critic and an architect associated with SITE, the architectural firm whose projects embody or exemplify many of his ideas.

2 John R. Searle, *Speech Acts: An Essay in the Philosophy of Language* (London, 1969), 51.

3 On the ambiguous position of architectural drawings see Margaret Richardson, "Architectural Drawings: Problems of Status and Value," *The Oxford Art Journal* 5, no. 2 (1983), 13–21.

CHAPTER 1 THE MONUMENT AND ITS ARCHITECT

1 "Exposé des motifs et projet de loi tendant à ouvrir un crédit spécial pour la translation des restes mortels de l'Empereur Napoléon," *Chambre des Députés, Session* [12 May] *1840*, no. 150 (Paris, 1840), 337–38.

2 Before the complex was completed Charles II of England requested that Louis XIV provide him with plans of it. The French king obliged by having drawings by both Bruant and Hardouin-Mansart engraved and publishing a description to accompany them. See Le Jeune de Boulencourt, *Description générale de l'hostel royal des Invalides* (Paris, 1683). The engravings were done by Jean Marot. In 1687, engraver Pierre Le Pautre was paid for another set of engravings of plans, sections, and elevations that were completed before the dome was finished. On these early plans see Patrick Reuterswärd, *The Two Churches of the Hôtel des Invalides* (Stockholm, 1965).

3 The problematic union of the two disparate buildings was a subject of discussion even in the eighteenth century. See abbé Gabriel Pérau, *Description historique de l'hôtel royal des Invalides* (Paris, 1756), iii.

4 Little had been written about the architect or his career until the recent exhibition catalogue *Louis Visconti, 1791–1853*, ed. Françoise Hamon and Charles MacCallum, *Délégation à l'Action Artistique de la Ville de Paris*, Paris, 1991. This catalogue contains essays on various aspects of Visconti's career by an inter-

national team of scholars as well as my catalogue essay on the tomb of Napoleon. During work on the exhibition many of the personal papers of Visconti were uncovered for the first time in the Archives of Count du Périer de Larsan.

5 See "Autobiographie," *Visconti, 1791–1853,* 23.

6 "Actualités-souvenirs," *L'Artiste,* ser. 2, vol. 8, livraison 25 (1842), 162–63.

7 See Charles MacCallum, "Les Hôtels," *Visconti, 1791–1853,* 189.

8 Visconti was involved with the plans to create a national library there during the Second Republic, before Louis-Napoleon became emperor. On this project see Emmanuel Jacquin, "La Reunion du Louvre aux Tuileries" and David Van Zanten, "Visconti et Le Nouveau Louvre," both in *Visconti, 1791–1853,* 220–39 and 248–53.

9 On the nature of this position see David Van Zanten, "Visconti architecte-voyer," in *Visconti, 1791–1853,* 66–71.

10 François Loyer, "L'immeuble, l'ordre et la fantaisie," in *Visconti, 1791–1853,* 206.

11 Adolphe Lance, *Dictionnaire des architectes français,* vol. 2 (Paris, 1872), 333–34.

CHAPTER 2 POLITICS OF REPRESENTATION AND LOCATION

1 Elected a deputy from Bergues in 1834, Lamartine consistently fought for liberal causes throughout his tenure in the Assembly despite the fact that he was a philosophical legitimist and pragmatic supporter of the constitutional monarchy of Louis-Philippe.

2 See Alphonse de Lamartine, "Discours sur la loi relative aux restes mortels de Napoléon," in *Oeuvres complètes de M. de Lamartine,* vol. 8 (Paris, 1842), 383–93. See the account of the debate in *Le Moniteur universel,* no. 148 (27 May 1840), 1188–90. An official account of the proceedings, which omits the names of the speakers, is found in the *Procès-verbaux des séances de la Chambre des Députés: Session 1840,* vol. 7, annexes 152–92 (Paris, 1840), 10–19. In reconstructing parliamentary debates both of these printed sources must be employed.

3 Charles de Monalembert, "Discours sur les travaux exécutés aux monuments religieux," reprinted in *Revue du Monde Catholique,* no. 5 (4 August 1847), 85.

4 "Sculpture," *Almanach populaire de la France* (Paris, 1840), 99, 105. This was published by the radical republican activist Laurent Pagnerre. David's essay was republished in its entirety and vigorously condemned by the *Journal des Artistes* (hereafter *J.A.*), ser. 2, vol. 1, livraison 38 (15 December 1844), 427–32. The periodical's attack on the sculptor continued in the "Actualités" section on 22 December 1844, 443.

5 Letter to Adrien Maillard, undated, in *David d'Angers et ses relations littéraires,* ed. H. Jouin (Paris, 1890), 255–56. The drawing was reproduced and discussed for the first time by Jacques de Caso, *David d'Angers: L'Avenir de la mémoire* (Paris, 1988), 175–76.

6 "Napoléon," reprinted in *Oeuvres complètes de Edgar Quinet*, 11 vols. (Paris: Librairie Pagnerre, 1857–70), 7:308. This poem was originally published in *Revue des Deux Mondes* in 1834.

7 On the political implications of this topos see Nina Athanassoglou-Kallmyer, "Sad Cincinnatus: *Le Soldat laboureur* as an Image of the Napoleonic Veteran after the Empire," *Arts Magazine* 60, no. 9 (May 1986), 65–75.

8 Quoted by Charles Nisard, *Des chansons populaires chez les anciens et chez les français*, vol. 2, Paris, 1867.

9 This was approved by the censor on 10 November 1840, but the register lists no "graveur," only Villain as the publisher. See the Archives Nationales (hereafter A.N.), F.18.VI.22, no. 4008.

10 For an extended discussion of the political context see my "Singing the *Marseillaise* in 1840: The Case of Charlet's Censored Prints," *The Art Bulletin* 69, no. 4 (December 1987), 606–25.

11 *1815 et 1840*, reprinted in *Oeuvres complètes de Edgar Quinet*, vol. 10 (Paris, 1858), 13.

12 *Lutèce*, reprinted in *Heinrich Heine: Werke, Briefwechsel, Lebenszeugnisse*, vol. 19 (Berlin-Paris, 1977), 87–88. On the attitude of the different strata of the bourgeoisie towards a possible war see the analysis of Adeline Daumard, *Les Bourgeois de Paris au XIXe siècle* (Paris, 1970), 342–43.

13 See A.N., F.18.VI, no. 17; ibid., VI.22, no. 3677.

14 On the relationship of Charlet and Thiers see D. Halévy, *Le courrier de M. Thiers d'après les documents conservés au département des manuscrits de la Bibliothèque Nationale* (Paris, 1921), 115–18.

15 See, for example, the anonymous article "Un peu de tout," in *L'Artiste*, ser. 2, vol. 5, livraison 20 (1840), 349.

16 Jean Boisson, *Le Retour des cendres* (Paris, 1973). See also the recent catalogues commemorating the 150th anniversary of the retour des cendres: *Napoléon: Le Retour des Cendres (1840–1990)*, Musée Roybet-Fould, Courbevoie, 1990, and *Napoléon aux Invalides: 1840, Le Retour des Cendres*, Musée de l'Armée, Paris, 1990.

17 This catafalque differed significantly from one conceived by Visconti. For a reproduction of Visconti's drawing of a much more austere, classical structure see Barry Bergdoll, "Metteur en scène des fêtes de juillet et des fastes du IIe Empire," in *Visconti, 1791–1853*, 157.

18 For information on this project and reproductions of the column and the statue that was partially destroyed in World War II see P. A. Wimet, *La Colonne de la Grande Armée à Boulogne-sur-Mer* (Port-de-Briques, 1954).

19 The print was authorized for publication on 30 November 1840. See A.N., F.18.VI.22, no. 4205.

20 See his *Chants du crépuscule* in *Victor Hugo: Poésie*, ed. Bernard Leuilliot, vol. 1 (Paris, 1972), 328–31. In 1827 Hugo had published an earlier ode to the column and to Napoleonic glory.

21 Lamartine, "Discours sur la loi," 391–92.

22 Ibid., 392.

23 The engraving by Seurre served as a plate in Ambroise Tardieu, *La Colonne de la Grande Armée d'Austerlitz*, 2d ed. (Paris, n.d.). The complete program for the 1831 contest was published by *J.A.*, 5th yr., vol. 1, no. 16 (17 April 1831), 293–94.

24 Alexandre Goujon, *Pensée d'un soldat sur la sépulture de Napoléon* (Paris, 1821), 8. The pamphlet went through six editions in the first year of publication.

25 On his career see Harold March, *Frédéric Soulié: Novelist and Dramatist of the Romantic Period (New Haven, Conn., 1981)*.

26 Frédéric Soulié, *Le Tombeau de Napoléon* (Paris, 1840), 21.

27 See A.N., F.18.VI.22, no. 3477.

28 Pierre Cuisin, *Les Lunes poétiques des deux-mondes: Contemplations philosophiques, historiques, morales et religieuses* (Paris, 1840). This book was published in installments from 1836 until 1840. The text illustrated by the plate is found on p. 133. Idem, *Le Triomphe des royalistes et de la cause ou la chute du tyran* (Paris, 1815), 1.

29 Rémusat papers, Archives municipales, Toulouse, 5.S.181, carton 7, no. 54, "Police III." The report from the agent is dated 21 May 1840. Ibid., no. 55, 22 May 1840.

30 See David H. Pinkney, *Napoleon III and the Rebuilding of Paris* (Princeton, N.J., 1958), 10–11.

31 This passage is quoted and discussed by David Van Zanten, *Designing Paris: The Architecture of Duban, Labrouste, Duc, and Vaudoyer* (Cambridge, Mass., 1987), 204–5.

32 "C", "Dialogue entre la colonne de Juillet et la colonne Vendôme," *Almanach populaire de la France* (Paris, 1840), 93–95.

33 *Notice historique sur l'obélisque de Luxor* (Paris, 1836), Bibliothèque Nationale, Fol. Lk7.7528. It was printed by the firm of Chassaignon and illustrated with beautiful wood engravings by Fleuret.

34 For a discussion of the circumstances behind the commission and its program see my "Eclecticism and Ideology in the July Monarchy: Jules-Claude Ziegler's Vision of Christianity at the Madeleine," *Arts Magazine* 56, no. 9 (May 1982), 119–29.

35 Charles Forster, *La Tombe de l'Empereur* (Paris, 1840), 44. For another pamphlet advocating the same location, but without discernible Bourbon sympathies, see Edouard Péclet, *Napoléon où sera le tombeau?* (Paris, 1840).

36 César Daly, "Le tombeau de Napoléon à la Madeleine," *Revue générale de l'architecture* (hereafter R.G.A.), vol. 2 (1841), col. 639–40.

37 Jacques-Ignace Hittorff, *Considerations sur l'Eglise de la Madeleine* (Paris, 1834), 1. This first appeared as a series of articles in *Journal des Artistes* in May and June 1834.

38 Lamartine, 391.

39 See Neil McWilliam, "David d'Angers and the Panthéon Commission: Politics and Public Works under the July Monarchy," *Art History* 5, no. 4 (December 1982), 426–27.

40 An engraving and description of this project is found in J. D. Thierry, *Arc de Triomphe de l'Étoile* (Paris, 1845), 15, plate 5. The group was based on a design of Emile Seurre. On the many projects to crown this monument see Louis de Fourcaud, *Francois Rude, Sculpteur, Ses oeuvres et son temps (1784–1855)* (Paris, 1904), 206–17, and Sheila Gaudon, "James Pradier, Victor Hugo et L'Arc de Triomphe de l'Étoile," *Revue de l'Histoire littéraire de la France*, no. 5 (September–October 1968), 715–25.

41 See Roger van Lancker, "Napoléon et l'abbaye de Saint-Denis," *Revue de l'Institut Napoléon* 72 (July 1959), 97–100.

42 This petition is in A.N., C.806, dr. 25.

43 On the plans during the Empire and Restoration see Tabariés de Grandsaignes, "Un plan du Palais du roi de Rome et de la région, vers 1811," *Bulletin de la Société historique d'Auteuil et de Passy* 7, no. 72 (1910–12), 86–89.

44 The original watercolor for the print is in the Musée Carnavalet, Paris.

45 For a reproduction and discussion of this project see the catalogue entry by F. Boudon and H. Loyer, *Hector Horeau, 1801–1872* (Paris, 1972), 31.

46 "Le Tombeau de Napoléon," *Revue des Deux Mondes* 23 (1 September 1840), 768–81.

47 "Exposé des motifs," 337–38.

48 Louis de Carné, "De la popularité de Napoléon," *Revue des Deux Mondes*, ser. 4, vol. 22 (1 June 1840), 865–66. Carné's proposal for a tomb was an enormous, undecorated granite pedestal supporting a colossal eagle that would have held a globe in its claws.

49 Eugène Pelletan, "Le Tombeau de Napoléon," *Revue indépendante* 1 (1 December 1841), 513–14. The editors of this journal were Pierre Leroux and George Sand.

50 Charles de Rémusat, *Mémoires de ma vie*, 5 vols. (Paris: Librairie Plon, 1958–67), 3:319–20. See the Archives municipales, Toulouse, 5.S.181(6). Duban's letter is dated 25 May 1840. His program limited the sculpture to two figures, representing "le peuple" and "l'armée," and a standing figure of Napoleon. He also included a separate equestrian monument in the package, apparently designed to be placed in the courtyard of the Invalides. The estimate of the cost for this statue was 260,000 francs or roughly one-third as much as the tomb, to which he would have allocated 900,000 francs.

51 Rémusat, *Mémoires*, 3:320.

52 Letter to Hippolyte Fortoul, Fortoul papers, 30 July 1840, A.N., 246AP14. This letter is briefly discussed and the sketch reproduced in Van Zanten, *Designing Paris*, 208, fig. 72; letter to Fortoul, Fortoul papers, 5 August 1840, A.N., 246AP14.

53 On the sculptor's career see Marco Calderini, *Carlo Marochetti: Monografia con ritratti facsimile e reproduzione di opere dell'artista* (Turin, 1928). The tomb project is briefly mentioned on pp. 28–29. For a short discussion of it see Marcel Vicaire, "Le projets de Marochetti pour le Tombeau de l'Empereur Napoléon," *Bulletin de la Société de l'histoire de l'art francais* (1974), 1975, 145–52. For a discussion of Marochetti's equestrian monument to Wellington at Glas-

gow and the latter part of his career in England see Philip Ward-Jackson, "Carlo Marochetti and the Glasgow Wellington Memorial," *Burlington Magazine* 132, no. 1053 (December 1990), 851–62. Marochetti's political involvements remain to be investigated, but he was elected mayor of Vaux in 1830 and still served in that capacity in 1848. See his "profession de foi" written during his campaign for the Assemblée Nationale in 1848 in the Bibliothèque Nationale, no. Le.64.1253.

54 The most favorable response to this statue was an eulogistic essay by Count de Fortis, *Notice sur la statue équestre d'Emmanuel Philibert, Duc de Savoie* (Paris, 1838).

55 On Thiers's method of awarding commissions and his interest in public monuments see my "Eclecticism and Ideology in the July Monarchy," 120–21. On Thiers's acquaintance with Marochetti see the entry of 14 August 1840 in *Mémoires de Madame Dosne, l'Egérie de M. Thiers*, vol. 1 (Paris, 1928), 169. That Rémusat himself was only lukewarm in regard to Marochetti's participation might be inferred from his comment in his *Mémoires*, vol. 3, p. 319, that while Marochetti was not greatly skilled as a sculptor, at least he had ideas. On the purported amorous relationship of Marochetti and Madame Dosne, see Vaudoyer's Letter to Hippolyte Fortoul, Fortoul papers, A.N., 246AP14.

56 Ottin's and Bonnassieux's letters are reproduced in Antoinette Le Normand, *La Tradition classique et l'esprit romantique: Les sculpteurs de l'Académie de France à Rome de 1824 à 1840* (Rome, 1981), 122, 171.

57 See Rémusat, *Mémoires*, 3:320. For first-hand descriptions see "Chronique," *Mémorial de la littérature et des Beaux-Arts* (25 July 1840), 286, and "Chronique," *Petit courrier des Dames* 39, no. 4 (20 July 1840), 30. Thierry Issartel reproduces as the first project of Marochetti a lithograph of an aedicular tomb for Napoleon that appeared in an anonymous brochure in 1840. However, this image does not match the descriptions of the first project published in the press. Thierry Issartel, "Les projets pour le tombeau de Napoléon," in the exhibition catalogue *Napoléon aux Invalides*, Musée de l'Armée (Paris, 1990), 140.

58 A lithograph was published in *L'Artiste*, ser. 2, vol. 5, livraison 21 (1840), opposite p. 372 and an engraving in *Journal des Artistes* 2, no. 22 (29 November 1840).

59 The allegorical figures at the corners may have been intended to recall those of the equestrian monument of Henri IV on the Pont Neuf, which was destroyed during the Revolution. For engravings of that monument see the B.N., Cabinet des Estampes, Marolles Coll., Pe. 16.

60 See "Rapport fait au nom de la Commission chargée d'examiner le projet de loi relatif à la translation des restes de l'Empereur Napoléon," *Chambre des Députés, Session 1840*, no. 150 (23 May 1840), 447–52. Clauzel had been a representative from the Ardennes since 1829 and was allied with the liberal opposition. He fought in North Africa from 1835 to 1837, but was relieved of his functions after the disastrous retreat from Constantine.

61 A recent discussion of the debate alleges that Thiers made no attempt to rebut the critics of the Clauzel report and consequently misinterprets his role in the matter. See Michael Marrinan, *Painting Politics for Louis-Philippe: Art and Ideology in Orléanist France, 1830–1848* (New Haven, 1988), 187.

62 Antoine Etex, *Souvenirs d'un artiste* (Paris, 1877), 325. Along with the drawing Etex wrote a detailed program and executed a model. The program, accompanied by an illustration, was published as a brochure, *Première idée du Tombeau de Napoléon dessiné sur bois d'après l'esquisse composée et jetée en plâtre le 15 mai 1840 par Etex statuaire* (Paris, 1840).

63 This change coincides with a pamphlet published by Etex, *Deux mots sur l'article de David, au mot Arc du dictionnaire politique* (Paris, 1840), in which he argued that classical drapery harmonized better with architectural monuments than modern military uniforms.

64 Bosio received a commission for a marble statue in January 1816, but it was changed to bronze in 1819. Almost no scholarship exists on the work of Bosio. For a survey of his career and the complete review see L. Barbarin, *Etude sur Bosio: Sa vie et son oeuvre* (Monaco, 1910), 91–93. On the statue of Louis XIV see Robert W. Berger, "Bernini's *Louis XIV Equestrian*: A Closer Examination of its Fortunes at Versailles," *Art Bulletin* 63, no. 2 (June 1981), 232–48.

65 See *Le Moniteur universel*, no. 148 (27 May 1840), 1188.

66 Mansart's role in commissioning and directing these projects is discussed by Michel Martin, *Les Monuments équestres de Louis XIV: Une grande entreprise de propagande monarchique* (Paris, 1986), 74–81.

67 The tomb of Colleoni was known, for example, to Ingres, who executed a pencil study of it sometime before 1840, which is in the Musée Ingres at Montauban, inv. no. 867-4066. For critics' complaints, see the article signed "H," "Monument de Napoléon," *J.A.*, no. 25 (21 June 1840), 396.

68 This tomb was illustrated and discussed shortly after Marochetti's project was conceived. See "Tombeau de Louis de Brézé dans la cathédrale de Rouen," *Magasin pittoresque* 11 (1843), 301–2 and Erwin Panofsky, *Tomb Sculpture: Four Lectures on its Changing Aspects from Ancient Egypt to Bernini* (New York, 1964), 83–85.

69 "Exposé des motifs," 337.

70 See George Laviron, "Le Tombeau de Napoléon: Deuxième projet de M. Marochetti," *L'Artiste*, ser. 2, vol. 6, livraison 17 (1840), 264–65; "Monument de Napoléon," *J.A.*, 16th yr., vol. 2, no. 16 (18 October 1840), 245–48.

71 Rémusat, *Mémoires*, 3:320.

CHAPTER 3 THE "CONTEST"

1 Various reports, letters, and documentation for this debate are found in the Bibliothèque Nationale, Deloynes Collection. See George Duplessis, *Catalogue de la collection des pièces sur les beaux-arts imprimés et manuscrits* (Paris, 1881), nos. 1695–797.

2 See *Procès-verbaux du Comité d'instruction publique de l'Assemblée législative*, ed. J. Guillaume (Paris, 1889). On Quatremère's views of contests see Yvonne Luke, "The Politics of Participation: Quatremère de Quincy and the Theory and Practice of 'Concours publiques' in Revolutionary France, 1791–1795," *The Oxford Art Journal* 10, no. 1 (1987), 15–43.

3 *Recherches sur l'Art statuaire considéré chez les anciens et chez les modernes, ou Mémoire sur cette question proposée par l'Institut national de France* (Paris, 1805), 538–39.

4 On the Madeleine competition see A.N., A.J.52.493. The six contestants were Pradier, Jacquot, Lemaire, Desboeufs, Gayrard, and Guersant. On the contest for the Place Louis XV, the committee to judge the submissions chose Destouches's project but also awarded the design of the fountains to Lusson. See Jean-Marie Bruson, "La Place de la Concorde," in the exhibition catalogue *Hittorff, 1792–1867*, Musée Carnavalet (Paris, 1986), 75–77. Significant for the discussion of the equestrian monument in chapter two, the plan of Hittorff included four symmetrically placed equestrian statues representing the four dynasties in the French monarchy. For the contest's program see the *Journal du génie civil, des sciences et des arts* (July 1829), 323.

5 On the three contests for history paintings see Albert Boime, "The Quasi-open Competitions of the Quasi-legitimate July Monarchy," *Arts Magazine* 59, no. 8 (April 1985), 94–105, and Marrinan, 79–94. Details concerning the contest for the statue of Napoleon and the list of entrants are found in A.N., A.J.52.493.

6 With the installation of the Soult government on 11 October 1832, the Ministre des Travaux publics was given power over commissions for public monuments formerly belonging to the minister of the interior.

7 "Monument pour les victimes de juillet—Concours," *J.A.*, 5th yr., vol. 2, no. 6 (7 August 1831), 97; see the *Procès-verbaux des sèances de la Chambre des Députés, Session 1832*, vol. 1 (Paris, 1833), 187–89.

8 "De l'action du gouvernement sur les arts," *Revue de Paris* 22 (January 1831), 81.

9 L.-C. Arsenne, *Manuel du peintre et du sculpteur*, vol. 1 (Paris, 1833), 174.

10 On this contest see my " 'Et la lumière fut' ": The Meanings of David d'Angers's Monument to Gutenburg," *The Art Bulletin* 73, no. 3 (September 1991), 367–68; "Monument de Kléber à Strasbourg," *L'Artiste*, ser. 1, vol. 8, livraison 8 (1834), 82–83.

11 "C.B.," "Concours pour le monument Kléber; Exposition des modèles," *Courrier du Bas-Rhin*, no. 27 (31 January 1835), 1. The complete documentation for this exemplary contest is found in the Archives municipales de Strasbourg, div. VI, 180. There were thirty-one entries in the early stages of the contest and nineteen in the exhibition, including a number of artists who were later to compete in the contest for the tomb of Napoleon. The sculptor chosen to execute this monument, which was inaugurated in June 1840, was Philippe Grass, a native son living in Paris. This choice, of course, tended to undermine the notion of contests as unbiased.

12 The papers and *procès-verbaux* of the organization are in the collection of the Bibliothèque historique de la Ville de Paris (hereafter B.H.V.P.), ms. C.P. 4051–65. See, for example, the minutes for the *séances* of 20 January and 20 December 1831, B.H.V.P., ms. C.P. 4051.

13 "Mémoire adressé par la Société libre des Beaux-Arts à la Commission spéciale nommé par M. Le Ministre de l'Intérieur," *Annales de la Société libre des*

Beaux-Arts 1 (1831), 71–103; B.H.V.P., ms. C.P. 4062, dr. 10 contains the supporting documentation for the report.

14 This should be contrasted with the account of the result found in Marrinan, p. 80: "A few months later—and with the hindsight of experience—almost no one wanted to renew the competition experiment."

15 See the *procès-verbal* for the meeting of 25 December 1831, published in J.A., 6th yr., vol. 1, no. 1 (1 January 1832), 4–5. A copy of the society's petition is in B.H.V.P., ms. C.P. 4063. It was approved unanimously on 20 December 1832 at a *séance* during which forty-eight members appear on the "feuilles de présence." The architect J. I. Hittorff was the president at this meeting and signed the petition in that capacity.

16 For the discussion see *Procès-verbaux des séances de la Chambre des Pairs, Session 1832*, vol. 2 (Paris, 1833), 750–53. The vote occurred on 15 February 1833. For the response of the Société libre des Beaux-Arts see Guyot de Féré, "Monument de la Bastille; Projet de loi passé à la Chambre des Pairs," J.A., 7th yr., vol. 1, no. 7 (17 February 1833), 119–21.

17 Charles de Farcy, "Concours pour le second tableau destiné à la Chambre des Députés," J.A., 5th yr., vol. 1, no. 6 (6 February 1831), 106.

18 "Du concours en fait d'ouvrages d'art et de travaux publics," *Revue de Paris* 20 (1830), 177–92; ibid., 21 (1830), 14–24.

19 "Beaux-Arts: Réunions des artistes, Concours," *Journal des Débats* (21 October 1830), 1–2.

20 Eugène Delacroix, "Beaux-Arts; Lettre sur les concours," *L'Artiste*, ser. 1, vol. 1, livraison 4 (1831), 49–51; Paul Huet, "Notes adressées à Messieurs les membres de la Commission chargée des modifications à apporter aux réglements de l'Ecole des Beaux-Arts et de l'Académie de France à Rome," Ibid., 52.

21 François Guizot, *Mémoires pour servir à l'histoire de mon temps*, 2 vols. (Paris, 1859), 2:69, 71.

22 Meeting of 16 June 1840. B.H.V.P., ms. C.P. 4068. There were twelve members on the original committee.

23 The brochure was published anonymously under the title *Sur la nécessité de mettre au concours le monument de Napoléon* in 1840. La Fage was a major figure in the revival of Plain Chant in France and a prolific historian and musicologist. He was also the grandson of the architect Nicolas Lenoir. For more biographical information see R. D. Denne-Baron, *Adrien de La Fage*, Paris, 1863. Also, see J.A., 2, no. 11 (1840), 172–74; 189–92, 205–7, and no. 14 (1840), 213–16.

24 Hippolyte-Louis Durand (Reporter), "Opinion de la Société libre des Beaux-Arts sur la nécessité de mettre au concours le monument à élever à Napoléon," *Annales de la Société libre des Beaux-Arts* 10 (1841), 30–38.

25 See, for example, B.H.V.P., ms. C.P. 4069, minutes for meetings of 20 July 1841 and 17 August 1841. At the latter séance a letter from the minister of the interior responding negatively to the group's latest petition for a written program was read aloud. Duchâtel did, however, accede to their demand that the deadline for submitting projects be extended from the first of September to the first of October.

26 "Revue," *Journal des Beaux-Arts* 18 (17 May 1840), 276–77 (hereafter *J.d.B.-A.*).

27 Hittorff was, in fact, an original member of the Société libre des Beaux-Arts committee charged with investigating the question of the contest for the monument. See B.H.V.P., ms. C.P. 4068 (16 June 1840).

28 [Ulysse Ladet], "Appel aux artistes pour le monument de Napoléon," *L'Artiste*, ser. 2, vol. 8, livraison 2 (1841), 19–20. The issues of the periodical are not dated at this time, but from the context it appears to have been published in late March or early April.

29 *Procès-verbaux des séances de la Chambre des Députés, Session 1841*, vol. 5 (Paris, 1841), 407, Projet de loi no. 147.

30 See *Le Moniteur universel*, no. 138 (18 May 1841), 1378–79. After passage by the Chamber of Deputies, Duchâtel introduced the bill at the Chamber of Peers with the same vague description of the competition. Once again, the committee's report was favorable and the bill was approved by this Chamber and signed by Louis-Philippe on 25 June 1841. See ibid., no. 154 (3 June 1841), 1584.

31 Rémusat, *Mémoires*, 3:320: "He persuaded Duchâtel to put the project to a contest, hoping . . . to make the project of his protégé Visconti triumph." On the close personal bond between Vitet and Duchâtel, dating from the 1820s, see Vitet's eulogy "Le Comte Duchâtel," *Revue des Deux Mondes* 86 (1 April 1870), 512.

32 This appeared on 17 July 1841, p. 1842. It stated that the contestants had until 1 September to depose their projects. The only specification as to the type of tomb required was that its cost should not surpass the "credit allocated by the law of 25 June 1841."

33 *J.A.* 2, no. 7 (15 August 1841), 100; ibid., no. 17 (24 October 1841), 265; *J.d.B.-A.*, no. 4 (10 August 1841), 62.

34 *J.A.* 1, no. 15 (10 October 1841), 233–35. Toussaint also announced that an engraving of his project was to be published in a supplement to his series of works, entitled *Mémento des architects*, which dealt with architectural history and practice. This supplement appears never to have been published.

35 *J.A.* 2, no. 16 (17 October 1841), 244–45. Allier (1793–1870) was a cavalry officer before becoming a sculptor. He was elected as a deputy from Embrun (Hautes-Alpes) in the place of his father in 1839. His lithograph was entered in the Dépôt légal register of approved prints on 19 April 1841. See A.N., F.18.VI.24, no. 1373. This project was also described in detail before the contest opened in "Nouvelles d'art," *L'Artiste*, ser. 2, vol. 8, livraison 7 (1841), 111.

36 "Exposition des projets de tombeau pour Napoléon," *R.G.A.* 2 (1841), col. 521–28; reprinted in *La France littéraire*, ser. 3, vol. 7 (1841), 237–43, and *La Phalange*, ser. 3, vol. 7, no. 35 (19 November 1841), cols. 572–76.

37 On his complex political and social allegiances see Hélène Lipstadt, "César Daly: Revolutionary Architect?" *Architectural Design* 48, nos. 11–12 (November–December 1978), 18–28, and Richard Becherer, *Science Plus Sentiment: César Daly's Formula for Modern Architecture* (Ann Arbor, Mich., 1984), 72–81.

Daly was to continue to proselytize for contests throughout his career and finally published a booklength polemical essay in 1861 entitled *Des concours pour les monuments publics dans le passé, le présent et l'avenir*. Strangely enough, it was dedicated to Prosper Mérimée, who was an undisguised foe of contests. *Profession de foi de citoyen César Daly* (Paris, 1848). Bibliothèque Nationale, no. Le.64.952.

38 "Concours pour le Tombeau de Napoléon," *La France*, no. 317 (13 November 1841), 2; Délécluze, "Concours pour le Tombeau de Napoléon aux Invalides," *Journal des Débats* (31 October 1841), 2–3.

39 *La Caricature*, no. 45 (7 November 1841).

40 Daly, "Exposition des projets," *RGA* 2 (1841), col. 525. The same charge appears in the anonymous article in J.A. 2, no. 17 (24 October 1841), 265: "it is unfortunate, as we have said a thousand times, that the choice appears to have been made in advance."

41 A.N., A.J.52.493 contains a letter from Cavé, the directeur des beaux-arts, authorizing Dédéban's work to be hung in the corridor.

42 The inscription under the 1836 drawing reveals the sympathies of the architect for Louis-Napoléon: "Sous le règne de Louis Napoléon III, ce monument a été érigé à Napoléon Ier par son fils le Comte Léon de Louisbourg." Thus, the drawing was executed in 1836, the year of Louis-Napoleon's first attempt at a coup-d'état, and predicts the revival of the Empire fifteen years later. It also could be seen as an act of advocacy for the overthrow of the government of Louis-Philippe. Count Léon de Louisbourg, named in the caption, was Charles Léon Denuelle de la Plaigne, the illegitimate son of Napoleon Ier. With the death of the Roi de Rome, Napoleon's only legitimate heir, in 1832, this illegitimate son became a pretender to the Empire. Needless to say, all this makes the special treatment of his project even more mysterious.

43 The breakdown of the contestants, a list of which is found in Appendix B, was 41 architects, 29 sculptors, 5 painters, and 6 persons who do not fall into these categories, or at least are not found in any of the standard artistic dictionaries, professional annuaries, or reference works for the period. All appear to have been of the male gender. It should also be noted that several of the entrants claimed expertise in more than one profession and that they have been included in the category for which they were best known.

44 J.A. 2, no. 20 (14 November 1841), 308. See Bidon's program, dated 28 September 1841, in A.N., A.J.52.492, n. 22.

45 Bidon also exhibited another project (no. 34) for the tomb. In this proposal two bronze allegorical figures were suspended from the cupola. They placed wreaths on the sarcophagus of Napoleon at the center of the dome. For a description see A.N., A.J.52.493, nr. 22. After the conclusion of the contest Bidon published a pamphlet with yet another imaginative program for the monument. See his *Projet de mausolée à élever à la mémoire de l'Empereur adressé au Ministre de l'Intérieur en 1842 et envoyé en 1843 à M. Sapey. Rapporteur de la commission de la Chambre des députés, chargée de sanctionner les travaux de MM. Marochetti et Visconti* (Paris, 1844).

46 See the letter of Cavé to Vinet, the registrar for the contest, dated 26 October 1841 in A.N., A.J.52.493. No reason is given for the instructions to retire this and two other works from the competition.

47 P.-F. Geslin, *Brevet d'invention. Notice de la pendule industrielle ou Histoire philosophique de la nature* (Paris, 1841), 35. His drawing and description are in the archives of the Institut nationale de la propriété industrielle, Paris, brevet no. 11.211, delivered 31 August 1841. The drawing is signed and dated 1831.

48 Geslin's letter of 20 September 1841 and Cavé's order rescinding his decision to bar the work are in A.N., A.J.52.493.

49 Daly, col. 627.

50 On Daly and his relationship to the "Néo-Grec" aesthetic being formulated by a few radical members of the Ecole des Beaux-Arts, such as Nicolle and Danjoy, see Van Zanten, *Designing Paris*, 205.

51 Daly, col. 602.

52 This interpretation of Rougevin's proposal was made by P. F. Sagaret, "Concours pour le tombeau de Napoléon," in *Almanach et annuaire des bâtiments* (Paris, 1842), 644 (hereafter Sagaret). Vernet's painting, now in the Wallace Collection, London, was executed shortly after the death of Napoleon. Jazet made a mezzotint after it in 1830, and the present lithograph was executed by the German artist Joseph Völlinger sometime after that date.

53 This is described in the anonymous brochure *Notice historique sur le Palais des Beaux-Arts; Exposition des projects ou plans pour le tombeau du Grand Napoléon* (Paris, 1841), 9. The author of the project, whose name is listed as Dennier, is unknown.

54 Sagaret, 650–51.

55 Described in detail in ibid., 652–53. Duquesney's detailed written program is found in A.N., A.J.52.493, no. 67. It states that "everything ought to be historical in the composition of the monument."

56 Huard, "Concours," *J.A.* 2, no. 19 (7 November 1841), 292.

57 "Concours pour le monument de Napoléon," *L'Artiste*, ser. 2, vol. 8 (1841), 275 (hereafter "Concours," *L'Artiste*).

58 Sagaret, 655–58; "Concours," *L'Artiste*, 275–76.

59 For the complete program and photographs of his maquette see M. H. Fauvez, *Projet de Tombeau pour l'Empereur Napoléon Ier par Louis Auvray, Statuaire* (Paris, 1861). The photographs taken by Marville are missing from the copy in the Bibliothèque Nationale but are included in the version in the Bibliothèque Municipale, Valenciennes. The Musée de Valenciennes formerly possessed the maquette, but it is now missing or destroyed. The museum does have eleven drawings of allegorical figures that were apparently executed in connection with his project.

60 Sagaret, 651.

61 Seurre's written program is in A.N., A.J.52.493. Daly, col. 593–95. Daly began his discussion of the individual projects with Duban's entry.

62 See A.N., A.J.52.493, no. 76.

63 See Alfred Mettrier, *Pierre Petitot et son fils Louis Petitot* (Langres, 1867), 53–54. Cartellier's statue had originally been intended for the Place de la

Concorde, but its destination was changed when Petitot was given the commission to finish it after the sculptor's death in 1831.

64 Louis Moreau, *Considérations sur les Beaux-Arts* (Paris, 1831), 13.

65 Criticism devoted to this project generally attended the concept involved, instead of specifically discussing the model or the drawing. However, both Daly and Sagaret describe a project that conforms to the drawing in the Musée des arts décoratifs in Paris rather than the model now in the Musée Girodet at Montargis in that the former includes a sarcophaguslike structure between the base and the *lit de mort* of Napoleon.

66 Other drawings by Triqueti executed for the tomb are also found in the collection of the Musée des arts décoratifs, Paris, FO.4., CD.6195.

67 Triqueti received the Madeleine commission in 1834 and completed it in 1841. On the project see Leroy-Jay Lemaistre, "L'Eglise de la Madeleine de la Restauration à la Monarchie de Juillet: Un Mécénat d'Etat," in the exhibition catalogue. *La Sculpture française au XIXeme siècle*, Grand Palais (Paris, 1986), 201–4.

68 Daly, cols. 611, 612.

69 Undated letter in the Rémusat papers, Archives municipales, Toulouse, 5.S.181, carton 3A.

70 Confusion exists as to the number given to this project since the register indicates that the artists submitted two projects jointly (nos. 7 and 72) and Maindron entered one project (no. 77) solely under his name. It is also unclear whether plaster models of drawings were exhibited under these numbers.

71 "Concours pour le monument de Napoléon," J.A. 2, no. 17 (7 November 1841), 291: "We recommend it to Mister Devoir and Pourchet for one of their future acts."

72 A detailed program and statement of their intentions is found in A.N., A.J.52.493. The project is discussed by Jules Duval, *Raymond Gayrard, graveur et statuaire* (Paris, 1859), 51–53, and models for it are listed in their appended catalogue (p. 143), but no location is indicated. A recent thesis (1980) on Gayrard by Hélène Du Mesnil, done at the Ecole du Louvre, may contain further information, but my efforts to secure permission to read it have been unsuccessful.

73 Délécluze began his review with Cannissié's project because, in his opinion, the architect was one of the few individuals in the contest to realize that the center of a church should never be the site for a tomb.

74 This appears to be the only drawing for the contest in the collection of the Musée de l'Armée at the Invalides. See inventory no. Fd 816 (A5113).

75 A MM. *les Députés, membres de la commission du monument de Napoléon* (Paris, 1843). A copy exists in A.N., C.2772.

76 Daly, cols. 597–98, discusses Horeau's project at length and specifies the way his model differed from this engraving. Although Daly claims that Horeau had published his engraving in July 1840, the Dépôt légal register in the Archives Nationales indicates that it was approved on 3 October 1840; see F.18.VI.22, no.

3594. This engraving was included in the recent exhibition catalogue *Hector Ho-reau, 1801–1872*, Musée des arts décoratifs, Paris, 1979, 30.

77 The proposal accompanying the project in A.N., A.J.52.493 states that an architect named Sievert was his collaborator, but the latter's name is not listed in the registers for the contest.

78 Daly, cols. 609–10. The letter published by Daly states that he was also sending the drawing discussed here.

79 Although the crypt and the entrance to it, which would have been closed by a movable floor slab, are not shown in this drawing, they are mentioned in his description of the project. See the four-page brochure in the Bibliothèque Nationale, no. Z.285(4).

80 The project of Labrouste is briefly discussed by Pierre Saddy in the exhibition catalogue *Henri Labrouste, architecte, 1801–1875*, Caisse nationale des Monuments historiques, Paris, 1977, 23–24. Daly, cols. 613–14. "Concours pour le monument," *J.A.*, 292. The critic continued, "Mr. Labrouste is one contestant, and perhaps the only one, who has departed from vulgarity and the routine."

81 Lemaire's detailed description of his project is found in A.N., A.J.52.493. Daly, col. 619, discusses the Charpentier/Klagmann project in detail.

82 Edouard Isabelle, *Notice sur le Tombeau de Napoléon* (Paris, 1841).

83 This commentary of the architect is largely quoted verbatim by Daly, cols. 615–16. It is also mentioned in the *J.d.B.-A.*, no. 15 (11 Nov. 1841), 182. I thank Mme. de Puylaroque, custodian of the family archives, for all her efforts to find this lost drawing.

84 Visconti's original program is in the Archives de l'Armée, Vincennes, Carton 35, dossier 1, "Invalides." The drawing itself was formerly in this dossier but has been missing since 1974. The tracing is found in A.N., F.21.728 and is accompanied by a letter of Visconti refuting accusations that the crypt would fill with water in the event of the flooding of the Seine. On the tracing he indicated the highest level to which the Seine was ever known to have risen.

85 Daly, cols. 619–25.

CHAPTER 4 THE PROCESS

1 Documentation for the procedure at the meetings is in A.N., A.J.52.493.

2 A.N., A.J.52.493. After Duc the rank order was Duban (10 votes), Labrouste (9 votes), Lassus (8 votes), Isabelle, Gayrard and de Ligny, Triqueti, Danjoy (7 votes). No record survives to indicate how individual members voted.

3 Letter to Léonce Lavergne, *Prosper Mérimée: Correspondance générale*, ed. M. Parturier (Paris, 1961), 136–37, letter no. 554bis. This is undated, but the context would place it in June 1840.

4 Ibid., 458, letter no. 613bis addressed to Etienne Conti and dated 28 February 1841.

5 "Rapport à M. le ministre de l'intérieur, au nom de la commission chargé de l'examen des projets du monument à la mémoire de l'empereur Napoléon," *Le Moniteur universel*, no. 16 (16 January 1842), 778.

6 Daly, cols. 578–81.

7 It should be noted in the handwritten draft of the report in A.N., F.21.728, there is a paragraph crossed out that indicates that on the first vote on the type of crypt, eight voted for one that was closed.

8 "Autobiographie," in *Visconti, 1791–1853*, 33.

9 See A.N., F.21.575 for a history of the negotiations and transcript of Vitet's report. This project was a collaborative effort between the State and the city of Paris.

10 "Autobiographie," 30, 33. Also see the appendix, 267, where Vitet's name appears on a list, found in the Archives du Périer de Larsan, of Visconti's private clients. Visconti performed an unknown service for Vitet in 1841. Louis Vitet, "Le Nouveau Louvre et les nouvelles Tuileries," *Revue des Deux Mondes*, 2d per. (1 July 1866), 57–93.

11 Vitet, 776–77.

12 A.N., F.21.729, transcription of a letter from Ingres dated 17 May 1848. This was intended to support Visconti in his legal battles that year. Ingres's sketch and the accompanying text are in the collection of the Musée Ingres, Montauban, cahier 9, fol. 53. The text has been published in H. Lapauze, *Les Dessins de J.-A.-D. Ingres du Musée de Montauban* (Paris, 1891), 214.

13 *Les Carnets de David d'Angers*, ed. André Bruel, vol. 2 (Paris, 1958), carnet 37, 94. The editor dates this as 1841, but from the dated entries preceding and following it, it was apparently written between 14 February 1841 and 5 July 1842. From the nature of the comment it was probably closer to the latter date.

14 Ibid., carnet 33, 31. This entry is undated, but the editor dates the notebook in which it appears as 1838.

15 In Fontaine's recently published *Journal, 1799–1853*, 2 vols. (Paris, 1987), there is a lacuna between the dates 1841 and 1844. Thus, there are no comments relative to his service on the commission. More details concerning this period may become available when papers still in private hands are published.

16 Charles De Spoelberch de Lovenjoul, *Histoire des oeuvres de Théophile Gautier*, 2 vols. (Paris: G. Charpentier et Cie, 1887), 1:232–36.

17 For Duchâtel's letter conferring the honor on him see *Théophile Gautier: Correspondance générale*, ed. Claudine Lacoste-Veysseyre, 7 vols. (Geneva: Librairie Droz, 1985–92), 1:292–94.

18 This correspondence is in the Rémusat papers, Archives municipales, Toulouse, 5.S.183 (3a, b). That Lingay was determined to extract this special favor from Rémusat is also seen in a letter he sent to Gautier on 22 October 1840: "I won't permit Mr. de Rémusat to leave office without paying his debt." See *Théophile Gautier, Correspondance générale* (Geneva, 1985), 1:222.

19 Archives municipales, Toulouse, 5.S.183 (3a). This letter is undated but Rémusat himself placed it chronologically in this period in the index he made of his correspondence.

20 Ibid. Letter dated 22 November 1841.

21 Eugène Pelletan, "Le Tombeau de Napoléon," *Revue indépendante* 1 (1 December 1841), 515; Daly, col. 615.

22 "Réclamation de M. Visconti," *R.G.A.* 3 (1842), col. 38.

23 *Le Charivari*, no. 24 (24 January 1842), 2. The artesian wells at Grenelle, an area that became part of the city of Paris in 1860, were considered to be engineering marvels when finished in 1840.

24 "Le Tombeau de Napoléon d'après Théophile Gautier," *Le Charivari*, no. 7 (13 February 1842), 1.

25 "Monument de Napoléon," *J.A.* 1, no. 10 (6 March 1842), 150.

26 The government made no official announcement but instead gave the information to the press. It was reported in *J.A.* 1, no. 14, (3 April 1842), 213. The only official document confirming the date of the commission appears to be a letter in the Archives du Périer de Larsan, dated 25 March 1842, that indicates that it had been given to the architect on 22 March.

27 This is one of four large architectural drawings in the archives of the Assemblée Nationale, "Session de 1843, N.V. Crédits, Loi de 1 juillet 1843," no reference number. They were signed and dated by Duchâtel, 1 December 1842. A letter from the minister of the interior to Visconti, dated 17 August 1843, indicates that he was paid for seven drawings to be deposited at the Chambre des Députés as well as at the Chambre des Pairs and the Ministry of the Interior. See the Archives Visconti, Archives du Périer de Larsan. The present location of the latter is unknown. Tracings of these drawings exist at the Archives Nationales, Plans et cartes, 67A.J.15.

28 "Rapport fait au nom de la Commission chargée d'examiner le projet de loi tendant à ouvrir un crédit de 1,500,000 fr, sur l'exercice 1843, en addition à celui de 500,000 fr. déjà ouvert pour la construction du tombeau de l'Empereur Napoléon par M. Charles Sapey," *Chambre des Députés, Session de 1843*, no. 129, Paris, 1843.

29 A.N., F.21.728. Letter dated 10 December 1842; A.N., F.21.735. Letter to Duchâtel dated 29 March 1843.

30 A.N., F.21.735. Letter dated 10 June 1844. This drawing was countersigned by Visconti with the note that it had been given to him by Marochetti on 10 June 1840. The present location of the original drawing is unknown, but the tracing reproduced here, is found in ibid.

31 Ibid. Visconti's letter is dated 28 November 1844.

32 This drawing is reproduced but wrongly attributed to Marochetti and incorrectly dated by Vicaire, "Les Projets de Marochetti pour le tombeau de l'Empereur Napoléon," 148–49.

33 These tracings of his drawings accompany his letter to the Minister of the Interior dated 19 April 1845. See A.N., F.21.735. They were approved by Duchâtel on 22 April.

34 Letter of Visconti to Duchâtel dated 16 August 1843, A.N., F.21.734, dr. 2, nr. 52.

35 A.N., F.21.734. Commission awarded 15 September 1843.

36 "Des Practiciens et de M. Pradier," *J.A.*, ser. 2, vol. 2, livraison 52 (21 December 1845), 472–73; "Nouvelles et faits divers," *Bulletin de l'Alliance des arts*, 2d yr., no. 5, 25 August 1843. This journal was directed by Thoré, who

supplied most of the criticism and commentary. Since the comments are in keeping with his social views one can assume that he wrote it.

37 On this fountain, inaugurated in January 1844, see Jacques de Caso in the exhibition catalogue, *Statues de chair; Sculptures de James Pradier (1790–1852)* (Geneva, Paris, 1985–86), 194–97; "Autobiographie," 30.

38 A.N., F.21.734, dated 30 November 1844. Correspondence cited in regard to this affair is all in this dossier unless otherwise indicated.

39 These are in the Musée Fabre, Montpellier, Inv. Claparède, nos. 224 and 224bis. For other sketches by Pradier for these figures see Claude Lapaire, in *Statues de chair*, 310–11.

40 See Visconti's letters dated 11 April and 13 May 1847, A.N., F.21.734; *Les Carnets de David d'Angers* 2:269–70. He also states that Pradier was someone who did not realize that one cannot produce good work by having practiciens enlarge small, hardly finished sketches.

41 Letter of the Directeur des Beaux-Arts to the Minister of the Interior, 25 August 1851. The members of the commission were Vitet, Fortoul, and Cottreau; Pradier's letter to the minister is undated but was obviously written soon after the commission was formed. See A.N., F.21.734 for both.

42 Report by Cottreau, dated 19 February 1852, ibid. It should be noted that Visconti had no such problems with Duret over the caryatid figures for the doorway to the crypt, even though the models when installed in situ were found to be faulty in their proportions and had to be completely redone. On this mistake, for which Duret was given additional compensation, see the letter from Duret to Visconti, dated 25 December 1846, ibid.

43 In justification of Visconti's negotiations with Lequesne the Directeur des Beaux-Arts wrote to the Minister of the Interior on 10 December 1852 stating that before Pradier's death he expressed his desire that Lequesne finish the figures. Lequesne was paid for his services on 20 June 1853. It is impossible to say how extensive his modifications were since the original plasters no longer exist.

44 Regarding the commission, see letter to Triqueti, dated 8 December 1843, A.N., F.21.729. For Triqueti's own summary of the mosaic experiment see his letter to the Minister of the Interior dated 19 March 1848, ibid. This was written at the time an investigation was underway on the expenses the project generated.

45 The surviving drawing, in the Archives du Périer de Larsan, is reproduced by François Legrand, "L'Echec des 'tarsias' aux Invalides," in *Louis Visconti, 1791–1853*, 181.

46 The plaster original for this statue is presently in the Church of the Madeleine, Montargis; Letters of Visconti to the Minister of the Interior dated 12 March 1846, 21 January 1852 and 19 January 1847, A.N., F.21.734.

47 Letter of Visconti dated 6 December 1844, A.N., F.21.728. A finished drawing of the crypt illustrating how the mosaic decoration might have looked exists in the Archives du Périer de Larsan.

48 A.N., F.21.739, dated 6 December 1845. Those proposed to execute the works were Triqueti, Simart, Ottin, Husson, Jouffroy, Jallery, Desprez, Villain, and Desboeuf.

49 It requires little understanding of human nature or the cultural milieu of the 1840s to foresee the future of this proposal. For a succinct discussion of the social implications and differences between *practiciens* and sculptors—or workmen and artists—at the time see Anne Middleton Wagner, *Jean-Baptiste Carpeaux, Sculptor of the Second Empire* (London, 1986), 8–10.

50 This demand is documented by the many letters in A.N., F.21.734 from deputies and other influential people recommending one of the reliefs be given to a particular sculptor.

51 The commission is dated 10 June 1846. A careful chronology of the various communications and official acts regarding the commission for the bas-reliefs is found in ibid. dr. 2, no. 32. Simart received the commission for the standing figure of Napoleon on 17 March.

52 Letter in ibid., no. 50, dated 7 April 1847. Addressed to Cavé, Directeur des Beaux-Arts.

53 See Visconti's letter to Cavé dated 11 May 1847 in the Fonds Doucet, Bibliothèque d'Art et d'Archéologie, ms. 213. Simart was awarded 16,500 francs for each relief, or a total of 165,000 francs. Letter in A.N., F.21.734, dr. 2, no. 64. It was stipulated that the assistants were to be paid from this sum.

54 Théodore Bra, "Dernière et prochaine grande distribution des travaux de l'Etat," *J.A.*, ser. 3, livraison 20 (16 May 1847), 177; idem, "Monument de l'Empereur," *J.A.*, ser. 3, livraison 24 (13 June 1847), 214. The other two installments of the article were published on 23 and 30 May.

55 "Monument de l'Empereur; Solution ministérielle," *J.A.*, ser. 3, 2d part, livraison 1 (4 July 1847), 1–3. The same charges were repeated in other articles appearing on 18 and 25 July.

56 Arsène Houssaye, "Le Tombeau de Napoléon," *L'Artiste*, ser. 4, vol. 9, livraison 13 (30 May 1847), 194; "Chronique," *L'Artiste*, ser. 4, vol. 8, livraison 14 (6 June 1847), 223; Paul Lacroix, "Chronique," *Bulletin des arts* 5 (10 June 1847), 416. This journal had as a co-editor the radical republican Théophile Thoré.

57 A.N., F.21.729, letter of 4 June 1849 from Cavé to Simart approving his choice of five sculptors to execute the works after his models. They were Auguste-Louis-Marie Ottin, Nicholas-Victor Vilain, Louis Chambard, François Lanno, and Jean-Claude Petit (who had not won the Prix de Rome, but who was substituted for one laureat who declined to participate). Chambard, a student of both Ingres and David d'Angers, won the Prix de Rome in 1837.

58 A.N., F.21.734, dr. 2. Letter of Chambard dated 9 September 1850, response by the director dated 25 September.

59 Simart to Visconti, ibid., dated 30 December 1850.

60 Visconti to the Minister of the Interior, ibid.

61 Letter of Félix Cottreau, Inspecteur des Beaux-Arts, dated 29 September 1851, and those of Visconti of 29 November 1851, all in ibid.

62 Adolphe Lance, *Jules Bouchet, Architect: Notice sur sa vie et ses travaux* (Paris, 1860), 6–7.

63 The artists on the committee were Jeanron, David d'Angers, Barye, Drolling; the architects were Henri Labrouste, Albert Lenoir, Louis Charpentier; representing the world of letters were Gustave Planche and Hippolyte Delaunay; other members of nonartistic professions, whose full names are not known, were Maret, Labouret, Girardière, Rondelet. See A.N., F.21.729.

64 "Commission Ledru-Rollin: Rapport sur les travaux exécutés au Tombeau de l'Empereur Napoléon aux Invalides," A.N., F.21.729, 29 May 1848, 4.

65 On these contests see Albert Boime, "The Second Republic's Contest for the Figure of the Republic," *The Art Bulletin* 53 (1971), 68–83; Marie-Claude Chaudonneret, *La Figure de la République*; *Le concours de 1848* (Paris, 1987); for Ledru-Rollin's program see *Le Moniteur universel*, 28 March 1848.

66 "Rapport sur le tombeau de l'Empereur Napoléon," *Démocratie pacifique* no. 159 (25 September 1848).

67 It approved an expenditure of 2,119,000 francs rather than 3,130,238, which had been requested.

68 Letter to the Minister of the Interior dated 20 May 1848. See A.N., F.21.739; *L'Artiste*, ser. 5, vol. 1 (1848), 106–7.

69 Documentation on the search in France, particularly in the Vosges, is found in A.N., F.21.728.

70 The paper was fined and forced to print a retraction. See *L'Ere nouvelle: Journal de la Corse*, no. 63, 17 May 1849. In a letter to his lawyer, dated 1 October 1848, Visconti made it clear that he believed the wounded "amour-propre" of David d'Angers lay behind these accusations and that he had tried to avoid this circumstance by attempting, without avail, to have the July Monarchy give part of the sculptural commission to the artist. Archives Du Périer de Larsan, no number.

71 This report is found in A.N., F.21.729. Along with it was included a report that differed with the conclusions of the majority and urged that funds be allocated for rapid completion of the project.

72 The members were de la Rochejaquelein, Aubry (Nord), Renouard, Danjoy, Faveau, de la Grange (Gironde), Druet-Desvaux, Martel, Vitet, Lespérut, de Luynes, de Kératry, Monet, Fortoul, de Mouchy.

73 Copies of the report are found in A.N., F.21.729 and F.21.735. It was also published in *Le Moniteur universel*, no. 159 (8 June 1850) 1984–85; the transcription of the debate was published in *Le Moniteur universel*, no. 164 (13 June 1850), 2036–37.

74 Letter to Charles Blanc dated 6 March 1848, A.N., F.21.735; letters of Visconti to the Minister of the Interior, 10 June 1848, A.N., F.21.739, and 25 August 1848, A.N., F.21.729.

75 Letter of Visconti to the Ministre des Travaux publics, 27 October 1853, asking who will be charged with maintenance of the completed tomb.

76 Letter from duc de Persigny, the Minister of the Interior, dated 20 March 1852, A.N., F.21.735. The new subjects for the reliefs were to be La Belle Poule returning to Cherbourg with the body of Napoleon, on one side, and the Funeral cortege of 15 December 1840, on the other; letter from Charles Gaudin to Marochetti, 8 July 1853, and letter from Marochetti to Gaudin, 11 July 1853, both in ibid.

77 The major equestrian monuments to Napoleon outside of Paris are Levéel's statue of him in military dress, inaugurated at Cherbourg in 1859, and Barye's statue of him in roman toga at Ajaccio, begun in 1861 and dedicated in 1865.

78 On his participation in this project see Stephen Bayley, *The Albert Memorial: The Monument in its Social and Architectural Context* (London, 1981), 57–63.

79 This equestrian statue was not placed on the monument until long after Stevens's death. On the multifaceted career of Stevens see the catalogue *Alfred Stevens, 1817–1875*, Victoria and Albert Museum, London, 1975.

80 Letter from Félix Cottrau to Dr. Conneau, n.d. This letter, apparently found in the office of Napoleon III in 1870, is reproduced, with no sources given, in the article by A. Vacquier, "Deux bas-reliefs des Invalides," *Bulletin de la Société d'histoire et d'archéologie VIIe arrondissement de Paris*, no. 7 (April 1910), 20–24. See also the letter of Visconti to the Minister of the Interior on 18 June 1852 announcing that they had just been removed. A.N., F.21.734.

81 Letter from Valette, secretary of Jérôme Bonaparte, to Visconti dated 21 June 1852. Archives du Périer de Larsan. Brian (1805–64) was a former student of David d'Angers who had won the Prix de Rome in 1832. Letter from the Directeur des Beaux-Arts to Visconti dated 15 July 1852, A.N., F.21.734.

82 Emile de Labédollière, *Le Nouveau Paris: Histoire de ses vingt arrondissements en 1860* (Paris, 1860), 100–101. This was illustrated by Gustave Doré.

83 See "Séance de la Commission chargée de l'examen et de la réception des travaux du tombeau de l'Empereur Napoléon," 8 June 1853, A.N., F.21.728.

84 In the Archives du Périer de Larsan one finds a letter from the minister of war dated 24 October 1853 notifying Visconti that his drawings for this ceremony, which was to have been held on 4 May, could be picked up at his office. There is no indication of a possible future date for the inauguration and no reason for its postponement. Oudiné was paid two thousand francs for the execution of the medal on 17 March 1853. See A.N., F.70.183.

85 "Une Visite aux Invalides," *Almanach de Napoléon* (Paris, 1852), 65. The same assertion was made by Georges Guénot, "Le Monde artistique," *Revue des Beaux-Arts* 4 (20 March 1853), 114.

86 For a description and depiction of the statue see "Fêtes du 15 août," *L'Illustration* 22, no. 547 (20 August 1853), 119–23.

87 Antoine Etex, *Souvenirs d'un artiste* (Paris, 1878), 270–71.

88 The tomb of Vauban was commissioned to Etex 7 June 1843 and finished in 1852. See Etex, 231–32; letter of Bouchet, 10 May 1858, A.N., F.21.810.

89 Quoted by Raincelin de Sergy, *Revue historique des notabilités*, vol. 2 (Paris, n.d.), 7. The original source is the *Revue de l'Occident français*.

90 *Mémoires du Duc de Persigny*, ed. Henri de Laire (Paris, 1896), 191–92.

91 The petition, an extract of the deliberations by the Municipal Council, and correspondence relevant to it are found in A.N., F.21.728.

92 Georges Guénot, "Le Monde artistique," *Revue des Beaux-Arts* 4 (30 April 1853), 147. One should note that even after the tomb at the Invalides had been inaugurated it was proposed by an important French historian that Napoleon's heart be retained at the Invalides while his body be removed to Saint-Denis. See

Amédée Gabourd, *Histoire contemporaine comprenant les principaux événements qui se sont accomplis depuis la révolution de 1830 jusqu'à nos jours*, vol. 4 (Paris, 1865), 363–64.

93 This document was published with little comment by Jules Formigé, "Un Projet de transfert du tombeau de Napoléon Premier des Invalides à Saint-Denis en 1853," *Académie des Beaux-Arts* (1958–59), 1959, 47–52.

94 This crypt no longer exists, having been destroyed in the course of archaeological excavations in our own century by the architect Jules Formigé.

95 The ceremony is described in *Le Moniteur universel*, no. 92 (April 1861).

96 This decree and the political events of 1861 are discussed in detail by Emile Ollivier, *L'Empire libéral*, vol. 5 (Paris, 1900), but strangely enough the inauguration of the tomb at the Invalides was never mentioned. The same lacuna is found in all other histories of the Second Empire.

97 See A.N., F.21.IV.77.

98 "Napoléon, son tombeau," *Le Charivari*, no. 265 (18 September 1840), 3.

99 Maurice Barrès, *Les Déracinés*, vol. 1 (Paris, 1897), 234.

CHAPTER 5 AUTHORSHIP, MEANING, AND METHOD

1 Originally underneath the effigy of Visconti was a bronze bas-relief by Louis Villeminot showing the new Louvre and the Tuileries in aerial perspective. The present whereabouts of this relief is unknown.

2 This sculpture makes an archaeological reference to the *statues accoudées* of Etruscan tombs, examples of which were to be found in the Campana Collection in the Louvre, and also appears to be based on a masterpiece of Germain Pilon, the funeral effigy of Valentine Balbiani (wife of the Chancellor René de Birague), which was completed around 1580 and sent to the Louvre after it was pillaged during the Revolution. See Jean Babelon, *Germain Pilon* (Paris, 1927), 67.

3 On the relocation of this tomb as an example of the upward climb of certain families in France see Antoinette Le Normand-Romain, "Les cimetières: un musée de sculpture en plein air," in *Rencontres de l'Ecole du Louvre: La sculpture du XIXe siècle, une mémoire retrouvée* (Paris, 1986), 310.

4 Ironically, the original portrait bust was by David d'Angers, a nemesis of Louis Visconti during the Second Republic. The original bust was commissioned by the minister of the interior in 1818, and the plaster for it was exhibited in the Salon of 1819. The marble is in the vestibule of the Institut de France.

5 A full account of the subscription and the role of the family is found in an article by Georges Guénot, "Monument à Visconti," *Revue des Beaux-Arts* 3, livraison 3 (1854), 35–38.

6 The first call for a monument to honor Visconti was by Félix Pigeory, "Visconti, sa famille et ses oeuvres," *Revue des Beaux-Arts* 5, livraison 2 (1854), 17–23. This article included a letter by Théodore Lejeune advocating a public subscription.

7 The design of the monument was by the architect Pigeory.

8 This essay has recently been republished in a collection of his writings entitled *L'art et les mystères grecs* (Paris, 1985), 51–117. For the only modern article on Ravaisson's archaeological interests see Meredith Shedd, "Félix Ravaisson's *Musée Grec* in Paris in 1860," *Gazette des Beaux-Arts* 105 (April 1985), 155–70.

9 This letter quoted in E. de Robillard de Beaurepaire, *Notice biographique sur Le Harivel-Durocher* (Caen, 1879), 25–26. It was published originally in the account of the trial in *Gazette des Tribunaux* on 17 March 1874.

10 Reproduced in *Realism and Tradition in Art, 1848–1900: Sources and Documents in the History of Art*, ed. L. Nochlin (Englewood Cliffs, N.J., 1966), 37.

11 Ayn Rand, *The Fountainhead* (New York, 1943), 683.

12 Thomas Hobbes, *Leviathan* (London, 1931 edition), 83–84.

13 Rand, 78.

14 El Lissitzky, "Ideological Superstructure," translated and reprinted in Sophie Lissitzky-Küppers, *El Lissitzky, Life, Letters, Texts* (Greenwich, Conn., 1967), 371–72.

15 The term derives from an essay by Michel Foucault, "What Is an Author?" *Language, Countermemory, Practice*, ed. D. Bouchard (Ithaca, N.Y., 1977), 113–38. He describes the author-function as a legal and regulatory necessity in modern industrial society, and authors as those who perform this role. However, like Hobbes, he believes that this function is tied to the institution of property, which poses problems in applying the term to this architectural monument financed by the State.

16 For a complete description and engravings of the monument see Léon Visconti, *Fontaines monumentales construites à Paris et projetées à Bordeaux par Ludovic Visconti, architecte de S. M. l'empereur Napoléon III* (Paris, 1860). The administrative difficulties that Visconti encountered in constructing this monument are chronicled by Françoise Boudon, "Visconti et le décor urbain: les fontaines parisiennes," in *Visconti, 1791–1853*, 88–91.

17 Edward Shils, *Center and Periphery; Essays in Macrosociology* (Chicago, 1975), 3–4. It should be noted that there is a strong similarity between Shils's ideas and those in *Le Mythe de l'Eternel Retour, Archétypes et répétition*, Mircea Eliade's discussion of the symbolism of the center (Paris, 1949).

18 Clifford Geertz, "Centers, Kings, and Charisma: Reflections on the Symbolics of Power," in *Culture and its Creators*, ed. J. Ben-David and T. N. Clark (Chicago, 1977), 152–53.

19 Michel Foucault, *Discipline and Punish: The Birth of the Prison*, trans. A. Sheridan (New York, 1977), 208–9.

20 See Bruno Foucart, "Architecture carcérale et architectes fonctionnalistes en France au XIXe siècle," *Revue de l'art*, no. 32 (1976), 37–56, for a discussion of prison designs during this period and illustrations of the plans of Blouet and Harou-Romain. That the design of the tomb was influenced by the panopticon scheme was suggested to me by Neil Levine of Harvard University.

21 On the public reception of this monument see Dore Ashton, "Paris Publicized and Privatized: Daniel Buren in the Palais Royal," *Arts Magazine* 61, no. 1 (September 1986), 18–20.

22 For complete documentation on the controversy surrounding the work and a compilation of the discourse it provoked see *Public Art, Public Controversy: The Tilted Arc on Trial*, foreword by R. Porter (New York, 1987). James Wines's *De-architecture* is unsympathetic to the cause of the sculptor, arguing that he has little understanding of public art and that "No matter what his rationales, most of Serra's aesthetic preoccupations become meaningless outdoors" (89).

23 The architect was George Keller and the sculptor of the effigy was Alexander Doyle. The statue was installed against the architect's wishes. On this project see Marianne Doezema and June Hargrove, *The Public Monument and Its Audience* (Cleveland, Ohio, 1977), 47–50. The placement of this figure in the center of a rotunda provides a precedent for the Jefferson Memorial, which was inaugurated in 1943 and contains a nineteen-foot-high standing figure of the third president of the United States that is mounted on a base six feet in height. The sculptor, Rudulph Evans, won the commission after a contest in 1938 in which more than one hundred designs were submitted.

24 On the building and the contests for it see David M. Kahn, "The Grant Monument," *Journal of the Society of Architectural Historians* 41, no. 3 (October 1982), 212–31.

25 There was no contest for the memorial because Philip Johnson, a friend of the Kennedy family, donated his services as did the construction firm. The memorial commission raised two hundred thousand dollars for this monument and the Kennedy Library in Cambridge, Massachusetts. On the circumstances behind this monument see the *Dallas Morning News*, 25 June 1970, 1.

26 There is a further similarity between these two works, widely separated in place and history. Like the original proposal of Visconti for the tomb of Napoleon and the recommendation of the Sapey report of 1843, the only inscription on the structure is that of the person being commemorated. Decorative detail is reduced to a bare minimum. One might note that plans for a Kennedy Memorial were begun shortly after the assassination in 1963, only three years after a huge contest, with 574 designs entered, was held for a memorial to Franklin Delano Roosevelt. The myriad of proposals for this monument, which was never erected, provides a spectrum of imaginative possibilities for funeral monuments in our century. On this aborted project see Thomas H. Creighton, *The Architecture of Monuments: The Franklin Delano Roosevelt Memorial Competition* (New York, 1962), and Hélène Lipstadt, "Transforming the Tradition: American Architecture Competitions, 1960 to the Present," in *The Experimental Tradition: Essays on Competitions in Architecture*, ed. H. Lipstadt (New York, 1989), 97–98.

27 See the *Dallas Morning News*, 3 December 1963. The proposal was by Mike Mckool, a local attorney and prominent figure in the Democratic party.

28 On this statue and the memorial see Michael Richman, *Daniel Chester French, An American Sculptor*, exhibition catalogue, Metropolitan Museum of Art, 1976, 171–86. One should remember that this monument does not house Lincoln's tomb. The monument in which his tomb is located is in Springfield, Illinois, and was based on the designs of Larkin G. Mead. It was inaugurated in 1874.

29 After its removal from the Rotunda, it was placed on the grounds of the Capitol but was eventually displaced to several other locations. Today it has found refuge in the National Museum of American History, Washington, D.C.

30 The classic statement of the importance of the penis in gender definition and the concept of penis envy is Sigmund Freud, "Analysis Terminable and Interminable," in *Standard Edition of the Complete Psychological Works of Sigmund Freud*, ed. James Strachey, vol. 23 (New York, 1964), 250–52. Writing from a poststructuralist perspective, the most emphatic denial of the universal character of the Oedipal complex and castration anxiety is that of Gilles Deleuze and Félix Guattari, *Anti-Oedipus: Capitalism and Schizophrenia*, trans. R. Hurley, M. Seem, and H. Lane (Minneapolis, 1983). These authors would maintain that a Freudian reading of this monument is simply superimposing a theory invented in our century and devised to support the capitalist economic system to a work of an earlier period.

31 Another reason for the aptness of the caricature might derive from Richard Nixon's private discourse, as revealed by the Watergate tape recordings, in which the phallus as metaphor played a central or obsessive role. Other psychological implications in Kliban's caricatures are discussed by Norman N. Holland, "Why Ellen Laughed," *Critical Inquiry* (Winter, 1980), 345–71.

32 Sigmund Freud, *Beyond the Pleasure Principle*, trans. and ed. by James Strachey (New York, 1961), 8–12. In this regard one might note that Jacques Derrida, in his deconstruction of Freud's discussion of the fort/da game, has claimed that this discussion is autobiographical in that it is a representation of Freud's own play with presence and absence as it appears in his process of writing and argumentation. See "Spéculer—sur Freud," *La Carte postale* (Paris, 1980), 362.

33 This kind of quandary does not seem to bother Leo Bersani. In his *The Freudian Body: Psychoanalysis and Art* (New York, 1986), 51–78, he discusses the Freudian theory in *Beyond the Pleasure Principle*, and then proceeds to apply his deconstructed version of it to a group of Assyrian bas-reliefs, in which he believes it is manifest. Nowhere in his formal analysis of the works is there an indication as to what their historical purpose was or any attempt to insert them into their historical context.

34 This is a central dilemma addressed by Hubert L. Dreyfus and Paul Rabinow, *Michel Foucault: Beyond Structuralism and Hermeneutics* (Chicago, 1982). Although sympathetic to Foucault's method, they ultimately fail to resolve this problem.

Selected Bibliography

The literature on the cult or legend of Napoleon and the return of his body to France is enormous and will not be dealt with here. In contrast, works discussing his tomb and its process of construction are few. Therefore, I will list below the locations of the most important archival documents pertaining to this monument and the secondary works in which it is discussed. The many references to periodical literature contemporaneous with the monument and official reports pertinent to it, found in the endnotes of this book, will not be repeated. A short list of the most important works dealing with the July Monarchy, the historical period in which the tomb was constructed, concludes this bibliography.

PRIMARY ARCHIVAL SOURCES

Archives Nationales, Paris

67.A.J.(1-26). "Agence des Invalides." Plans et cartes Division. Many tracings of drawings for the project submitted by Visconti to the Conseil des bâtiments civils.

2.A.P.6. Archives privés Division. Documents on the career of Duchâtel, including a dossier on the tomb of Napoleon.

246.A.P.14. Archives privés Division. Papers of Hippolyte Fortoul.

332.A.P.4. Archives privés Division. Papers of Victor Baltard.

A.J.52.493. Extensive documentation on the contest of 1841 and the actions of the commission appointed to report on it.

F.18.1864. Letter of Destouches proposing to convert the Panthéon into a tomb for Napoleon.

F.21.728–29. Documents containing miscellaneous information about the tomb.

F.21.730–33. Miscellaneous correspondence relating to the tomb and data on its construction and use of materials.

F.21.734. Documents regarding the mosaic decoration and the decorative sculpture.

F.21.735. Documents concerning Marochetti's equestrian monument.

F.21.736. Documentation for Triqueti's statue of the Crucifixion.

F.21.737. Documentation regarding the temporary sculpture commissioned for the retour des cendres.

F.21.739. More data concerning the sculpture commissioned for the retour. Correspondence and reports on the status of the monument in 1850.

F.21.740. Documentation on the tombs of Generals Duroc and Bertrand, on either side of the entry to the crypt.

F.21.810. Miscellaneous information concerning the monument, 1853–79.

F.21.871. Miscellaneous information concerning the monument, 1854–80.

F.21.1839. Miscellaneous information concerning the monument.

F.21.1463–64. Miscellaneous data on the tomb prior to 1851.

F.21.1675. Miscellaneous data on the tomb, 1850–58.

F.21.2753. Documents concerning the expenses of construction and maintenance.

F.70.183. Payment records for 1853 and 1854.

F.70.288. Various decrees concerning the tomb, 1852–64.

Archives de l'Assemblée Nationale, Paris

An album entitled "Session 1843, N.V. crédits, loi du 1 juillet 1843" contains the official, approved drawing of the tomb by Visconti.

Archives Hervé du Perier de Larsan, Paris

Visconti Papers. These private documents and drawings in the possession of Visconti's descendants have been inventoried by Emmanuel Jacquin, but they have not yet been catalogued.

Archives de l'Armée, Vincennes

Carton 35, dossier 1. "Invalides" contains the original of Visconti's program for the contest of 1841.

Archives municipales, Toulouse

Papers of Charles de Rémusat, carton 5.S.181

Bibliothèque historique de la Ville de Paris, Paris

Papers and procès-verbaux of the Société libre des Beaux-Arts in which the monument is discussed, mss. C.P.4051–4069

Bibliothèque du Musée des arts décoratifs, Paris

Mss. 289 and 290 contain copies of the major reports on the project.

SECONDARY SOURCES

Boime, Albert. *Hollow Icons: The Politics of Sculpture in Nineteenth-Century France*. Kent, Ohio: Kent State University Press, 1987.

De Caso, Jacques, *David d'Angers: L'Avenir de la mémoire: Etude sur l'art signalétique à l'époque romantique*. Paris: Flammarion, 1988.

Driskel, Michael Paul. "By Competition or Administrative Decree?: The Contest for the Tomb of Napoleon in 1841." *Art Journal* 48, no. 1 (Fall 1989): 46–52.

———. "Le tombeau de Napoléon: Louis Visconti, createur et administrateur." In the exhibition catalogue *Louis Visconti 1791–1853*. Paris, 1991: 168–80.

Durey, Philippe. "Le tombeau de Napoléon Ier aux Invalides: Les inscriptions de la gloire." In the exhibition catalogue *La Sculpture Française au XIXe siècle*. Paris, 1986: 76–182.

Etex, Antoine. *Souvenirs d'un artiste*. Paris, 1877.

Eyriès, Gustave. *Simart: Etudes sur sa vie et sur son oeuvre*. Paris, 1860.

Formigé, Jules. "Un Projet de transfert du tombeau de Napoléon Premier des Invalides à Saint-Denis en 1853." *Académie des Beaux-Arts* (1958–59), 1959: 47–52.

Issartel, Thierry. "Les projets pour le tombeau de Napoléon." In the exhibition catalogue *Napoléon aux Invalides: 1840, Le Retour des cendres*. Paris, Musée de l'Armée, 1990: 121–45.

Legrand, François. "L'échec des 'tarsias' aux Invalides." In the exhibition catalogue *Louis Visconti 1791–1853*. Paris, 1991: 181–83.

Léouzon Le Duc, Louis. *Le sarcophage de Napoléon Ier aux Invalides*. Paris, 1873.

Lenoir, Albert. *Le Tombeau de Napoléon Ier aux Invalides*. Paris, 1855.

Marrinan, Michael. *Painting Politics for Louis-Philippe: Art and Ideology in Orléanist France, 1830–1848*. New Haven: Yale University Press, 1988.

Noix, Gustave Léon (General). *Napoléon et les Invalides*. Paris: Delagrave, 1911.

Poisson, Florence. *Le retour des cendres*, exhibition catalogue, Courbevoie, Musée Roybet-Fould, 1963.

Vacquier, A. "Deux bas-reliefs des Invalides." *Bulletin de la Société d'histoire et d'archéologie VIIe arrondissement de Paris*, no. 7 (April 1910): 20–24.

Van Zanten, David. *Designing Paris: The Architecture of Duban, Labrouste, Duc, and Vaudoyer*. Cambridge, Massachusetts: MIT Press, 1987.

Vicaire, Marcel. "Le projets de Marochetti pour le tombeau de l'Empereur Napoléon." *Bulletin de la Société de l'histoire de l'art français* (1974), 1975: 145–52.

Visconti, Louis. *Tombeau de Napoléon Ier erigé dans le dome des Invalides.* Paris, 1853.

HISTORICAL CONTEXT OF THE JULY MONARCHY

Bezucha, Robert J. "An Introduction to the History." In the exhibition catalogue *The Art of the July Monarchy, France 1830–1848.* Columbia, Missouri, 1989: 17–48.

Blanc, Louis. *Histoire de dix ans (1830–1840).* 5 vols. Paris, 1846.

Charlety, Sébastien. *La monarchie de Juillet.* Vol. 5. In the series *Histoire de La France contemporaine,* ed. Ernest Lavisse. Paris: Hachette, 1922.

Collingham, Hugh. *The July Monarchy: A Political History of France 1830–1848.* London, New York: Longman, 1988.

Gabourd, Amédée. *Histoire contemporaine, comprenant les principaux événements qui se sont accomplis depuis la révolution de 1830 jusqu'à nos jours.* 4 vols. Paris, 1865.

Lucas-Dubreton, Jean. *The Restoration and the July Monarchy.* Trans. by E. F. Buckley. New York: G. P. Putnam's Sons, 1929.

McWilliam, Neil. "David d'Angers and the Panthéon Commission: Politics and Public Works under the July Monarchy." *Art History* 5 (December 1982): 426–46.

Nouvion, Victor de. *Histoire du règne de Louis-Philippe Ier.* 4 vols. Paris, 1857–61.

Pinkney, David H. *Decisive Years in France, 1840–1847.* Princeton, New Jersey: Princeton University Press, 1986.

Ponteil, Félix. *La Monarchie parlementaire, 1815–1848.* Paris: Colin, 1949.

Regnault, Elias. *Histoire de huit ans, 1840–1848.* 3 vols. Paris, 1851.

Rémusat, Charles de. *Mémoires de ma vie.* Vols. 3–5. Paris: Plon, 1958–67.

Rittiez, François. *Histoire du règne de Louis-Philippe, 1830–1848.* 3 vols. Paris, 1855–58.

Seignobos, Charles. *Histoire politique de l'Europe contemporaine.* Vol. 1. 7th ed. Paris, 1870.

Thureau-Dangin, Paul. *Histoire de la monarchie de Juillet.* 7 vols. Paris, 1884–92.

Weill, Georges. *La France sous la monarchie constitutionelle (1814–1848).* Paris: Société française d'éditions d'art, 1912.

Index

Alavoine, Jean-Antoine, 42
Albert Memorial (London), 166
Allevy, Achille, 95
Allier, Antoine, 88
Amadeo, Giovanni, 71
Arc de Triomphe (Paris), 51, 60
Arsenne, L. C., 79
Auvray, Louis, 102–3

Bacon, Henry, 199
Baltard, Victor, xvi, 124–26, 129
Barrès, Maurice, 177–78
Basilica of Saint-Denis, 52, 62, 73,
    171, 172, 173–75, 177
Bentham, Jeremy, 190–91
Bertrand, General, 12
Bidon, Théophile, 94–95, 100
Blanc, Charles, 164
Blanc, Louis, 164
Blouet, Abel, 191
Boisson, Jean, 30
Bonaparte, Jérôme, Prince, 167, 173
Bonino da Campione, 71
Bonnassieux, Jean-Marie, 61
Bosio, François, 32, 68, 70
Bouchet, Jules, 1–3, 157–58, 171
Bra, Théodore, 154
Brézé, Louis de, 73, 113
Brian, Jean-Louis, 167
Bruant, Libéral, 1, 3, 123, 124,
    130, 151
Buhot, Louis, 116
Buren, Daniel, 192–93

Cannissié, Philippe, 113
Carné, Louis de, 56–57

Cavé, Hygin-Auguste, 92, 95,
    97, 139
Chambard, Louis, 156
Champfleury, Jules, 183
Charles X (king of France), 77
Charlet, Nicolas-Toussaint, 21, 26–
    28, 39, 68
Charpentier, Théodore, 123
Chasseriau, Charles-Frédéric, 100
Chasseriau, Théodore, 100
Chenavard, Paul, 160
Church of Saint-Sulpice (Paris), 14
Church of the Madeleine (Paris),
    46–49, 60, 77, 110
Clauzel, Bertrand, 52, 64–65
Colin, Alexandre, 95
Colleoni, Bartolommeo, 71, 113
Coquereau, Félix, 12
Courbet, Gustave, 183
Cuisin, P., 40–42

D'Angoulême, Duc de, 51
Daly, César: criticism of the admin-
    istration of the contest, 89–90,
    92; criticism of entries in con-
    test, 97–98, 103–5, 110–11,
    116, 120; criticism of Visconti's
    plan, 127–28, 138–39; theory of
    monuments, 131; tomb of Napo-
    leon at the Invalides, 48–49
Dantan, Antoine, 113
Daumier, Honoré, 140
David, Jacques-Louis, 82, 95
David d'Angers, Pierre-Jean, 18–20,
    51, 129, 136–37, 148, 158
Delacroix, Eugène, 82–83

Delaroche, Paul, 46, 48
Delaunay, Hippolyte, 160
Des Longrais, Armand, 65
Dédéban, Jean-Baptiste, 92
Délécluze, E.-J., 82–83, 90–91
Devéria, Achille, 111–13
Duban, Félix, 58–60, 61, 105, 108
Duc, Louis, 42, 44, 129
Duchâtel, 86, 129–30, 138, 146,
    154, 158, 160, 191
Dumont, Augustin, 11, 61, 160,
    165–67, 177
Duncan, John H., 196
Duquesnay, François, 100
Duret, Francisque, 6, 146, 152

Emeric-David, T.-B., 77
Etex, Antoine, 65–66, 68, 69–70,
    110–11, 116–20, 171

Failin, Victor, duc de Persigny, 165,
    172, 173, 175
Fanelli-Semah, 100–101
Farcy, Charles de, 81
Feuchère, Jean-Jacques, 31
Foucault, Michel, 190–91, 204
Fountaine, Pierre, 54, 129, 137
French, Daniel Chester, 200
Freud, Sigmund, 202–3

Garfield, James, 196, 199
Gaudin, Charles, 165
Gauguier, Charles, 47–48
Gauthier, Pierre, 99
Gautier, Théophile, 129, 137–
    38, 140
Gayrard, Raymond, 113
Geertz, Clifford, 190
Geoffroy, Louis, 21–22
Geslin, P.-F., 96–97
Glais-Bizoin, Alexandre, 18, 70
Goujon, Jean, 73
Gouvion Saint-Cyr, General, 13
Grant's Tomb (New York City),
    196–97
Greenough, Horatio, 201
Guersant, Pierre, 101–2
Guizot, François, 28–29, 83

Hardouin-Mansart, Jules: design for
    the Invalides, 1–3; relation of
    contest entries to his design,
    113–15, 122–27, 132–37
Heine, Heinrich, 25–26
Hittorff, Jacques-Ignace, 49, 84
Hobbes, Thomas, 184–87
Hollier, Edouard, 170
Horeau, Hector, 54–55, 116, 191
Houssayne, Arsène, 155
Huet, Paul, 82–83
Hugo, Victor, 33

Ingres, J.-A.-D., 46, 129, 130, 134–
    36, 153, 155
Isabelle, Edouard, 124

Johnson, Philip, 198
Joinville, Prince de, 12, 30, 34, 167
Jouffroy, François, 12, 160, 162,
    166, 167

Kennedy Memorial (Dallas), 198–99
Klagmann, Jean-Baptiste (Jules), 123
Kléber, Jean-Baptiste, 79
Kliban, Bernard, 202

La Fage, Adrien de, 83–84
Labédollière, Emile de, 168
Labrouste, Henri, 32, 120–22, 158
Labrouste, Théodore, 122–24
Lacroix, Paul, 155–56
Lamartine, Alphonse de, 17, 18,
    35–36, 49
Lance, Aldolphe, 15, 157–58, 181
Las Cases, Count de, 21, 68
Le Harivel-Durocher, Victor,
    182–83
Ledru-Rollin, Alexandre-Auguste,
    158–59, 160, 161, 164
Lejeune, Théodore, 182
Lemaire, Victor, 123
Lemud, Aimé, 32–33, 35, 100
Lequesne, Eugène, 150
Lévêque, Edmond, 116
Lévi-Strauss, Claude, xv
Ligny, Louis de, 113

Lincoln Memorial (Washington, D.C.), 199–201
Lingay, Joseph, 138
Lissitzky, El, 185–86
Louis XIV (king of France), 2, 3, 39, 68–69, 107, 137, 158
Louis XV (king of France), 77
Louis XVI (king of France), 29, 46
Louis XVIII (king of France), 69
Louis-Phillippe (king of France): political opposition, 79; politics of the July Monarchy, 28–30, 37–38, 44–45, 49–50, 57, 83, 202; relationship with Thiers, 28; Retour des cendres, 12, 30, 144
Louvois Fountain (Paris), 14
Luynes, Alfred, Duc de, 161–62

Maindron, Hippolyte, 111–13
Marochetti, Charles: first project for tomb, 58, 60–64, 66–67, 69–75, 76, 85, 146–47; relationship with Thiers, 60–61; unfinished equestrian monument, 141–45, 159, 165–66
Marshall, William Calder, 166
Mehemet Ali (pasha of Egypt), 24–25, 28, 46
Mérimée, Prosper, 130
Moitte, Jean-Antoine, 75
Molière Fountain, 133–34, 147
Montalembert, Charles de, 18
Moreau, Louis, 108–9
Moret, Camille, 54

Napoleon 1er (emperor of France): choice of burial site, 67, 132, 171; debate over location of tomb, 35–58; exile and burial, 11, 19, 21, 88, 99–100, 167; myth and legend, 20–23, 95, 169–70; reputation as despot, 18–19; retour des cendres, 12, 17, 24, 30–35; uses of his image during the "Eastern Question," 24–28
Napoleon III: attempt to move the tomb, 171–77; delay in inaugurating the tomb, 168–71; dislike of Visconti's design, 171

Nicolle, Joseph, 98
Nixon, Richard, 202

Ottin, Auguste-Louis, 61, 157
Oudiné, Eugène, 168

Palais Royal (Paris), 192–93
Panthéon (Church of Sainte-Geneviève), 49–51, 76, 137, 160
Pelletan, Eugène, 57, 138
Percier, Charles, 12, 54
Petitot, Louis, 106–7
Philibert, Emmanuel, Duke of Savoy, 74
Pigeory, Félix, 182
Place de la Bastille, Paris, 78, 81
Place des Victoires, Paris, 68, 70
Pradier, James, 8, 130, 146, 147–50, 152, 153, 159, 183
Pruche, Clément, 91

Quatremère de Quincy, Antoine-Chrysostome, 76–77
Quinet, Edgar, 20

Raffett, Denis-Auguste-Marie, 21, 25, 95
Rand, Ayn, 184–86
Ravaisson, Félix, 182–83
Rémusat, Charles: announcement of the Retour des cendres, 1, 35, 56, 64, 74; choice of an architect, 58–60; service on the committee to judge the contest, 133; Triqueti's letter to him, 111
Restoration Government, 21, 46, 51, 78, 109
Rivoulon, Antoine, 116
Rochejaquelein, Henri de la, 162, 165, 166
Rochet, Louis, xvi
Rougevin, Auguste, 98–99
Rude, François, 51

Sagaret, François, 100, 101, 103
Saint Paul's Cathedral (London), 166
Saint-Helena, Island of, 1, 6